The Language of Planning

THE LANGUAGE OF PLANNING

Essays on the Origins and Ends
of American Planning Thought

Albert Z. Guttenberg

FOREWORD BY Lewis Hopkins

University of Illinois Press
Urbana and Chicago

© 1993 by the Board of Trustees of the University of Illinois
Manufactured in the United States of America
1 2 3 4 5 C P 5 4 3 2 1

This book is printed on acid-free paper.

Library of Congress Cataloging-in-Publication Data

Guttenberg, Albert Z.
    The language of planning : essays on the origins and ends of
American planning thought / Albert Z. Guttenberg.
        p.   cm.
    Includes index.
    ISBN 0-252-02003-0 (cl.). — ISBN 0-252-06307-4 (pbk.)
    1. City planning—United States—History. 2. Land use—United
States—Planning—History. 3. Regional planning—United States—
History. I. Title.
HT167.G88   1993
307.1′2′0973—dc20   92-41286
                                                                          CIP

To Mariella

Contents

Foreword

Students and scholars continue to ask, What is planning? How is it different from other activities? How can we determine whether it is worthwhile? How can we deal with the tension between planning and democracy? What, if anything, differentiates planning as it has evolved in the American context from planning elsewhere? Does planning bring its own perspective to understanding the city and the region?

These essays focus on the language of planning and the history of planning in order to distinguish a planning perspective from other perspectives, to consider the city from such a planning perspective, and to place this perspective in the American cultural context. They avoid simplistic answers; they do not resolve the issues. Rather, they demonstrate how careful thought can be effective in understanding and using the tensions in these questions to inform and energize planning practice.

Although a few of the essays in this volume are readily available—indeed, influential—in the field, others are difficult to find and little known because of the range of perspectives that Albert Guttenberg achieved and the various forums in which his writings were presented. The present volume performs an important service by making his insightful essays available to a wider audience of planners and related professionals. Bringing them together reveals an underlying conceptual design that has an impact greater than that of the sum of its original parts. They are organized here so that the cumulative contributions of individual essays to the two major subjects, planning as a language and planning as social invention, are mutually reinforcing.

The conceptual framework of these essays is a stimulating change from the usual. It is a cultural framework rather than a design, political, economic, or sociological framework. Although influenced by the roots of traditional planning literature in design and social reform as well as by the social sciences, Guttenberg's scholarship, with its examination of the meaning of words, its focus on the way discourse forms communities, including the community of planners, and its search for the historical sources of contemporary planning thought, is closer to the humanities than to the social sciences. Thus, his essays exemplify an interpretation of planning that is underrepresented in the planning literature. The approach integrates a wide range of planning concepts. Guttenberg addresses cities from a perspective specific to planning, planning itself as a cultural phenomenon, and the cultural context that forms the city and the profession and that in turn is formed by them.

The essays carefully establish fundamental concepts and at the same time reach very pragmatic results. Guttenberg's multiple-dimension approach to land use classification, for example, is the conceptual basis for current work in the field. His essays on land use classification attain the specificity of a technical manual. The dimensions of classification are, however, grounded in a concept of humankind as transformer of the environment in the light of human ideals. They include not only categories capable of describing existing land use, but also categories for evaluating land use and categories for representing possible actions necessary for realizing those values. Thus, the interests of the traditional scholar in the humanities and the technician of geographic information systems meet.

Two themes are important throughout. The first helps one to understand how planning relates to cities. The second helps to understand how planners relate to the norms of their culture.

In the first case, Guttenberg maintains that because planning is action-oriented, a profession rather than an academic discipline, there should be and is a planning perspective that is different from the perspective of any one of the social sciences. There is a way to look at and understand the social and physical structure of a city that is peculiar to the questions a planner ought to ask and must address. A planner should understand a city in a way that leads to social inventions—changes in the city. Land use classification must include categories describing not only what is but also what can and should be. Similarly, concepts of form must address how form changes and how it can be changed intentionally. The creation of a language of land use, a grammar for land use planning, thus becomes a task specific to the planning perspective.

As a society and a profession we are perennially asking, "What is the purpose of planning?" and "What does a planner do?" Guttenberg's answer is of particular interest: The planner is a social inventor. This is a new role created in part from the combination of the roles of social scientist, reformer, and designer. A social invention is a new concept that often arises from the mental intersection of known concepts. It is not simply an additional cumulation of known elements, but a new structure. A planner as inventor thus brings things to society, not merely guides or coordinates members of society. The intellectual and professional excitement comes from the tension between the culture that forms the planners and their inventions and the reciprocal effect of these inventions and their inventors on the culture.

The second theme concerns the dilemma of planning in a democratic society. How does a planner, a believer in the benefits of professional expertise, reconcile such expert intervention with the fundamental commitment to the intelligence of the common people? A strong commitment to the "American experiment," to a constitution in which we believe, must be reconciled culturally with reliance on expertise. This is not, for Guttenberg, a question of political theory or procedure, but of formative actions to create and sustain institutions and relationships in physical space that respect both these ideas. It is not a question of class structure, but of the cultural structures that shape the relationships of individuals to society and individuals to themselves and of the material and institutional effects of that culture. For example, experts can become part of a community of citizens by living in the community, or citizens can become experts through wide dissemination of pertinent knowledge.

In a time of rapid social change and confusion, when all professions are shaken to the extent that they wonder about their identity and purpose, this volume makes a significant contribution to strengthening the planning profession's sense of identity and the uniqueness of its task. It demonstrates that a close relationship can exist between society's built environment and its ideals. What it offers is especially valuable to planning students and aspiring practitioners—a vision of the high role they can play in realizing that relationship.

Lewis Hopkins

Preface

Although the essays in this collection span more than thirty years of writing, I have thought it best to organize them hierarchically rather than chronologically by publication date, especially because the publication dates do not strictly reflect the order in which they were written. More important, although I would not deny that a certain development has occurred in my thinking over time, this development has consisted largely in extending a method and a set of concepts from one field of application to another and in refining those concepts rather than generating additional concepts in a linear pattern. I believe also that even the earliest essays have a contemporary relevance that outweighs any value they may have as examples of how planners thought about cities and regions at a particular time and place in the past.

Fitting these essays together required careful editing and adapting. For the sake of continuity, conciseness, and to reduce overlap, I found it necessary to cut here and there and to supply some connective text and commentary. In a few cases I also ventured to modify titles where this seemed to enhance the meaning of the essay or for stylistic reasons.

Most of the work—and most of the pleasure—of preparing this volume lay in bringing to the surface the underlying themes that have given my writing its unity over the years. I say pleasure quite deliberately, because this endeavor has given me the opportunity to revisit imaginatively the places where I learned and the persons at whose feet or at whose side I learned. No one can claim to be the product of one's self alone, and this applies as well to one's intellectual self. Thought, as Mary Parker Follett taught, takes place best not within the confines of a single mind, but between minds. It is essentially a social affair, a dialogue or a debate among friends.

Many years ago, when I worked for the Philadelphia City Planning Commission, my friends were also my colleagues. Most of us had arrived in the mid-1950s. Our reason for being together was to make a comprehensive plan for the year 1980. We considered ourselves professionals, not planning mechanics. We spent a good deal of our own time

discussing what, precisely, as comprehensive planners, we were trying
to do and why we were trying to do it. Naturally, we all had our own
compasses, our own directions. What interested me most was to discover order in the urban environment—city planner's order, not social scientist's order. I believed that urban planning was more than applied
urban economics plus applied urban sociology plus applied political
science, so there must be a concept of urban structure that correspond-
ed specifically to urban planning. The quest soon led to related inquiries: What is planning? What are its ends? What are its means? and What
is land use? Many of the essays in this collection have their roots in that
formative period between 1956 and 1961.

One of the valuable things I learned in Philadelphia was an admira-
tion for cities and a spirit of hopefulness for their future—an attitude
very unlike the one that prevails today. Now, cities are compared with
cancers. They spread malignantly across the landscape. They merge and
form supercities. They make the air foul and the waters loathsome.

The image of the cancerous city is not unfounded, although it probably owes something to our present national mood. Admitting that our
cities are in serious difficulty, the first rule for righting them is to understand them in positive terms. The way to a creative understanding of the
nature of the city is to ask what cities do for people rather than what
they do to them.

The city is not disease, nor is it a haphazard or accidental phenomenon. It is an intricate system whose parts bear a necessary and under-
standable relationship to each other. It is also a place where grave social
problems manifest themselves, but this is no reason for despair. The
modern Western city began as an association of free people, and to this
day retains its capacity for self-direction.

Because cities are a product of impersonal social and economic forces and free human will, theoretical interest in the city is divided between
social scientists and social reformers—between those who want to know
what a city is and how it works and those who want to use it to create a
just and prosperous social order. The planner learns from both camps
but has to be wary of both. As with the centipede, too much scientific
attitude, too much thinking about the city as a determined object,
numbs the sense of human control and can end in paralysis.[1] On the other hand, to be too much of a reformer, to be a visionary or a revolution-
ary, is to risk losing all sense of the real restraints upon action. What often follows is a fatuous, even dangerous, utopianism.

If urban planners are neither social scientists nor social reformers nor
utopians, what are they? A concept is needed to express the planner's
responsibility to reality as well as that confidence to go beyond the
merely existent, which is the hallmark of true planning.

Planners are social inventors, experimenters with, and builders of, new social forms.[2] The forms may be physical, social, legal, political, economic, or all of these. Their newness consists in the combining of elements that, heretofore, have seemed mutually exclusive on various grounds—logical, cultural, or geographical. The following examples, familiar to most planners, indicate the nature and wide variety of social inventions.

Transfer development rights (TDR) is a social invention. It combines (regulates or adjusts) two kinds of value, market value and the value emanating from nature or culture (environment, history). It also has a physical aspect: sending and receiving districts

The agricultural assessment district is a social invention. It is a device that regulates two levels of land value, urban and agricultural, and two ways of life, permitting them to coexist.

The impact fee is a social invention. It is a new way of linking private resources with public benefits.

Congregate housing is a social invention. It combines private living with institutional living.

Social invention can be simple, combining two elements or a few elements (e.g., the garden apartment combines urban-style, multifamily structures with a little rural amenity, open space), or it can be a complex fusing of many elements. One of the most ambitious inventions of the past was Ebenezer Howard's Garden City, which aimed at combining town and country, agriculture and industry, management and labor, people and nature, and many more apparently opposed qualities. The city itself is an ancient social invention of the most complex sort. The *jumelage* [sister city] idea (chapter 7) is a social invention for connecting whole cities in different countries. Contemporary Roman planners are seeking to connect three different cities separated in time: ancient Rome, the medieval city of the popes, and the present-day capital of Italy.

Social invention is not whimsy or caprice. It is not a question of the "What shall I invent today?" variety. It is a culturally guided program with definite civilizational objectives. Historically, social invention has aimed at the reconstitution of the integral human personality (real or mythic) shattered by the Industrial Revolution. Lately, its main thrust has been to assert the social unity of humankind by overcoming the barriers that race, gender, class, creed, stage of life, occupation, or geographical distance impose on human fellowship. But, as the preceding illustrations show, social invention may also have much lower-level objectives, and its products may consist of new means as well as new ends.

If a planner is a social inventor, the inverse is also true. A social inventor is a planner, regardless of the inventor's formal professional identification, if any. Some of the inventor heroes and heroines of the essays in the second part of this volume were never members of the official planning fraternity. M. L. Wilson was an agricultural economist; Benton MacKaye was a forester; Elwood Mead was an engineer; Wilbur and Elsie Phillips were social workers; Prestonia Mann Martin was a socialite, an intellectual, and a housewife; and Mary Parker Follett was a political theorist. This anomaly is explained in part by the nebulousness of the planning movement, especially in its early years. When the American Institute of Planners was founded in 1917, it drew a boundary between reformers who were otherwise quite close to each other in spirit and purpose. Thus, my view of planning as social invention is, in a sense, a harking back to an earlier epoch when planning was a broad social movement. It is still a social movement. The profession is an institutional crystallization of the movement, but it is not identical with it.

This collection of essays is organized into two major parts: Part 1 concerns land use planning as a language, Part 2 is about planning as social invention from a variety of perspectives. The two are intimately related. The understanding of planning as social invention is a conclusion I came to by degrees through a long-term inquiry into the linguistic sources and factors of land use planning. Part 1 is the record of that odyssey.

The inquiry began about 1959 as a consequence of a chance assignment. The city of Philadelphia was preparing for a real estate inventory, and it fell to me to attempt to devise categories for summarizing the data in land use terms. Fortunately, there was no need to start from scratch. The basis had already been laid by others. I was familiar with John Rannell's study on "the core of the city," and I had taken courses at the University of Pennsylvania with Chester Rapkin, coauthor with Robert Mitchell of the pathbreaking work on urban traffic and land use. And behind all stood the seminal thought of Robert Murray Haig. Although these men had identified the major strands in the land use concept, it seemed to me that they had not done so with sufficient clarity or consistency. Furthermore, their tendency was to narrow the meaning of land use by highlighting the categories "activity" and "type of establishment" and downplaying the others. My purpose was to broaden the concept by capturing and systematizing as many of its senses as seemed justified by the actual usage of the term.

I proceeded by assigning the myriad terms describing real estate in the city records to their various referents. Some were building terms, some referred to the activities conducted on the parcels, others to economic functions that the buildings and activities served. Some pertained to the density or intensity of use, and others to the environmental effects, the spatial range of influence, and the rhythm of the use. I entitled the result of this process "A Multiple Land Use Classification System." Not only did this system make practical sense, but it also had theoretical grounding in the work of such cultural anthropologists as Bronislaw Malinowski, with his analysis of human culture into a number of "concrete isolates" that included "material apparatus," "activities," and "functions."[3] It was an advance in two respects. It facilitated—potentially at least—more precise communication among land use planners, and it stimulated research on the interrelationships among the various land use dimensions.

In focussing on the several dimensions of urban land use and their mutual influences, multiple land use classification was implicitly a theory of urban structure. Since its appearance, the theory has undergone periodic amplification and evolved into a theory of land use planning based on a comparison of planning with language. Here, too, it was never a matter of generating concepts in a vacuum, but rather of synthesizing the insights gained from many sources. As an undergraduate at Harvard College, it had been my good fortune to come under the intellectual influence of I. A. Richards, the British literary critic, and through him the American philosopher Charles Morris. Both men were pioneers in the study of the functions of signs. I was particularly impressed by the usefulness of Morris's classification of the modes of signifying into identifiers, designators, appraisers, and prescriptors, and I adapted them very liberally to the classification of the significations of the term *land use*. In the light of Morris's typology, it was clear to me that multiple land use classification, because of its sole focus on "what is," was only one mode of speaking about land use—the scientist's mode. The identification of additional modes soon followed—the reformer's modes of appraisal and prescription. Still, there was an X in the system, an unknown I had difficulty in identifying with precision. Because human language has, among its functions, prayer, prophecy, and poetry, I reasoned that the language of planning must have a corresponding creative or transcendent mode. I termed this unknown, this X, the *optative mode*, a term borrowed from Richards. Its subject is the ideal element in the language of land use planning, the reaching out for something more than making things a little better. For a long time the precise nature of the unknown continued to elude me. It was only after 1970, when I began my research into the history of planning, that I was able to substitute for X an actual value in more than the most general terms. That value was land use planning as social invention.

The idea of publishing these essays as a book had its origin at two sessions of a national conference of the Association of Collegiate Schools of Planning that were devoted to discussing my contributions to the literature of urban and regional planning. For this purpose a panel of scholars was selected: Robert Begg, Eugenie Birch, Barry Checkoway, Leonard Heumann, Andrew Isserman, Lewis Hopkins, Carl Patton, Peter Schaeffer, and Michael Teitz. They have my profound thanks for the encouragement they gave me and and for their incisive and creative comments. I am particularly indebted to Andrew Isserman, who conceived the whole project, and to Lewis Hopkins, who generously made himself available as guide and counselor. Whether it was an abstract question of conceptual design or the details of manuscript preparation, his advice was always ready and immensely helpful. I owe a special debt of gratitude to the John Simon Guggenheim Foundation. Without the opportunity for research that it provided through a fellowship in 1970, none of the essays on planning history could have been written. I am also grateful to the reviewers, known and unknown, who contributed so much to improving many of these essays at the time of their original publication.

Notes

1. "The centipede was happy quite until the toad for fun / Said, 'Pray, which leg comes comes after which?' / This worked her mind to such a pitch / She lay distracted in a ditch, considering how to run." The verse is taken from Frank W. Cushwa and Robert N. Cunningham, *Ways of Thinking and Being* (New York: Charles Scribner's and Sons, 1936), 340.

2. The first use of the term *social invention* that I have been able to discover was by Louis D. Brandeis, associate Supreme Court justice, in the second decade of this century.

3. Bronislaw Malinowski. 1944. *A Scientific Theory of Culture.* Chapel Hill: University of North Carolina Press. See especially 53.

PART 1

Linguistic Sources and Factors in Planning

The state of its language reveals much about a profession, about its preoccupations, about the social, political, economic, and scientific forces that bear down upon it, and also about its readiness to confront those forces effectively. Too many planners use their language unreflectingly. Some worry about its impreciseness. A few, Richard Hedman, for example, have tickled us by poking fun at the planner's jargon. The following seven essays view planning terminology not as an object of amusement or derision, but as offering an opportunity to shed light on the nature of the American planning movement and to help bring greater order to planning discourse.

In the first two essays, a vision of planning begins to unfold. The starting point is the ambiguity of words: "in the literature of planning one notes a bewildering change from one context to another in the meaning of the key terms. *City* and *planning* are themselves the supreme examples, but there are many others of a lower order: *open space, neighborhood, slum, blight,* to name a few. Such disagreements are not to be ignored, nor should they be dismissed as signs of confusion. If planning terms are ambiguous, it is because they are the meeting grounds of tremendous pressures coming from rival word-users."

Each term in the planning lexicon is an arena where the great ways of thinking about cities and regions, that is to say, about societies, engage each other. The essays in Sections A and B are voyages into the meaning of three key terms in the planner's lexicon: *planning, land use,* and *region.*

The first two essays demonstrate the use of word analysis as a method of penetrating and comprehending the philosophical and sociological complexity of planning discourse. The essays in Section B advance to the systematization of that discourse in the interest of improved technical communication among planners, as well as effective public communication. The concluding two essays extend and expand the method used in the dissection of *land use* to the term *region.*

The Semantics of Planning

The two essays in this section demonstrate that the way we describe what we do ascribes value to what we do. A physical planner uses physical changes to achieve social ends, yet is viewed negatively, or as irrelevant, by some planners. What does it mean to create the concept of a social planner in contrast to a physical planner? That is, what are its consequences? Does it distinguish by ends or means, or confound its own value as an idea by confounding ends and means? How does it change our conception of what we do and why we do it? If we wish to distinguish a focus on changing physical forms from a focus on changing institutional forms, can we do so without implying a difference in intended ends? The questions raised in this section are perennially pertinent because this issue surfaces frequently in the profession. The resurgence of concern with physical planning in the 1990s is only one indication of the persistence of this theme in planning discourse.

1

The Social Uses
of City Planning

I regard the minute exploration of the meanings of
the primary words we use in discussing public affairs
as an intellectual operation absolutely necessary to
any fruitful and effective consideration of vital issues
in our Republic.

—CHARLES A. BEARD

The meaning of a word is its use.

—LUDWIG WITTGENSTEIN

Ideally defined, city planning is an attempt to better the human lot by
perfecting the urban environment. Like every idealistic enterprise, however, it soon becomes involved in the realities of social structure—actual methods of government, property relationships, special interests of all
kinds. Indeed, only by coming to terms with these real forces does it
have any hope of gaining its objectives, although in the process much of
its original élan is lost.

The questions to be raised here concern the effect of the socialization
process on the city planning ideal. Specifically, what uses other than
those appearing in professional declarations of purpose does North
American society make of city planning? What uses do planners make
of their profession other than to serve society?

These are fundamental questions in the sociology of planning. Our
approach to them, however, will depart from the usual methods of sociological inquiry. Rather than focussing on the actual planning process or
any particular instance of it as in a case study, we propose to make use of
certain concepts and methods developed and applied with good results
in other fields, notably linguistic philosophy and literary criticism.

Philosophers of language tell us that if we want to know what a word
means we have to pay attention to the circumstances surrounding its
use. This dictum seems so obvious as to be hardly worth mentioning,

yet it stands in marked contrast to the point of view that has prevailed throughout the greater part of the history of Western thought. If one had to epitomize the difference between the modern and the traditional philosophies of language, it would be thus: Whereas the traditionalists believe that behind each key word (e.g., Beauty, Truth, Justice, etc.) there stands one right meaning, the modern viewpoint is that the meaning of a word is no more than the way it is used in a particular situation. Let the situation change, and the use of our word is likely to change with it. Insofar as the word has many different uses, it has many different meanings, but for none of them can it be said that it is the one true meaning.

The doctrine that the meaning of a word is no more than the collection of its various uses is still a subject of considerable argument in the philosophic world (Gellner 1959). Two aspects of this doctrine, however, have some bearing on our subject: it fits very well with our earlier suggestion that this one term, *city planning*, represents a variety of real (as opposed to ideal) social functions; moreover, it suggests a method of identifying these multiple functions.

In the literature of planning one notes a bewildering change, from one context to another, in the meaning of the key terms. *City* and *planning* are themselves the supreme examples, but there are many others of a lower order: *open space, neighborhood, slum, blight*, to name a few. Such disagreements are not to be ignored, nor should they be dismissed as signs of confusion or error on the part of one or another of the parties to the dispute. If planning terms are ambiguous, it is because they are the meeting points of tremendous pressures coming from rival word-users, each of whom would like to appropriate the word for his own purposes. It is precisely from the clash of meaning within ambiguous words that we can get an inkling of the different roles which city planning plays in North American society, that is, its different social functions. Consequently, a primary aim here is to take account of some of these meanings.

More than just exploring the ambiguity of city planning terms, however, we propose to look for a systematic connection between different uses (meanings) of the same term. Is there an underlying pattern observable in the way in which ambiguous planning terms acquire or change their meanings? The question is of more than academic interest. An affirmative answer would have practical application, for it would indicate that semantic variability is not random but systematic, so that when a new term is introduced in to the planner's vocabulary it may be possible to foresee some of the turns it will take, the uses that will be made of it.

One can imagine ingenious experiments or painstaking studies of past and present usage which might show that ambiguous planning terms do indeed acquire their meanings according to a regular pattern. There is good reason, however, for asserting on rational grounds alone that regularity, or what amounts to the same thing, predictability, is by no means out of the question. For to say that meaning is predictable is only to say that it develops out of a general sociocultural background whose main features and general dynamics are familiar to us. Word use is an act, and like every act is subject to environmental influences. To learn what a word means, one looks at the social context in which it is used, and to learn about systematic meaning change, one must observe the word against a background of systematic changes in social context.

Four tendencies of change in the meaning of planning terms are tentatively identified in the following pages which are called social, political, technical, and professional dynamics. They operate simultaneously, but each one operates more deeply and over a longer period of time than the one which follows it. No more than the briefest sketch of each dynamic is attempted here, with whatever illustration comes to mind. However, I believe that this first try may serve to lay down some profitable lines of future inquiry into the nature and dynamics of the city planning movement.

The Social Dynamic

"Living language," observes a noted writer, "is always in flux" because thought, conditioned by the changing social and economic environment, can never be quite the same at any two moments" (Robinson 1962, 53). It is above all the tendency of planning words to reflect changes in social and economic perspective which constitutes the social dynamic.

The modern critique of the American city began with social and economic conflict. Mutual distrust had always dominated town and country relations. These hostile feelings, however, were greatly aggravated by the tide of industrialization which swept the nation in the last century and permanently altered the balance of political and economic power between its urban and rural sectors. Agrarian resentment found expression in the farmers' fight to save their way of life, but it also took the form of vituperation directed against the city as the stronghold of international financiers and other "parasites." As Richard Wade, the urban historian, observes, "William Jennings Bryan's famous 'cross of gold' speech caught the conflicting forces and embodied the Populist notion of the primacy of rural America: 'the great cities rest upon our broad and fertile prairies. Burn down your cities and leave our farms and your cities will spring up again as if by magic; but destroy our farms and grass will grow in the street of every city in the country'" (1963, 70–71).

Populism left a permanent mark on American social thought. Even today many city planning terms, when viewed collectively, seem to convey an anticity bias, or a response to it. Thus, there are the terms which suggest the odious or menacing nature of urban expansion (*tyrannopolis, exploding metropolis, overspill, sprawl*); terms which suggest what the spreading city leaves in its wake (*slums, slurbs, blight*); nostalgic terms recalling lost rural conditions (*neighborhood, community, open space*); planning devices to restore the ancient balance (*neighborhood unit, garden city, green belt, greenway, conservation*).

In the early days of the present century, the principal contest was no longer between the farmer and the urban industrialist, but between the native urbanite and the immigrant (Wade 1963, 72). As the older inhabitants retreated to the suburbs, they never abandoned their economic stake downtown. Consequently, criticism of the city, although continuing, was no longer so sweeping as in the heyday of populism. *Dirty, vice-ridden, parasitic*—terms once used to damn the whole city—were now reserved for parts of the city, the ethnic ghettos encroaching on the downtown commercial enclaves of the well-to-do. To prepare the way for action, a more practical medical terminology soon replaced the sweeping moral invective: slums are *sore spots*, they *fester* and require *treatment*, sometimes by *surgery*. In the same vein, urban redevelopment becomes the "cleaning out of pockets of blight," and urban renewal, a precautionary measure against the "spread of infection." Without this imagery the arguments for public action would no doubt have lacked much of their force.

In our own day the civil rights movement is probably the most fertile source of ideology in planning language, as witness the appearance of certain euphemisms, such as *underserved areas* and *disadvantaged people* for slums and slum-dwellers. Parallel changes are occurring in the meanings of the older terms. Only fifteen years ago slum was defined as "an overpopulated part of the city inhabited by the poorest people, destitute or criminal classes" (*Words and Phrases* 1953, 526). In a later edition it is defined as "an area which does not provide an environment . . . in accordance with an accepted standard of urban neighborhood life" (*Words and Phrases* 1966–67, 42). The stigma of the slum is shifting from the people to the environment.

The self-improvement of the Negro is unimaginable without his power to seize and redefine words. The underclass naturally argues for an environmental theory of "slum," "blight," "crime," and "poverty" to counter the moralistic or genetic theory of its opponents ("the slum is in the people"). But even when all parties agree that the fault is environmental, the liberal is more likely to include the institutional environment, while the conservative stops with the physical environment; hence the current debate of "social planning" versus "physical planning."

One might add to these examples indefinitely without changing the essential point: planning terms direct the imagination along lines favorable to those who produce and define them, and in this way they function as instruments of class policy. The same struggle to control words and their meanings, however, can also be seen within and between individuals of the same class. One doesn't ordinarily think of the traditional land use categories ("industrial," "commercial," etc.) as serving special interests, and yet they promote a view of city land as an economic factor. Lately, the idea has been gaining ground that cities are places to be enjoyed and savored. It is not surprising, then, to find urban structure beginning to be described in terms of ordinary household activities, such as eating, sleeping, working, etc., rather than in terms of economic functions such as manufacturing, wholesale trade, retail trade, and so on (Chapin and Hightower 1966).

The tendency for a single class to split along lines of interest can also be observed in the case of normative terms, such as *standard* and *substandard, urban design,* or *balanced* land use or transportation. One hears in these words at least three different meanings which correspond to three distinct interests: amenity and convenience, representing the interest of the consumer; profitability, representing the entrepreneurial interest; and social impact, representing the public interest. To the land-user, a "substandard area" is one disagreeable to live in; to the owner or investor, it means risky in the financial sense; to the taxpayer, it means imposing an excessive burden on the public treasury; to the public official, it means not conforming to local codes and ordinances. These are contemporary meanings of almost equal importance (Guttenberg 1967).

The Political Dynamic

People use planning terms to express their present dissatisfactions (*slum, blight,* etc.) or to symbolize their aspirations (*open space, neighborhood,* etc.). They will then attempt to arouse and organize public sentiment in their behalf and to win votes for a public action program. In the process such terms acquire a set of typical functions, i.e., meanings. This is the political dynamic, a mere eddy in the broader social currents.

Suppose the term in question (let us refer to it as X) is a negative one (*slum, blight, poverty,* etc.). Since those who are most concerned constitute only a portion of the total population, the first step will be a characterization intended to secure agreement that X is bad. This means placing it in a context in which it appears to contradict the ultimate values of the total society; hence X is said to be "un-Christian," "undemocratic," "un-American." At the same time it will be characterized in more mundane terms so as to appeal to the real as well as the ideal motives of the general community. Not only is X un-Christian, un-democratic; it is also wasteful of our material and human resources ("our most precious asset") and inexpedient ("gives comfort to our enemies at home and abroad"). X also threatens you, personally. Here is the appeal to the particular as opposed to the general interest. X "spreads like cancer," threatens *your* health, *your* safety, *your* property.

The negative characterization of X does not go uncontested. As an effort to bring about real changes in the status quo, it always engenders countercurrents of evaluation. X is said to be a false issue (red herring; excuse for a federal power grab; attempt to impose middle-class standards, etc.); or an exaggerated issue (poverty is a form of hazing through which all newcomers to the society must pass); or an eternal issue (useless to worry about, since it will always be with us).

In the political phase of its development, as a result of constant reiteration in these various contexts, X also becomes practically synonymous with the forms of action which are supposed to bring relief. X means "march," "fight," "vote." In other quarters it may become "legislate" or "educate."

The Technical Dynamic

What the public sends forth as a symbol of its hope or discontent has to be returned to the public in the form of a practical definition. It is the process of rendering a vague idea more precise which I have called the technical dynamic to distinguish it from other major tendencies of meaning change which have their source in real transformations of the social and economic environment, or in the pros and cons of political debate.

The fight for X (e.g., for "open space") or against X (e.g., "slums") may never become the subject of a government program. However, if it does this event will hasten its entry into the technical phase of its development. It is at this point that the professional planner usually appears. Criteria are needed to distinguish X from non-X, otherwise how can it be fought (or promoted) effectively? The planner is hired to provide these criteria.

The planner's job is to deal with X as a real thing in the world, to take its measure. But the planner soon discovers that it is not so easy to identify as was commonly supposed when X was still in its slogan or symbol stage. Take "open space." Is it to be conceived in negative or in positive terms—as the presence of something or the absence of something? Or "slums." Is the essential phenomenon human or physical? Now ambiguity ceases to be just an interesting fact about words and becomes an actual impediment to action. Consequently, the demand for definition grows more insistent. What does X really mean?

This question, when it arises, creates an opportunity for two types of bureaucratic planner to enter the picture with their own meanings for X: the administrative planner, whose contribution is a clear-cut rule or standard for action (e.g., "poverty" means receiving less than $3,000 a year in income); and the analyst, whose function is to provide a more elaborate or scientific rationale for action.

The technical phase is often characterized by conflict between these two types which can never be fully resolved because of the different positions they occupy in the total structure of action and the different functions they perform. For the administrator, the analyst is the bottleneck who holds up the program by forever making simple things complex, while for the analyst, the administrator is the "terrible simplifier."

In the hands of the analyst the meaning of X undergoes further development. Not only must he render vague words more precise by attaching them to real things in the world and delving into the hidden causes of these things. He must also attain this greater precision without disturbing the broad agreement which may have attended the use of the term in its pretechnical phase. Therefore, of all possible specifications of X only the blandest survive, those which are least controversial. Perhaps it is this double need—for specificity and wide acceptance—which accounts in large part for the long-standing emphasis in city planning on the physical element as that element in the total city which is at once most easily identified and specified and least likely to occasion controversy. Men first talk about slums in physical terms for the same reason that they talk about the weather—to put off more difficult or touchy subjects.

The same principle can also be seen in the case of more positive terms, such as *neighborhood*. Originally, the term was used to invoke an ideal of small-scale community life, such as can be found only in vestigial form in the modern city and whose principal attributes are a shared territory, common facilities, cultural homogeneity, and social intimacy (Powdrill 1961, 41). It is the latter two which are most admired. However, by some, such as Isaacs, the neighborhood has come to be regarded as an instrument of social exclusiveness, and by others as an instrument of unwelcome social integration. It is not surprising, therefore, to find that the controversial social elements have been all but washed out of the technical planning definition of neighborhood. The concept has survived, but only as a physical design ideal stressing spatial rather than social relations, and safety and amenity rather than fellow-feeling (Gallion and Eisner 1963, 51).

The Professional Dynamic

The professional dynamic is best illustrated by an account of what is happening today in the United States to the term *city planning* itself.

A generation ago many planners would have considered it unnecessary to add the terms *social* and *physical* to *planning*. All city planning was social inasmuch as it served social objectives. Thus, in 1940, Russell V. Black and S. R. DeBoer wrote as follows: "the city, state, or regional plan has, by necessity, the outward appearance of a so-called 'physical plan' . . . there should be no necessity of labeling regional plans with social and economic objectives. What other reason have they for being?" (102).

Today, no point of view could be more out of date. American city planning is said to be in a state of flux between two major phases of its career—a passing "physical planning" phase and an emerging "social planning" phase. The popularity of this notion is not difficult to explain. A slogan is needed to express current dissatisfactions with both the present range of planning objectives and the present range of means employed for meeting them. The phrase "social versus physical planning" serves this purpose. Paul Davidoff puts it this way: "The fact what many of us have called for . . . social planning is, I believe, a way of asserting that we think it time that planners . . . take a more active role in correcting the abuses which plague our society." He adds: "The great substantive issue before us at present is how to fulfill the goal of equality of opportunity" (1964, 127).

Social planning, then, means not planning for social objectives—city planning has always done that. Rather, it means planning for certain objectives which planners have either neglected, or which they have pursued mainly through changes in the physical environment rather than through changes in the nonphysical environment. To the extent that this implied extension of the meaning of city planning is a response to the civil rights movement, it exemplifies the working of the social dynamic. However, it seems likely that the readiness of many American city planners to accept this extension is also to be explained in part by the prospect of dwindling opportunities for jobs and contracts which would be offered to mere land use planners under the Demonstration Cities Act and other federal programs. The observation gains point when we consider that the turmoil in the cities is demanding a new profession, or rather an "inter-profession," and that the lead in creating it might as easily be taken by social workers, economists, or public administrators as by city planners.

The tendency of planning terms to change their meanings, then, cannot be entirely understood apart from the politics and economics of professionalization. In the past, city planning has lived under the necessity of differentiating its product from those of its nearest competitors, architecture and engineering. It found this product in the "comprehensive arrangement of land uses." Now the threat to its economic future is from another quarter, and it is responding by changing its product. Formerly, the city was defined in terms of physical facilities, densities, and their spatial patterns. Now, the real but invisible city of socio-cultural institutions occupies the forefront. *City* planning is becoming *society* planning, partly in response to the problems of the age, and partly in order for the social professions to capitalize on those problems.

Summary

This discussion has focussed on city planning terminology as a means of interpreting the American city planning movement and the social role of the planner. Methodologically, it suggests that more attention might profitably be paid to the ambiguities of planning language. One gains considerable insight into the principal issues that agitate both the society and the profession by disentangling the separate strands of meaning involved in ambiguous terms.

Substantively, it indicates that there may be little ground for the verbal realism which we often profess—the belief that corresponding to every noun such as *slum, blight, open space, neighborhood,* etc., there is something constant "out there," which can be identified and defined in its essence if only we look at it long enough, or reason about it, or collect enough statistics. Rather, the meaning or such terms is to be sought in a study of word usage as a mirror of the social process. If our interpretation is correct, planning terms reflect mainly attempts by contending groups to present their programs in the guise of disinterested social thought. Beyond this, they represent fears and aspirations in the public mind, as well as efforts by legislators, administrators, and technicians to render these emotions objective and therefore manageable by turning them into things.[1] In this way are born some of our more specific notions about what the city is, its ills, and, of course, the cure for those ills.

Special interest attaches to the roles of the planner in this process. On the job, as administrator or technician, his freedom to create or define

words is limited by bureaucratic accountability. Off the job, as a professional competing with other types of professionals, he is kept in line by
his dependency on government patronage. In both cases he appears to
be more controlled than controlling, a fact which contrasts oddly with
his public image as initiator and innovator.

Notes

This essay is adapted with permission from *Plan Canada*, the journal of the Town
Planning Institute of Canada, 9 (March 1968): 6–14.

1. For a more extended analysis of the political and bureaucratic uses of language and their effects, see Harold D. Lasswell et al. (1949) and Murray Edelman (1964).

References

Beard, Charles A. 1944. *The Republic*. New York: Viking Press.
Black, Russell Van Nest, and S. R. DeBoer. 1940. "Integration of a Regional Plan."
    Planners' Journal 6 (Oct.–Dec.): 102.
Chapin, Stuart F., Jr., and Henry C. Hightower. 1966. *Household Activity Systems:
    A Pilot Investigation*. Chapel Hill: Center for Urban Studies, University of
    North Carolina.
Davidoff, Paul. 1964. "The Role of the City Planner in Social Planning." *Proceed-
    ings of the 1964 Annual Conference*. Cambridge: American Institute of Planners,
    127.
Edelman, Murray. 1964. *The Symbolic Uses of Politics*. Urbana: University of Illi-
    nois Press.
Gallion, Arthur, and Simon Eisner. 1963. *The Urban Pattern*. 2d ed. New York: D.
    Van Nostrand, 251.
Gellner, Ernest. 1959. *Words and Things*. Boston: Beacon Press.
Guttenberg, Albert Z. 1967. *The Social Evaluation of Non-Residential Land Use–Sub-
    standardness Criteria*. Urbana: Bureau of Community Planning, University of
    Illinois.
Isaacs, Reginald. "The Neighborhood Theory: An Analylsis of Its Adequacy."
    1948. *Journal of the American Institute of Planners* 14 (Spring): 15–23.
Lasswell, Harold et al. 1949. *The Language of Politics*. New York: George W. Stew-
    art.
Powdrill, E. A. 1961. *The Vocabulary of Land Planning*. London: The Estates Ga-
    zette, Ltd., 41.
Robinson, Richard. 1962. *Definition*. Oxford: Clarendon Press, 53.
Wade, Richard. 1963. "The City in History—Some American Perspectives." In
    Urban Life and Form, ed. Werner Z. Hirsch, 70–71. New York: Holt, Rinehart
    & Winston.

Wittgenstein, Ludwig. 1953. *Philosophical Investigations*. Oxford: Basil Blackwell.

Words and Phrases. 1953. Permanent ed. St. Paul: West Publishing, 526.

Words and Phrases. 1966–67. Cumulative Annual Pocket Part 4. St. Paul: West
    Publishing, 42.

2

Social versus Physical Planning Revisited

Nowadays, it is commonplace to dismiss questions of terminology as being "mere semantics." In the long run, however, effective action depends on clear thoughts which, in turn, depend on clear words. Unfortunately, American city planning has never been sufficiently conscious of its language.

A case in point is "social versus physical planning." In the early 1960s a slogan was needed to rally support against the prevailing aims and methods of city planning, and "social versus physical" served this purpose. But not enough time was given to defining these words, let alone to asking if they were the right words.

Objections to "social versus physical" can be raised on many counts, but let's consider only the most obvious. First, there is the question of intelligibility. Isn't physical planning (e.g., playground planning) also social planning in the sense that it serves social objectives? Therefore, how can we logically speak of social versus physical planning?

Then there are the side effects of this terminology. Dennis O'Harrow observed, "there are few greater insults you can offer a man than to call him a physical planner" (1967, 58). Recently, someone has said of physical planning that it was shot to death in the streets of Watts. This comment is not surprising in view of a growing tendency to regard physical planning as intrinsically antisocial, a tendency attributable in part to the "social versus physical" slogan.

Nor are the effects of the slogan damaging to only one group or interest. To be sure, "social versus physical" injures the physical planning professions by implying that they are devoid of social content. But, by the same token, it sets back the cause of urban reform by seeming to deny the social relevance of the physical environment.

These considerations justify a reexamination of the social versus physical planning idea from the semantics standpoint. What is meant by these terms? Are they the right terms? If not, what should replace them?

The "Soft City" versus the "Hard City"

For some, social versus physical planning means no more than the planning of social welfare services—as for jobs, education, legal aid—as opposed to physical facilities planning, but the matter goes deeper than this. The meaning of city itself is at issue in the distinction between social and physical planning.

Traditionally, *city* is defined as a municipal corporation with definite legal boundaries. It is quite common, however, to apply the same term to the total local functional community without regard to legal limits. The difference is important to the planner since, in any particular case, it determines his jurisdiction. Does his authority stop at the municipal boundary, or does it cross that line? The context of this type of disagreement about the meaning of city is typically the metropolitan area composed of independent municipalities which are disposed to resist a definition prejudicial to local autonomy.

A quite different kind of argument concerns not the political limits of the city but its nature. What is the essential substance of a city? On this question opinion divides along professional lines. For planners with a physical design background (engineers, architects), the city consists of land, buildings, and other physical facilities, that is, of material objects and their spatial relationships. For those with a background in law, education, economics, and psychology, it consists of nonmaterial objects— beliefs, values, attitudes, rules, and habits of thought and behavior.

Given the city's basic duality, it is not surprising that a distinction should have arisen between two possibilities of city planning—a "physical planning" corresponding to the "hard" material environment, and a "social planning" corresponding to the "soft" nonmaterial or institutional environment. However, the meaning of "social versus physical" grows more complex when we take into account not only the nature of the city, but the objectives of city planning, as well.

Social Justice versus Esthetic Order

In the goals and objectives sections of our plans we are so accustomed to seeing long lists of abstract nouns strung together that we often forget that they include different ideals of urban order. Two of these ideals are especially prominent. The city should be planned to satisfy the sense of beauty, and it should be planned to meet the traditional moral demand for social justice. Although not in principle opposed, the two ideals may collide in practice. Esthetic goals pursued beyond a certain point may result in an unjust city, while the drive for social justice may lead to an ugly city. In many actual cases, therefore, justice and beauty appear as competing rather than as complementary goals.

So the American city planning concept is doubly ambiguous. On the one hand it embraces different ideals—esthetic order and justice. On the other hand, it includes two different definitions of the city. The expression "social versus physical" reflects these ambiguities. In some cases it is used to distinguish between planning the "soft city" and planning the "hard city." In other cases it refers to planning for social justice and welfare as opposed to esthetic planning.

The People as Subjects versus the People as Objects

More than giving people their fair share of material benefits, justice means regarding them as subjects rather than objects, as masters of their own fate; hence the demand for various types of local power. In this context, social planning connotes power to plan locally. It stands opposed to central planning in which people appear almost as physical objects even when the planning is in their favor.

The belief that planning should be by as well as for the people is not new. In the past, the same idea was represented by the term *citizen participation*. Lately, however, it has taken a more aggressive turn in the advocacy planning movement. Some planners have been pointing out that the spatial form and structure of the community represent an aspect of social cost and benefit distribution, and that questions of urban form can no longer be excluded from the realm of political controversy. This belief, in turn, is not without its effects on the planner's conception of his social role. A decade ago he was readier to see himself as representing a public interest. Now he shows a greater sensitivity to the conflicts that spring from diversity of interest in community spatial structure. He is urged to be an advocate for the weaker parties in this conflict, which requires, first, stirring them from their lethargic state as objects to the consciousness of subjects fully aware of their own interests. Indeed, the willingness to take on this task is regarded by most advocates of advocacy as the true measure of commitment to social planning.

Institutional Reform versus Physical Design

Because it puts the stress on the soft as opposed to the hard city, there are those who are inclined to see in "social versus physical" only an attempt by the educator, the welfare worker, the lawyer, to replace the engineer, the architect, and the land-use planner as the typical urban planning experts. In this charge there may be some substance, and we will return to it shortly. On the other hand, a movement so widespread as the one under discussion can hardly be laid at the door of interprofessional politics. If the old "hard" planner is losing ground, this is mainly because the means he disposes of are no match in themselves for the problems he faces. Here, the slogan "social versus physical" proclaims a more radical approach to the problem—the substitution of institutional reform for physical design measures.

A case in point is racial and economic segregation. Segregation has many causes, but in its modern phase it appears to be one result of metropolitan growth and expansion. While technological advances have made possible the organization of life on a vastly wider geographical setting, blacks have remained pinned to the inner city by discriminatory legal and social practices as well as by natural economic forces. The result has been racial and economic segregation at a metropolitan scale. By comparison, yesterday's smaller, more compact metropolis seems preferable, since at least it kept people of different race and class in closer touch, that is, less segregated, within the same fiscal and political boundaries, the boundaries of the central city.

The old city planning was hardly a champion of racial and economic justice but, to give it its due, it was opposed to the segregation process more than is apparent because it was seldom put in those terms. Rather, it was subsumed under a more general objective: How to save the central city? Class and race segregation at the metropolitan scale are only one of the results of the break-up of the central city. At one time it seemed possible that the social and economic disruption resulting from central city decline—blight, ghettoization, municipal insolvency— might be reversed or checked by physical measures, especially urban renewal. Now it is clear that in most northern cities the process has gone beyond the point of reversal and that for metropolitan social and functional unity to be restored, physical measures are not enough; hence the call for metropolitan government, open-occupancy laws, tax reform, and the like, all of which are matters of institutional reform, of reforming the soft city, of social planning.

Space limits prevent further elaboration of the meaning of "social versus physical," but even from this brief analysis certain conclusions can be drawn. First, "social versus physical" represents not one, but many cleavages within the planning profession. Insofar as these cleavages are based on real differences of philosophy or method, no amount of word-tinkering will resolve them. On the other hand, since even to disagree constructively we need precise language, it helps to identify the issues more precisely, rather than letting "social versus physical" stand for all of them.

Second, it seems clear that much of the odium which surrounds the term *physical planning* is verbal in origin. Thus, because *physical* refers sometimes to the planning of the hard environment and other times to planning for esthetic goals, there is a tendency to identify the work of architects, engineers, and land-use planners exclusively with esthetic and other "nonsocial" objectives, for example, efficiency. This is unfortunate. No doubt their means are physical but their ends need be no less humanitarian than those of health workers, educators, or lawyers, whose means are nonphysical. Nevertheless, by a trick of language they see themselves and their professions deprived of their reputations for social usefulness.

Considering its ambiguities and invidious uses, perhaps we should drop the phrase "social versus physical" and acknowledge with Paul Davidoff that "all public planning must be considered social planning. Our concern with the nature of the physical environment is social. We do not seek to alter that environment for any reason except to benefit society" (1964, 126). Hopefully, engineers, architects, and land-use planners will work to benefit society through changes in the material environment. Lawyers, educators, health and welfare workers, and economists may seek the same goals through institutional or attitudinal changes. The former are physical planners, the latter are nonphysical planners. Both are types of social planner.

This, it seems to me, puts the matter more constructively. It avoids invidious comparisons based exclusively on profession and, at the same time, makes the physical environment a matter of concern to all planners, regardless of their social philosophy.

Note

This essay is adapted with permission from *Planning* [American Society of Planning Officials newsletter] 35 (Aug. 1969): 112–14.

References

Davidoff, Paul. 1964. "The Role of the City Planner in Social Planning." *Proceedings of the 1964 Annual Conference.* Cambridge: Conference of the American Institute of Planners.
O'Harrow, Dennis. 1967. "Claim-Jumping: A Questionable Practice." *Planning* 33 (May): 57–58.

Toward a Grammar
of Land Use Planning

In a democracy, a stable and intelligible technical language is the foundation of good planning. The ability to make oneself clear, to understand and be understood, even by average people, is the indispensable basis of trust between planners and their client, the public. Nor, without a stable language, can there be effective technical communication between the planner and other professionals. Through careful definition and classification of the various senses of the term *land use*, the following essays arrive at the rudiments of a land use planning grammar, with its various parts of speech presented in great detail in Appendixes A and B. The last essay in this section points to the generalizability of the grammar across international boundaries.

Until the late 1950s, the prevailing land use categories were simplistic and scarcely able to cope with the multiple objectives and complex data requirements of modern land use planning. The concepts expressed in "New Directions in Land Use Classification" contributed to a major advance in land use analysis. In the words of Michael Teitz, they provided "the first clear conceptualization of the dimensionality of land use." They helped prepare the way for the entry of land use planning analysis into the computer age. Multi-dimensionality is now also the basis of much current land use classification work in geographic information systems.

3

The Elements of Land Policy

Land policy is the subject of much debate, but the quality of the debate suffers because the field remains in a state of conceptual disorder. What is land policy? What are its major parts? How can these parts be further defined into topics that can be discussed, analyzed, and decided upon? The purpose here is to contribute to improved communication in land policy and planning by laying the groundwork for a comprehensive classification of its elements. As an initial step, land policy is divided into five major subtopic areas—those pertaining to the land, the land unit, the land user, the land use, and to land relationships.

The Land

To the man in the street, the term *land* means terra firma, as opposed to the air or to bodies of water from ponds to oceans; the size does not matter. For economists, however, land is a synonym for natural resources, and this is the meaning intended here. Land includes not only water, but also everything else in the world other than man-made objects and man himself—wild animals, wild plants, "wild Nature in all its varieties" (Post 1927, 29). Many years ago, Louis Post, a former American secretary of labor, offered the following unpremeditated and somewhat poetic classification of land: "Trees grow in forests, minerals repose in the earth, the soil offers itself to the farmer, the sea to the sailor, solid ground to the builder. Together with the winds, the lightning, the snow, the rain and all the other subtle and mysterious forces of Nature, those Natural Resources respond freely to the multifarious energies, the broadening knowledge of natural law and the intensifying skill of Labor" (1927, 51–52).

From a policy standpoint, the term *natural resources* is not entirely satisfactory, implying as it does that nature exists only for human use. Recently, quite a different attitude has come to the fore, one that eschews treating the land as a mere object. It regards an animal, a tree, or even a stream as also a being, albeit not human, with whom men and women

Speaking of the Land (Land as Object)	Speaking to the Land (Land as Subject)
Dividing nature into discrete objects	All forms of direct address that recognize nature as comprised of fellow creatures
Naming, counting, mapping, dating the objects	All forms of behavior evincing regard for nature for its own sake
Ascribing monetary or other utilitarian value to the objects	Sharing the earth with other species (wilderness as a land use); animal advocacy; caring for wildlife (feeding, rescuing, braking for animals); sportsmanship toward game
Prescribing actions upon the objects	

Table 3.1. Land Policy as Communication

may occasionally enter into communion. "Saying you to the land" is the way one philosopher has characterized this interpersonal relation of man and nature, a phrase derived from the "I and Thou" philosophy of Martin Buber (Buber 1970; Tallmadge 1981). St. Francis was saying "thou" when he addressed the earth's luminaries as "Brother Sun" and "Sister Moon," poetry, perhaps, or mysticism, but a policy stance toward nature, nonetheless, which policy analysts must reckon with.

It is this policy mode which underlies the current inquiries into the constitutional rights of animals, plants, and even rocks. Now we are called upon to invent or discover categories of land policy which correspond to various forms of communion with the land. The taxonomic challenges are exhilarating, but they must be taken up with much prudence and common sense.

If land classification is a kind of language or speech, then speaking *to* the land is only one of its forms. The other, and a far more influential one it has been, is speaking *of* the land. In this context, land is indeed an object to be transformed in accord with human desires and purposes. Here belong those systematic classifications of the human energies that act upon the land. Clearing forests, draining swamps, irrigating deserts, dredging rivers, and damming streams are examples. But these are land control categories in almost the muscular sense of the term. They denote actual engineering activities which serve more general social purposes.

A higher level of classification representing those purposes is also needed, such as development, redevelopment, conservation, preservation,
reclamation, and the like. Beyond these, there are the various types and
subtypes of territorial order envisioned by land policy—esthetic, ethical,
and functional order. Classification must proceed at all levels.

The idea of land policy as communication with its two major branches is set forth in table 3.1. It constitutes the broadest conceptual framework for our research.

Note

This essay is adapted with permission from *Ekistics* 51 (Jan.–Feb. 1984): 13–18.

References

Buber, Martin. 1970. *I and Thou*. New York: Scribner's.
Post, Louis F. 1927. *The Basic Facts of Economics*. Washington, D.C.: Published
    privately.
Tallmadge, John. 1981. "Saying You to the Land." *Environmental Ethics* 3 (Win-
    ter): 351–63.

4

New Directions in Land Use Classification

In a recent article devoted to the changing law of land use, the author observes that it "would be intriguing to have . . . an analysis of the emotion-laden words 'private property'" (Cribbet 1965, 278). This comment deserves more than passing notice from planners. It reminds us that our own language, as well as the language of law, is studded with terms needing clarification.

This treatise is about one ambiguous planning term—land use. It undertakes to show what meanings are involved in it for planners and to demonstrate how these meanings can be used to construct a multipurpose land use classification system more comprehensive than any now in use.

Interest in the city has always been divided between two main camps, those who want to know what a city is and how it works, and those who want to use the city to produce beneficial social results—between social scientists and social reformers. The origins of city planning are to be found in both camps. In this study, however, it will be useful to look at city planning against a somewhat different background. If we ask about city planning not "what are its historical antecedents" but rather "to what can it be compared in certain fundamental aspects of its structure," one answer is human language. In some respects language presents us with a model of planning (figure 4.1).

A typical human utterance has two components. It contains a reference to an external object or event (the sense component) as well as an attempt to evaluate the object and to influence human behavior toward it (the gesture component). The referring and gesturing components of language are not necessarily a matter of which words are used, but rather of how they are used. Even a single word can perform all the functions of language at once. For example, the word *fire* uttered in a certain way indicates an objective event, but at the same time it gestures, that is, it expresses concern, sounds and alarm, summons help, and so on.[1]

In this respect planning resembles language. This is apparent if we

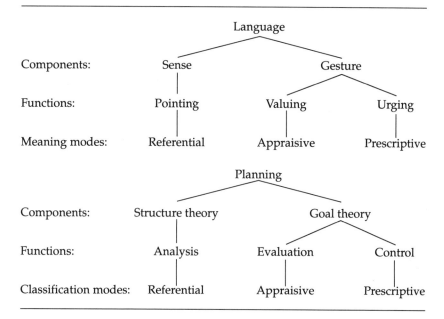

Figure 4.1. Language and Planning: A Structural Comparison

disregard for a moment its special content or subject matter and concentrate on its form and structure. Planning, too, has a sense component (urban structure theory) and a gesture component (goal theory). That is, it not only refers to a system of objects and objective relationships (the city), but it also evaluates these objects and urges people to do something about them. Like language, it analyzes (a more rigorous or scientific form of reference), evaluates, and proposes action.

Figure 4.1 throws some light on a perennial problem of planning, land use classification. In it, certain shortcomings in the current theory and practice of classification become more apparent. Language has modes—it refers, appraises, prescribes; one would expect planning, which is similar to language in its structure, to have well-developed classification modes that correspond to its major functions. However, most current land use classification schemes stay almost entirely within the bounds of a single mode—the referential. They are useful for describing or analyzing, but not for evaluating or prescribing. Consequently, the power of planners to use the full resources of their technical language is impaired.

In the remainder of this discussion, land use classification is put on a broader footing by extending it into areas where it has not yet been applied in a systematic manner, the areas of evaluation and control. "Land use" is seen successively in different lights. First, it is seen as an object or thing. Next, it appears as a set of values. Finally, it reappears as an act, or as an active planning relationship which the community takes to its own structure. Each meaning of land use is discussed in some detail, and an effort made to show how it provides the basis for a unique set of classifications.

Analysis: The Referential Mode

One function of language is to refer to an external object or event. In the case of planning language, this takes the form of reference to, or analysis of, the land use object. But what is the land use object? Or, more precisely, what is the object of land use classification? Does it consist of underlying, intangible things—economic processes, legal relationships, and the like? Or does it consist of things that can be seen, heard, touched, or smelled?

The same question can be asked about urban structure theory itself. Is it concerned with underlying causative factors—economic, social, legal, cultural? Or, is it concerned with the material effects of these factors—observable activities, facilities, and their surrounding sights, smells, and sounds? . . . It is concerned with both. The full range or scope of urban structure theory is outlined in table 4.1. Each element here is an object of interest in its own right: economic processes are the subject matter of the economic sciences; the physical framework of the city is the subject matter of architecture or of city planning conceived as architecture. Similarly, the relationships between some of these factors are areas of independent theoretical interest. . . . The broadest possible theoretical interest concerns the link between all underlying causative factors as a whole, and all tangible or material factors. The ultimate objective of urban structure theory is to explain how a world of economic and legal relationships translates itself into an actual world of sights, sounds, and hard objects in space.

The Major Elements of Land Use

The "elements" listed in table 4.1 may be thought of as being the fundamental components of the total city. However, if instead of the whole city, we take any part of it we shall find that even in the smallest part the same elements are present. Thus a single parcel is composed of a site, a site facility, a site activity, and an activity effect; these are the outward manifestations or observable elements of land use. Going deeper, we find an underlying set of legal and economic characteristics present but not directly observable. Knowledge about them can only be inferred from what is observable, or else it must be derived from other sources (as from written

Observable (caused) factors:
Adapted spaces (sites)
Physical framework (facilities)
Activity type
Activity effect (sight, sound, smell)

Underlying causative factors:
Economic processes (functions)
Legal relationships (ownership, etc.)

Table 4.1.   The Range of Urban Structure Theory

records). Both types of factor together comprise the full range of land use elements to be classified. Consequently, in the referential mode there are six subjects of land use classification: four *observable characteristics:* general site development; special site development (building type or other site facility); actual use (i.e., the type of activity on the premises); and activity characteristics (size, rhythm, realm, and material impact on the senses); and two *underlying characteristics (not directly observable):* economic "overuse" (the kind of economic function performed on the site) and type of ownership and other legal characteristics.[2]

Observable Characteristics

General Site Development

One important feature of a piece of land is what's on it, if anything. The land may have a structure on it or it may not. If it does have a structure, that structure may be temporary [in the physical, not in the economic sense] or it may be permanent (insofar as any structure can be called permanent). But if it doesn't have a structure, the parcel is not necessarily undeveloped; it may be developed or adapted in some other way, as in the case of land under cultivation. Considerations of this kind lead to a first possible classification in the referential mode, one based on general physical site development characteristics. A few suggested categories in this classification are: undeveloped land; developed land, without structure; developed land, with temporary structure; and developed land, with permanent structure.

Special Site Development (Building Type)

The classification of site development characteristics will tell whether or not a parcel of land has a building on it. This is significant because it bears upon the general availability of the parcel.[3] But the type of building, if one is present, is also a matter of interest because it indicates the form and quantity of internal space available to a user or potential user of the parcel. Hence, a second classification is desirable, one based on the building type and representing the utility of inside space, for example: hospital-type building, office building, row house, warehouse, etc.

Using such categories, it would be possible to make summaries of the total land area occupied by each type of building in a community, as well as the floor-area ratio, assessed value, or value per square foot.

Actual Use (Activity Type)

Building type limits internal activity but does not determine it. If a building did determine activity, there would be no practical need to distinguish between the two; knowing one, we would also know the other. But to some extent activities are adaptable, and perhaps each could use any building type although it would be most at home in a specific type. Familiar examples of activities "not at home" are the storefront church, the office in the loft, the embryonic industry in a household garage. By making activity a distinct subject of classification we are able to take note of what actually takes place at a site or building such as: household activity, school activity, vehicle parking, office activity, playing, etc.

These are a few categories from a third type of classification based on the element actual use. A parcel-by-parcel comparison of actual use with building type would show the degree to which the activities of a community inhabit makeshift or unsuitable space (or, similarly, the extent to which buildings have descended from original to substitute uses). In other words, it would show the extent to which the community has outgrown, or is outgrowing, its physical plant.

Activity Characteristics

Some activities pollute the atmosphere. Some generate a lot of traffic or a particular kind of traffic. Some activities draw people from an entire region; the influence of others is not felt beyond their own immediate environs. Some are daytime, others are night-time activities. We are considering here size, range, rhythm, and material impact on the human senses—characteristics of the activity at each site which make it a good or a bad neighbor to activities at surrounding sites. They are therefore the substance of many planning concerns having to do with the arrangement of the activities on the land, including zoning, neighborhood planning, and transportation planning. Each represents a distinct aspect of land use which also requires classification. The major subjects of the fourth classification, the last of the classifications concerned with the outward manifestations of land use, are: activity size, as represented by the number of people joining the activity daily, weekly, or for some long-er period of time; rhythm or time shape, the typical variation of size in the course of a day or week (e.g., the daily peak and low periods); realm or range of influence of the activity (such as neighborhood, citywide, or regional); and material effect on the human senses (such as noise, odor, or vibration).

Underlying Characteristics

Economic Over-use (Function)

Every activity which takes place on the land is carried on as part of an enterprise of some kind.[4] An enterprise may make goods, distribute them, perform a service (i.e., it has an economic function). The econom-ic function performed by an enterprise using a parcel is the economic over-use of the land as opposed to the actual use or activity. The latter can be directly observed; the former cannot. As an example of the dif-ference between these two aspects of land use consider two separate parcels on which are located two activities, both of them operated by the same manufacturing enterprise. On one parcel is a factory. On the sec-ond parcel is the company's administration building. Activity at the two sites is observably quite different. Nevertheless, both sites (as well as both activities) are employed in the service of the same manufacturing function. Or consider two parcels, side by side, with a warehouse on each. Activity is the same or similar on both, yet one is conducted by a manufacturing firm and the other by a wholesale distributor, and there-fore the economic over-use differs accordingly.[5]

The usefulness of the distinction between activity and function is apparent. First, it permits us to take account of all land employed in the service of a single economic function (e.g., retail distribution), regardless of what takes place on the land. Conversely, it enables us to take account of all the land used by a single activity type, despite the fact that the activity units or establishments serve different functions.

One of the purposes of planning analysis is to determine how much space and what kind of facilities a community will need for activities in order to perform its underlying economic functions. A parcel-by-parcel inventory of land use by both function and activity would show the kind and amount of space used by each function, would permit compar-isons among different communities in this respect, and would give some basis for deriving space and facility requirements from economic projec-tions, for example, the amount of store, storage, and office space to be expected from a given increment of wholesale trade.

These considerations warrant a separate classification of the land ac-cording to its economic over-use: manufacturing, wholesale trade, retail

Parcel	Development Status	Facility Type	Activity Type	Economic Function	Activity Characteristics			
					Size	Effect	Range	Time-Shape
W	developed, structure	multistory offices	office activity	manufacturing	medium	glare	more than local	3
X	developed, structure	produce warehouse	storage and handling	agriculture	medium	sound, odor	more than local	4
Y	developed, no structure	kiosk, pavement	parking	retail trade	large	sound	local	1
Z	undeveloped	none	play	recreation	small	sound	local	5

Table 4.2.   Patterns of Analysis

The examples show some of the ways in which the land use object can be described or analyzed (i.e., referred to). In each case, a hypothetical parcel is analyzed in terms of its more important dimensions. *Size* refers to the number of persons using the parcel daily or for some longer period. *Effect* refers to the type of impact the activity has on the surrounding environment. *Range* refers to the spatial extent of the impact. However, there is no intent here to judge the impact as being good or bad. This is the function of the appraisive mode.

The numbers in the Time-Shape column represent curves describing daily variation in the number of people and vehicles participating in the activities. The numbers are, like the activities in the table, hypothetical, as are the terms *medium, small,* and *large, local* and *more than local.* For a fuller discussion of these activity characteristic fields and their categories, see Appendix A.

Parcel W is owned by a national manufacturing company, although its activity on this site is exclusively administrative. The building is the tallest in town, and on a sunny day the flash of its glass and metal walls is noticeable to motorists at a considerable distance.

Parcel X is the in-town site of a produce warehouse operated by a large agricultural enterprise. Its effect may also be more than local, depending on wind velocity and direction.

Parcel Y is the downtown parking lot of a clothing firm. It is paved with black asphalt and has a small kiosk used by an attendant who supervises the lot during business hours.

Parcel Z is a tract of land overgrown with weeds. The lot, although vacant, performs an economic service (recreation) because it is frequently used by children and occasionally by adults for sports. It is classified in the Function column accordingly.

trade, services, agriculture, etc. But one retail distributor handles books and another handles liquor. In one service establishment hair is cut, in another clothes are cleaned. Insofar as possible, the classification should recognize the specificity of the economic over-use, thus: retail trade— food, clothing, etc.; services—hair cutting, pressing, etc.[6]

An overall view of the different subjects of land use classification in the referential mode is given in table 4.2. Each subject represents a different element of the land use object. Classified in terms of their variable characteristics, they can be used to analyze any parcel into its more important constituent elements. Many urgent planning problems are involved not so much with the individual elements as with the relationship among them.

Evaluation: The Appraisive Mode

To explain how a world of economic processes, legal relationships, and social relationships translates itself into an actual world of sights, sounds, smells, and hard objects in space is the ultimate task of urban structure theory.[7] To control these relationships in the interest of human welfare is the purpose of urban planning. Evaluation is one of the links between identifying and defining the object and controlling it. Some comments about evaluation in general will be useful in explaining the particular approach taken to land use evaluation in this section.

Value is not inherent, but depends upon the explanatory context in which an object or event is placed. Murder, for example, can be viewed in a moral context or in a medical context: Is the killer evil or sick? Depending on the answer, the attitudes evoked will be different, and the consequences for an offender will also differ. Where different evaluations of the same object or event are possible, not science but interest is [most often] the arbiter. This explains why the attempt to apply an appraisive classification, or even to construct one is often stoutly resisted. The referential mode is neutral—it simply takes an object apart (i.e., analyzes it). The appraisive mode, on the other hand, casts the object in the light of good or bad, desirable or undesirable. It touches real interests on all sides. Neither values nor interests are immutable—they change in company with changing circumstances.

Much of the material for an appraisive classification of land use already exists in the form of land use evaluation standards. These standards have their legal basis in American constitutional history, which has been a constant balancing, not only of particular interests with each other but of particular interests with the interests of the nation as a whole. The changing balance has determined which properties are looked at (evaluated) and the way they are looked at (the values applied).

Some recent history provides a good example of the effect of the shifting balance of interest. In the past two decades evaluation standards have been dominated by a single concern, the improvement of the residential environment. The great landmark in standards in this era has been the American Public Health Association's *An Appraisal Method for Measuring the Quality of Housing* (1945). This dominance is explained by the long-standing preoccupation with the problems of residential slums and slum-dwellers, a concern which has been a natural accompaniment of the industrialization process. But more recently, the effects of urban growth have been engulfing other important segments of the urban population in addition to the industrial laborers, including downtown merchants and landowners, suburbanites, industrial interests, and minority groups, all of whom have been making their concern and influence felt in the administration of national and local programs for urban relief and redevelopment.

Consequently, there has been a growing sense of the limitations of devices like the APHA technique accompanied by a demand for new ways of looking at old problems, as well as for the inclusion of some new problems into the bargain (e.g., nonresidential renewal). Formerly, it was enough to view any structure merely as a shelter for people and to judge it by its effects on health and safety. Now one sees the structure also in terms of its efficiency or inefficiency, as an element affecting the tax base and hence the well-being of the entire community. Also, there has been a deepening of interest, from concern with physical symptoms of disorder to investigation into their underlying social and economic causes. No wonder, then, that the terms *standard* and *substandard* are coming to include meanings which they never before possessed.

In this section some of these older and newer meanings are brought together in a fresh synthesis. Two noteworthy features of this synthesis are: 1) it gives equal consideration to the various public and private interests which meet in a single parcel of property, some of which have long been understated due to the continuing influence of APHA thinking; and 2) it makes a clear connection between each interest identified and the objective features of a property—both physical and nonphysical—which affect it.

The Dimensions of Land Use Value

Planning for change in an already developed area tends to make us more aware of what is wrong about a piece of property than what is right about it. Consequently, appraisal is more often conducted in negative rather than in positive terms, in terms of the substandard, rather than in terms of the standard. In both words, however, the notion of value is equally present. To say that a property is substandard is to say that it fails to measure up when judged by certain criteria. Our purpose is to discover what these criteria are so that they can be made the basis of a set of land use classifications in the appraisive mode.

If one attunes his ear to present usage, he will hear in the word *substandard* three different meanings (commingled to be sure, but distinct enough to be identified). The three meanings correspond to three general interests or viewpoints, although here, too, the correspondence is far from precise. They are: *quality* (or user benefits) in terms of overall physical condition and technological up-to-dateness; the core of the substandardness concept, it is now becoming only one dimension of a larger view; *economic durability,* representing the entrepreneurial interest in land use; and *social impact,* representing the public interest in the parcel and its use.

Quality

By quality, we mean a psychological condition as well as a physical condition, the sense of well-being or enjoyment which a user has because a facility is new, in good repair, and the last word in terms of design and equipment. Typically, this sense of well-being is lowered if the facility is old, run down or dilapidated, and lacking expected conveniences (e.g., air-conditioning). These are only a few broad categories from an appraisive classification based on quality.

As far as the hypothetical user is concerned, good quality is an end in itself, needing no further justification. The public, too, is interested in the well-being and satisfaction of its individual members. But is it justified in regarding a property as substandard if it doesn't meet the high quality standards of certain modern users of advanced taste and means? Perhaps, but there is risk in attributing substandardness to a facility solely on the grounds that it is old, of antiquated design, or lacking in modern amenities (as will be evident from the fact that such buildings are often in use, or even in great demand, and therefore can hardly be called substandard in the economic sense of the word). This brings us to a consideration of the second basic feature of a property—its economic durability.

Economic Durability

How long will the parcel continue to be useful in its present form of development? This question is of particular interest to the owner or investor. Economic durability sometimes becomes a public concern; if many properties are found to lack durability this can be seen as a threat to the community's economic base, its livelihood. Moreover, in the case of individual parcels, durability has meaning for public redevelopment action. A durable parcel, one sustained in its present state by normal market forces (not to be confused with one frozen in its present state by market impediments), is less takable than a nondurable parcel, even though the taking may be in the public interest. The durability of a parcel of property depends on the demand for a parcel of that type, or quality, or location; therefore, no one can say with any certainty that it is durable or not durable simply from an inventory of parcel characteristics and without a thorough knowledge of the local economy and its space requirements. On the other hand, it can hardly be claimed that the characteristics of a parcel have no effect on the demand for it.

One of the physical characteristics affecting demand is versatility of design. The more versatile the design of the parcel and its improvements, the greater the probable demand for it, and the greater the chances that it will continue to be useful in its present form. The importance of versatile design for durability is evident in the greater difficulty experienced—because the risk is greater—in financing even an up-to-date special purpose building such as a theater.

In addition to physical design, there are a number of other factors affecting risk. The property might be perishable (i.e., prone to destruction by fire or other causes); subject to legal disabilities (such as title defects and code violations); underserved by public facilities; and poorly located with respect to present use. These are items from an appraisive classification of land use representing economic durability.

Social Impact

In addition to possessing quality and durability, a parcel also bears some relationship to various social interests and public purposes, which is to say, it may favor these purposes or thwart them. In table 4.3 these are called "the public interest proper" because they unavoidably carry with them public responsibilities. Private individuals cannot or will not pursue them on their own since they lack the authority, or competence, or incentive to do so. The four cardinal social interests are: law enforcement; protection of non-owning property-users against loss and injury; environmental security (protection of neighboring users and their property); and conservation of social resources.

Law Enforcement   As a means of ensuring order in human affairs, law observance is a primary social interest. A property is out of order (i.e.,

Quality: The user's interest	Age, deterioration, deficient in basic utilities, lacking in modern amenities	Old, uncomfortable, outmoded
Economic Durability: The investor's interest	Physical perishability, unadaptable design, public service deficiencies, illegal status, title problems, owner incapacity (financial), poor management, local hostility to use, deleterious environment	Risky
Social Impact: The public interest proper	Nonconformity with law	Illegal
	Danger to life by fire, unsanitary conditions, otherwise unsafe, unhealthy	Unsafe, unhealthy
	Harmful material effects, unesthetic effects, antisocial effects	Costly to others
	Underdevelopment, overdevelopment, maldevelopment, maluse, site stagnation	Wasteful of social resources

Table 4.3.   Major Subjects of Land Use Classification: The Appraisive Mode

substandard), if it does not comply with the numerous codes, statutes, ordinances, regulations, and other official enactments that have to do with the physical structure of buildings, their maintenance, alteration, use, location, and occupancy regardless of the content or soundness of the enactments.

Protection of Non-Owning Property-Users against Loss and Injury   The ostensible purpose of local codes is to protect the property-user. Why, then, the distinction between code compliance and the protection of property-users? The answer is that codes have a dual purpose. On the one hand, they are meant to protect the property-user. On the other hand, they are meant to protect the owner by defining (i.e., putting a limit to) his legal responsibilities. Being a compromise between two sets of interests—those of the user and those of the owner—codes can fall short on both accounts. That is, in some respects, they may fail to give the user adequate protection, while in other respects, they may subject the owner to unfair or excessive responsibilities. Since the correspondence between legal standardness and interest of the user may be less than complete, a second look at property conditions is justified from the standpoint of actual fitness for human occupancy, rather than mere legal fitness.

Environmental Security (Protection of Neighboring Users and Their Property)   In addition to characteristics that affect its own habitability, every property has characteristics that make it a good or bad neighbor to surrounding properties (i.e., it has environmental effects). Such effects may stem from the natural features of the site (e.g., flooding), from the structure (e.g., fire hazards), or from the use of the structure (sight, sound, smell). Whatever their source, if these effects are so marked as to deprive a neighboring property of some of its value or habitability, then an uncompensated cost is imposed on a neighbor, or on the public itself, and in this sense, the offending property is substandard.

Environmental influences include moral as well as material effects. A property may be safe and sound but damaging to community morale because it is used for purposes contrary to the prevailing moral or social sentiments of the community. In one community it may be a beer parlor which offends; in another the offensive use may be a coffee house. The context has to be considered.

It will be apparent that not all forms of substandardness are structural and therefore, not all can be corrected by changing the physical make-up of the parcel. The gamut of appropriate corrective measures is much wider and includes forms of use control as well.

Conservation of Social Resources   To the society at large, even a private parcel is an asset to be conserved (i.e., used in such a way as appears likely to benefit the greatest number of people, living and unborn). The misuse of urban land can take several forms, but they are all forms of social waste, such as:

Underdevelopment: the waste of an important (e.g., central) location by
   using it for an insignificant (e.g., obsolete) service or facility;
Overdevelopment: the waste of an important facility by placing it at an insignificant (inaccessible) location;
Maldevelopment: the preemption of a rare natural or historic site by an establishment that could as well be located elsewhere;
Maluse: subjecting a historic site or facility to an unworthy use; destroy-
   ing scarce natural resources, such as topsoil, beach, etc.;
Site stagnation.

The last (site stagnation) is a special form of social waste and occurs as a
result of certain disadvantages to which an obsolete or other type of substandard property may be subject and which keep it off the market when
otherwise it might automatically (i.e., without public assistance) enter the
stream of social change. The chief factors contributing to site stagnation
are legal disabilities (as title defects); physical disabilities (as undersized
or odd-shaped lots); environmental handicaps (as excessive traffic); and
certain public or private restrictions (as zoning and covenants) which may
limit the marketability of the site. An overview of the major classes in [the
appraisive mode] is given in table 4.3. Table 4.4 illustrates the different
patterns of substandardness that individual parcels may exhibit.

Control: The Prescriptive Mode

Land use is not just something that happens "out there," of which the
community is only the passive observer. It also means an active and
purposeful replanning by the community of its own structure in order
to bring this structure into agreement with the community's goals and
objectives. Consequently, there ought to be a mode of land use classification which corresponds to this function. In fact, there is ample evidence in planning documents that such classification does exist, although in inchoate form. Here, for example, are some categories from a
typical urban renewal plan: clearance and redevelopment, housing code
enforcement, and private rehabilitation. These are categories in the prescriptive mode. They neither analyze land use into its fundamental parts
nor place it in a context of values. Instead, they classify use from the
standpoint of community action and control. The principal subjects of
classification in this mode are: the aim or end of planning action, the
means used to attain it, and the agent or actor.[8]

Ends and Means

Since our subject involves ends and means, we ought to make clear at
the outset what we mean by these words so as to avoid misunderstanding in subsequent discussion.

Parcel	Quality		Durability		Social Impact			
	Higher	Lower	Longer-term	Shorter-term	Danger to Life	External Costs	Social Waste	Market Impediments
Parcel A	x		x			x	x	
Parcel B	x			x			x	x
Parcel C		x	x		x	x		
Parcel D		x		x			x	

Table 4.4.   Patterns of Value

Parcel A, the site of a new ramp-type garage, is located on a busy thoroughfare. The long lines of cars moving in and out contribute to traffic congestion and create hazards for pedestrians. The gaping entrances mar the street facade and detract from the appearance of the street, which is a famous one. In fact, a formal community program is now under way to enhance its special character. From the standpoint of this public purpose, the garage appears substandard despite its high quality and long-term durability.

Parcel B, the site of a movie house still of good quality by modern standards. The advent of TV was a blow from which it never fully recovered, and recently it closed its doors for good. Being a special-purpose building and therefore difficult to adapt to other uses, it has remained vacant. Meanwhile, certain title problems have kept the site off the market and prevented private redevelopment. Despite the basic soundness of the structure and its modernity, the parcel is, therefore, substandard in two respects: (a) in its present form of development, it is wasteful of an important site; and (b) its redevelopment probably cannot occur without public assistance.

Parcel C is in a poor part of town and includes a ramshackle, one-story structure now used as a grocery store. The structure is bad in almost every respect—old, rundown, dirty, a fire hazard, and a neighborhood eyesore. Nevertheless, it meets a neighborhood need well, and there is little chance that its economic (and social) usefulness will soon be terminated. In this one respect, its functional role, it is quite standard.

Parcel D is the site of a large downtown office building several decades old. Inside, it lacks many of the features that tenants have come to take for granted, such as central air-conditioning, and already there are a number of vacancies. The individual air-conditioning units that protrude from some of the windows mar its otherwise pleasant exterior— the structure is built around a kind of front court. Realtors say this wastes space on expensive land, and they expect it will soon be replaced by a more efficient structure. In terms of quality and durability, the structure is substandard. However, nothing stands in the way of its replacement by private means. In this respect, it is standard.

Let us begin by distinguishing between ultimate and proximate ends. All practical social disciplines—the law, city planning, social work, etc.—have the same ultimate ends in view: to perfect the workings of human society and to promote the happiness of its individual members. Every social discipline represents but a different means to this same end. However, although all social disciplines have the same ultimate ends, each pursues them in characteristic fashion (i.e., with its own set of proximate ends). Thus, in the case of the law, the proximate end is just legal enactments; in the case of social psychiatry, it is the mental well-being of the community.

City planning is no exception in the possession of characteristic ends; one of the distinguishing features of city planning as a social discipline is that its proximate ends have always been beneficial changes in the material environment. Such changes may pertain to the site, to the site facility, to the activity which uses the site, or to the activity characteristics. What all these objects have in common is materiality. They can be touched, seen, felt, heard. Once the material or observable objects are changed in accord with some ulterior social purpose, then the city planner has made his contribution to the social welfare. Again, this is not to assert that such changes represent the end-all and be-all of his professional responsibility. City planning shares with all other social professions the ultimate goals; however, we are speaking here only of its proximate goals, and it is these which consist of material effects and which will be the first subject of classification in this section.

Types of Change

In the material or observable objects of the referential mode we have the basis for a typology or classification of planned change.

One possible object of change is the site itself (i.e., its natural features, including cover, ground water level, soil condition, and topography). Alterations in these features (site rehabilitation) by clearing, draining, grading, or landscaping change the actual or potential value of the site.

The primary object of change may also be the facility: to convert it to some other use, or to enhance its present usefulness as a human shelter or as a production facility, or both. Site readaptation (facility change) may range from the total replacement of the facility to mere surface treatment, such as cleaning and painting. Between these two extremes lie all degrees of repair, redesign, or partial reconstruction.

Change in the natural characteristics of the site, or in the site facility, may also bring about a change in how or by whom the parcel is used [activity and function]. For example, if a house is replaced by a factory, the new user will be a manufacturing enterprise rather than another family [and household activity will be replaced by factory activity, for example, heavy goods handling and processing]. However, actual use may be a more direct object of change, as in the case of the replacement of residential or religious activity in a store front, the conversion of a dump to a playground, or the extension of urban activity to areas now used for farming. In each of these cases there would be a change in the economic function (over-use) performed at the site, as well.

The user himself (i.e., his personal identity) can never be a deliberate and legitimate object of planned change, although such a change may come about as an incidental effect of other types of planned action, such as site readaptation. On the other hand, it is allowable to seek changes in operational characteristics of the parcel site which have their source in user behavior or practices, at least insofar as these practices give rise to disturbing environmental effects (noise, glare, vibration). To eliminate such effects is one of the fundamental objectives of planning action.

Not to be overlooked is the possibility of no change at all as an objective. A parcel may be left unaltered, not necessarily because it is perfect but because there is nothing to be gained by changing it in any respect.

Agents of Change

An essential function of land use classification in the prescriptive mode is to indicate not only the kinds of change required, but also how such changes are to be brought about and by whom (i.e., who is to be the responsible party, the agent of change).

In referring to agents of change the terms commonly used are *public* and *private*, but this classification is too simple. Strictly speaking, the term *public* applies only in the case of an action taken on government property, at government expense, and administered by public officials. Likewise, *nonpublic* or *private* should be reserved for cases in which there is total reliance on nonpublic initiative and resources. Only rarely, however, does a proposed action fall entirely into one class or the other. In most cases the type of agent is mixed, involving some sort of public-private interplay. This is an effect of our national constitution which divides the elements of power between people and their government, making it necessary for the two kinds of agents to come together into a working relationship.

The problem of agency classification is to find categories which express the variable nature of the relationship, the different forms it can take. Better results can be obtained by reframing the question we began with. Instead of asking, Who is the agent of change? it is more useful to ask, What means does the public agent employ in bringing about desired changes? The effect of this question is to focus attention on the possible forms of the public-private relationship rather than on the individual agents (public or private) involved.

Means of Change

Where there is only one legitimate agent—the state—all desired changes can be enforced directly. But in an economy where power is scattered, direct enforcement is often out of the question; more round-about methods have to be used. No one of these methods is entirely satisfactory, but each has an advantage which the others lack.

One way is to take a parcel into the public domain by ordinary purchase or by exercise of public sovereignty (eminent domain). However, ability to do this on a large scale is limited by law and by the inordinate expense that would be involved.

Public regulation (police power) is a second possibility, but here there are also serious limitations. If private power is to continue to mean anything, regulation has to stop at a certain point, and this point usually turns out to be short of what is required for effective control.

A third form of the public-private relationship is persuasion. Here, the object is to work on the motive of the private individual so as to confirm it in the public point of view. He is asked to believe that in the long run, self-interest is better served when it encompasses the public good. This is a doubtful proposition at best, and the subject isn't always easily convinced.

Tactics is a fourth possibility. The essential method here is not to divert the individual from his pursuit of self-interest, but rather to change the field in which he acts so that his actions are more likely to favor the public purpose. If, for example, the public purpose is to bring about the higher development of certain parcel sites now used as parking lots, tax policy may be changed so that the burden is shifted from the buildings to the land. In this case, the private agent is neither coerced nor exhorted, but the legal and economic environment conditioning his behavior is changed; in this way it is hoped that his use of the land will be altered in a manner favorable to the public purpose. The weakness of this form of public-private relationship is the difficulty of producing precise material effects using broad tactical means.[9]

Again, for the sake of logical completeness, we should include here the category: "no public means" (i.e., no public action). The latter can have either a positive significance, expressing confidence in the ability of the private sector to accomplish the desired changes, unaided and without prodding, or a negative significance meaning that the public is not able to act in any way, or is not interested in acting.

Proximate Ends (Types of Change):
No change
Change in operational characteristics
Use change (activity)
Facility change (site readaptation)
Site change (site rehabilitation)

Means of Change:
Appropriate (ordinary public purchase)
Expropriative (eminent domain)
Regulative (police power)
Persuasive
Tactical
No public action

Table 4.5.   Major Subjects of Land Use Classification: The Prescriptive Mode

A classification of parcels in terms of the categories listed in table 4.5 and in detail in Appendix B is useful for presenting the plan of action—as distinct from a goal plan[10]—for describing the landscape from the standpoint of community action and for comparing individual parcels as well as larger areas in terms of how heavy or light the public hand will weigh on them (table 4.6). In applying this scheme it would never be a matter of one parcel, one method, but rather of an appropriate mix of methods depending on the particularities of time and circumstance.

Perspectives

Having stated the basic idea and method of modal land use classification it will be helpful to look back briefly and see what has been accomplished conceptually by this system.

First, we have explored some of the dimensions of the land use concept. We have shown that it includes an element of evaluation and of action as well as of mere reference to what already exists.

With this enlarged concept as a framework we have identified at least three possible modes of land use classification.

By naming these modes and their component dimensions we have both expanded and refined the technical vocabulary of city planning. For example, for the simple term *land use classification* it is now possible to speak more precisely of referential classification, appraisive classification, and prescriptive classification.

Further, by making each mode the basis of a distinct set of classifica-

	Types of Change				Means of Change					
No Change	Operational Change	Activity Change	Facility Change	Site Change	Public Purchase	Eminent Domain	Police Power	Persuasion	Tactics	No Means
Parcel A		x	x		x					
Parcel B			x	x		x				
Parcel C		x		x				x	x	
Parcel D	x										x

Table 4.6.   Patterns of Action

By pattern of action, we mean here the combination of a specific type of material change sought (Proximate end) and a specific means for achieving it. The examples given below refer to hypothetical public actions taken with regard to the hypothetical cases used in the corresponding chart for the appraisive mode (Figure 4.4).

Parcel A is the new ramp-type garage which hampers pedestrian traffic and mars the street facade. In this case, changes are sought in both the activity and the facility, but no legal means for bringing them about exist, except ordinary purchase by the public power.

Parcel B is the good but abandoned movie house. The public purpose is to remove the house (facility change) and replace it with a sunken skating rink (involves a site change), an act which would take place normally except for the title problem. In this case, the means of change to be employed is condemnation (eminent domain).

Parcel C is the ramshackle but useful grocery store. The changes sought here are improved sanitation and safety measures (part operational and part facility change), and the means are the building code, the health code, and persuasive techniques.

Parcel D is the large downtown office building. Public policy requires no change, and consequently no means are required.

tions, we have made possible a systematic connection between the interests and concerns of planning and the form in which land use data is collected and organized.

Finally, a classification system has been presented which—in its design at least—has several of the features which would be required of a "standard" classification: it is expandable, it is flexible, and it is amenable to modern techniques of data manipulation.

It hardly needs to be pointed out that the system is still far from complete. The individual modes need stronger definition, especially the prescriptive mode which is the least developed of the three and which represents, as it were, the working edge of the system. Also, within each mode there are additional subdimensions to be defined and classified, such as the dimensions of ownership in the referential mode.

Looking further ahead, we must consider the possibility that there are yet other meanings at work in the land use concept which need to be identified. For example, nothing has been said in this study about the ideal element in land use and land using, sometimes badly represented by the term *urban form*. We have considered how a particular parcel might run afoul of certain interests, but beyond merely ceasing to offend, how can it be asked to excel? One can imagine a classification mode whose function would be to evoke or project the ideal element, although what its categories would be and how they would apply to individual parcels is harder to determine.

A final point concerns the limitations of this system as a kind of machine for automatic decision making, a function which, as it now stands, it can never perform. That is, one cannot automatically derive evaluations from descriptions or prescriptions from evaluations. There is a missing part which only the system user can supply.

An illustration will make this point and the reason for it clearer. Let us refer to Parcel C (the ramshackle grocery) in table 4.4. We have said that the structure is bad in every respect. But does it necessarily follow that the structure should be removed (i.e., "cleared")? Not at all, for we have also ascribed to this hypothetical structure a useful neighborhood function. It performs an irreplaceable social and economic service. Following one path in the evaluation process we may wish to clear the structure. Following the other path we may wish to retain it. Thus it will be seen that evaluations, although necessary for a determination of the course of action, are not sufficient. To act, one first has to weigh (i.e., to compare in terms of their relative importance) a number of possibly conflicting values. This higher evaluation is the essence of policymaking. It may be built into the system in the form of weights attached to individual items in the appraisive classification of land use, but only by the policymaker.

Notes

This study was originally published as a monograph by the American Society of Planning Officials in 1965. It is adapted with permission. It includes material that appeared in "A Multiple Land Use Classification System" (1959).

1. The basis for this statement on the functions of language can be found in a host of writings in linguistic theory, but I have relied most heavily on the works of C. K. Ogden and I. A. Richards (1938) and Charles Morris (Morris 1946, esp. 60–91).

2. No classification of ownership is provided here. To the author's knowledge, no satisfactory classification of ownership has yet been devised. [The remainder of this exposition of classification in the referential mode is derived from an earlier publication (Guttenberg 1959).]

3. The natural characteristics, legal characteristics, and economic development characteristics of a site often affect its availability more importantly than do its physical development characteristics. Some of the legal and economic aspects of site availability are covered in the sections "Evaluation: The Appraisive Mode" and "Control: The Prescriptive Mode," which follow.

4. In the case of residential activity or residing, the enterprise is a family or private household; in the case of play activity on a public playground, the enterprise is the community itself.

5. The distinction between the outward manifestations of an act (which are directly observable) and the underlying characteristics of the same act (those which are not directly observable) is a valid one and necessary for a full description of the act. Consider two persons sitting side by side, both of them typing. One is typing invoices, while the other is writing a poem. They are engaged in the same activity (typing), but they are performing different functions. The common activity can be directly observed, but the differing functions cannot.

6. The terms *pressing* and *haircutting* specify different economic functions performed. They should not be mistaken for types of activity. For a functional classification with different degrees of specificity see *Standard Industrial Classification Manual* (1957).

7. This section is based on a more detailed discussion found in an earlier work (Guttenberg 1964).

8. A fourth subject, the timing of the programming of specific actions, is omitted here because I have not been able to find a way of classifying it meaningfully.

9. It should be noted that the same or similar means of change are possible without public involvement. Thus a private individual or group may purchase a parcel in order to reshape it in accord with some public or private purpose. Or something like eminent domain can be used. A substantial number of states have legislation which makes the condemnation power available to a private redevelopment group when it is needed to compel the "holdout" to sell his property to such a group. Owners or occupants are sometimes held to certain standards of practice or behavior by deed restrictions, covenants, by leasing terms, or by the requirements of lending and insuring institutions. This represents a kind of regulatory power in private hands analogous to the police power. Private persuasive measures may range all the way from verbal inducement to setting an example with one's own property.

10. For a more complete discussion of an "action plan" versus a "goal plan," see the essay entitled "The Tactical Plan" in this volume.

References

American Public Health Association, Committee on the Hygiene of Housing. 1945. *An Appraisal Method for Measuring the Quality of Housing: A Yardstick for Health Officers, Housing Officials and Planners.* New York: A.P.H.A.

Cribbet, John E. 1965. "Changing Concepts in the Law of Land Use." *Iowa Law Review* 50 (Winter): 245–78.

Guttenberg, Albert Z. 1959. "A Multiple Land Use Classification System." *Journal of the American Institute of Planners* 25 (Aug.): 143–50.

———. 1964. "New, Old Criteria Explored in Search of Means of Evaluating Non-residential Properties." *Journal of Housing* 21, no. 2, 73–79.

Morris, Charles. 1946. *Signs, Language and Behavior,* 60–91. Englewood Cliffs: Prentice-Hall.

C. K. Ogden, and I. A. Richards. 1938. *The Meaning of Meaning.* New York: Harcourt, Brace.

U.S. Bureau of the Budget. 1957. *Standard Industrial Classification Manual.* Washington, D.C.: U.S. Government Printing Office.

5

Toward an International Classification of Land Use Planning Information

I came to the Netherlands a few months ago to study efforts by West European nations to improve their technical communications in land use planning matters. One phase of this inquiry concerns the prospects for developing a uniform classification of land use and land use planning information. The adoption of a standard system, if it could be achieved, would constitute more than a technical step forward; it would also be a significant political act insofar as it would contribute to common understanding and therefore to common action.

My work entails the collection and comparison of systems for classifying land use and land use information which are already in use or in the process of development. I hope to produce an inventory of these systems classified by various characteristics such as their scales, purposes, and subject matter.

Le Corbusier once used an arresting phrase. He spoke of the "poetry of classification." Too many [land use] classifications are devoid of poetry. Their categories are ill-defined and ambiguous. They appear to be dominated by short-term purposes, or by purposes other than land use planning acquired by incorporating what is immediately available. Expediency is the principle governing their construction. Classifications are supposed to be useful, but they also have another function, which is to reveal and clarify the nature of the subject or object classified, and it is in this sense that so many contemporary land use classifications fail to be poetic. Not aiming beyond usefulness, they end up by not even being useful.

Once having experienced the disorder, it is difficult not to ask, What is good order in the classification of land use information? This is a question which ought to be addressed by every serious researcher in the field.

Land Use Planning as Information

Since our subject is land use planning information, let us begin with a definition of land use planning and examine its relation to information.

There are many approaches to a definition of land use planning but perhaps the best approach is to ask what land use planners do. Ideally, they do three things. They engage in a study of existing objects and objective relationships: land use sites, the buildings or other equipment on the sites, the human activities in and around the buildings, and the environmental effects of the activities. They examine these objects and relationships from the standpoint of their effect on community goals and purposes. And if they find that the objects and relationships do not agree with community objectives, then they may proceed to change them. That is, land use planning is a form of social action which, like most of its other forms, consists of three clearly definable functions: scientific description and analysis, social evaluation, and social control.

A further step in the clarification of the meaning of land use planning is to understand that not only is it a form of social action, it is also action which achieves its effect through the use of signs and symbols. That is, land use planning is a language [see the preceding essay]. Ordinarily, we do not think of planning as language, and yet what else do planners use as tools of their trade if not words, mathematical notations, graphs, and lines on maps? These are all signs which are used either to represent existing reality or to give directions for changing that reality.

Insofar as land use planning is a language, it is also information. This is by no means to contend that to convey information is the only function of language. For example, when we meet a great person in the street, it would be difficult to argue that the salutation *hello* is information. On the other side one would be hard put to show that the conveying of information is not the main purpose of language, especially of technical language.

Language can be classified according to the various informational functions it performs. When a word, a number, or some other sign is used to refer to an existing object without attempting to evaluate that object or to change it, let us call that word *referential information*. When a word, or number, or some other sign is used to evaluate the object (as good or bad, safe or dangerous, ugly or beautiful), let us call it *appraisive information*. And when a word, or number, or some other sign is used to prescribe a change in the object or the situation of which it is a part, let us call the word *prescriptive information*. The three types of information are present in most instances of planning communication.

To illustrate, consider a simple sentence from land use planning about a fictitious restaurant called the Oval Barn: "The Oval Barn, this corner restaurant of Smith's, although very unsafe, is an architectural rarity; it ought to be repaired and preserved."

This is not the only type of sentence produced by planners, but it is one of the most familiar. At the present level of abstraction, what is significant in the sentence is not the specific words but the structure. "Residence" might replace "restaurant," "Jones's" might replace "Smith's," "a traffic hazard" might replace "unsafe," "removed" might replace "repaired." The sentence can sustain any number of such substitutions without a change in its structure, that is, its meaning. From a structural standpoint it can be resolved into three main information areas, thus:

> *Referential*
> The Oval Barn, this corner restaurant of Smith's,
>
> *Appraisive*
> although very unsafe, is an architectural rarity;
>
> *Prescriptive*
> it ought to be repaired and preserved.

The function of the first part is simply to refer to an object; the function of the second part is to evaluate the object in the light of social goals and purposes; the function of the third part is to prescribe, that is, to specify an appropriate action to bring a facet of the object into line with these purposes.

Just as the total sentence can be analyzed into three broad informational areas, so each area can be broken down into more specific informational fields, thus:

> *Referential*
> /The Oval Barn / this corner / restaurant / of Smith's/
>   (1)   (2)   (3)   (4)
>
> *Appraisive*
> /although very / unsafe, is an architectural rarity/
>   (6)   (5)
>
> *Prescriptive*
> /it / ought to be / repaired and preserved/
> (8)   (9)   (7)

The referential area includes at least four information fields. In our sample sentence the term *Oval Barn* represents the first of these fields, the nominative field. It names the use. Private dwellings only occasionally have names, but the naming of public or commercial uses is common practice (e.g., Mauritshuis, Hotel Centrale, etc.). At first sight it

seems unlikely that the mere name of a land use could constitute significant information, but for some purposes names are among the primary
means of identifying land uses, as any local tourist map will verify. In
referring to land uses, names also provide the single most important
link between the planner or other expert and the "man in the street," a
consideration not to be overlooked in an era which places such great
stress on communication and participation.

The locative field (2) is represented by *corner*. It locates the use in
space. How best to locate a use is still a matter of considerable research
and discussion among land use information specialists. Some of the alternative methods used or proposed are location by street address, by
coordinates, or by grid cell.

Referential field (3) is the substantive field, for identifying the land
use type. For illustrative purposes I have used the word *restaurant*, indicating a type of activity. Activity type, however, is only one of the substantive aspects of land use. A second aspect is the type of building
which houses the activity. A third is the economic function performed
by the activity (e.g., wholesale trade, retail trade, business service, etc.).
The environmental effects of the building and the activity (sound, odor,
traffic, etc.) must be counted among the substantive dimensions of the
land use.

Field 4 is the possessive field represented by *of Smith's*. To whom does
the use belong? Is Smith the owner, or the operator of the restaurant, or
both? Here "belong" is shorthand for that bundle of rights that informs
a use and which may be distributed among numerous "owners," including the public. One of the principle desiderata in the field of land use
information is a systematic and comprehensive classification of the legal characteristics of a use.

With the Field 5 we enter the appraisive area of the sentence. The
function of this field is qualitative, that is, it specifies the quality or value of the use, not only in monetary terms or from the owner's or operator's point of view but also from the standpoint of the user (convenience, comfort, amenity) and from that of the public in general (service
costs, environmental impacts, etc.). In our example, the Oval Barn is a
danger to its users, but is of great esthetic value to the public. This illustrates how land use evaluations can conflict.

Field 6 is a quantitative field. Not only is the Oval Barn unsafe, but it
is very unsafe. In place of *very*, numerical data might appear which
quantifies the degree of unsafeness.[1]

Field 7 is the main field in the prescriptive area of the sentence, the
active field. It states or proposes a remedial or preventive action. The
phrase *repaired and preserved* is a stand-in for all the types of action that

might be taken with respect to a use. With regard to a building, action might range all the way from complete replacement to mere surface treatment (e.g., cleaning, painting, etc.).

In the case of the Oval Barn, it is the building which is to be preserved, not necessarily the activity ("restaurant"). Action, however, need not be directed exclusively to the site facility (the building). It might additionally or alternatively be directed to the site itself (clearing, draining, grading, landscaping), or to the activity which uses the site. For want of a better term I have named that part of our sentence which contains this information the objective field (8), since it specifies those facets of the use which are the direct object of action.[2]

Field 9 is auxiliary to Field 7 in that it represents the time and mood of the action. The building "ought to be" repaired. This is quite different from stating that it "must be" repaired. The following is a tentative classification of tenses plus moods which pertain to land use actions:

1. Indicative: states a fact
   past (was repaired)
   present (is being)
   future (will be)
2. Optative: expresses a wish or desire
   past (ought to have been repaired)
   present and future (ought to be)
3. Imperative: expresses necessity
   present (must be repaired)
   future (shall be)
4. Indeterminative: expresses uncertainty
   past (may have been repaired)
   present (perhaps can be)
   future (perhaps will be)

These classes are familiar grammatical distinctions, yet they are important types of information which planners or other land use specialists may wish to convey to each other or to various publics concerning land use actions. In this sense they constitute land use information.

The major types of land use information are summarized in table 5.1.

Good Order in Land Use Planning Information

Suppose it is now agreed that there are three types of land use planning information. One might still wonder what is special about this classification. Why does its use constitute "good order"? After all, there are many possible logical divisions of the subject.

It is not enough for a land use planning information system to be log-

Field	Function
Referential:	
Nominative	Names the use
Locative	Locates the use
Substantive	Identifies the use types
Possessive	Identifies legal characteristic of use
Appraisive:	
Qualitative	Evaluates the use
Quantitative	Quantifies the use
Prescriptive:	
Active	Prescribes a remedial or preventive action
Objective	Specifies the target of action
Mood and Tense	Conveys mood and indicates time of action

Table 5.1.   Some Major Land Use Information Fields and Their Functions

ical. It must put data in a form which corresponds to the logic of planning. The system introduced here meets this requirement. It is not arbitrary. It is not imposed on planning. The tripartite classification corresponds to the functions of planning as evidenced in the planner's own language. The most I have done is to make this underlying structure more visible by bringing it to the surface. With this step the basis for a conscious grammar of planning is laid down, and further development of the grammar can proceed with the building up of a systematic vocabulary for each of its parts of speech.

On the one hand, the classification must conform to the logic of planning. On the other hand, it must respect the richness and semantic variety in its subject, land use. Too many would-be land use classifiers have failed because they have resisted this variety rather than accepting it gracefully and allowing it to determine the form and content of the land use classification system. Of what use is it to insist, as some do, that land use "really means" only "the activities that make use of the land," while many of the words they use to denote these "activities" refer instead to the type of building located on the land, the economic function represented by the buildings and activities, and the form of land tenure?[3] Better to recognize at the outset that we are dealing with a multidimensional concept, and to provide taxonomic space for each of its dimensions than to lay the term *land use* down upon a procrustean bed and lop off those meanings which do not fit an arbitrary definition.

Referential	Appraisive	Prescriptive
Substantive	*Qualitative*	*Active*
Dwelling	Unsafe	Demolish
School	Obsolete	Renovate

Table 5.2. Multidimensional Land Use Classification: An Example

There is yet another sense in which the classification of land use and land use information can display good order. It must contribute to the realization of the ideals of the day, or at least it must not stand in the way of those ideals.

In the democratic West, perhaps the most important social contribution that classification can make is to put land use data in a form which renders it serviceable to the greatest number of potential users. This is another requirement which many classifiers have been slow to recognize. In land use planning it is not uncommon to find as the basic elements in the classification system categories such complex classes as: unsafe dwellings to be demolished; or obsolete school buildings to be renovated.

Such classes may be perfectly adequate to the purpose at hand. One must foresee, however, the time when new purposes and new users will come along requiring information, for example, not only about unsafe dwellings to be demolished and obsolete school buildings to be renovated, but also about unsafe dwellings to be renovated and obsolete school buildings to be demolished. Eventually, the classification system may have to be revised to include eight classes: unsafe dwellings to be demolished; unsafe dwellings to be renovated; obsolete school buildings to be demolished; obsolete school buildings to be renovated; unsafe school buildings to be demolished; unsafe school buildings to be renovated; obsolete dwellings to be demolished; and obsolete dwellings to be renovated.

Time, energy, and money might be saved if, at the outset, one were to set up three parallel classificatory dimensions corresponding to the three information areas and their appropriate fields, allowing the users to specify their own, more complex, classes as needed (table 5.2).

The ordering principle in table 5.2 may be described as multidimen-

Referential		Appraisive	Prescriptive
(Locative)	*Substantive*	*Qualitative*	*Active*
(center)	dwelling	unsafe	demolish
(periphery)	school	obsolete	renovate
(suburbs)	(fire station)	(badly located)	(no action)

Table 5.3. Multidimensional Land Use Classification: An Expandable System

sional classification by the smallest meaningful units in the language. If it becomes necessary to enrich the language (expand the information handling capacity of the system), this can be accomplished with minimum disturbance by adding new units to existing dimensions or by adding entirely new dimensions. Words in parentheses in table 5.3 represent either new units or new dimensions.

This example allows us to glimpse what is involved in the structure of land use information classification systems (i.e., the complex relationship between its structure, its cost, its service capabilities, and its political implications). No one can be certain about such things but, on the face of it, the first method appears more authoritarian. It confronts all users with a rigid system that can only be modified at great cost. The superiority of the second method lies in its suppleness, its inherent capacity to respond to the needs of many users. Thereby, it promises the individual user greater representation in land use planning matters. In a sense it increases the chances of speaking for oneself rather than being spoken for by a central authority.

Finally, there is the responsibility to devise systems with an eye to the possibility of cooperation in classification; I would put the stress on the need for international cooperation. The essence of cooperation is communication. It is not simply that planners in different countries speak in their own national tongues. They also speak different dialects of the same technical language. If these dialects are to be harmonized, they first have to be compared. I would contend that the foregoing analysis provides the required meta-categories for the job. For example, how do English, Dutch, French, and German planners refer to (name, locate, typify) land use in their respective countries? What appraisive categories do they employ for designating its adequacy to the owner, the user, and the public? What are the principal prescriptive categories for effecting change? The comparative analysis of land use classifications could lead not only to a refinement and extension of classificatory systems in each country, but also new insights on all sides as we learn each other's planning language. Such an enterprise must constitute the first step toward a workable international classification system. The task would no doubt be long and laborious, but not until it is underway can we look forward to a new era of international land use planning.

Notes

This essay is adapted with permission from the Proceedings of the Conference of the Gesellschaft für Klassifikation, Frankfurt-Hoechst, Germany, April 7, 1978. I wish to thank my colleagues of the Afdeling der Geodesie, Technische Hochschule, Delft, The Netherlands—M. Bogaerts, M. Creusen, and A. van Lamsweerde—for their helpful and insightful comments as it was being prepared. The theme of the conference was cooperation in classification.

1. Field 5 is only one of several possible quantitative fields. A quantitative field may also be associated with each of the following substantive dimensions of land use: the site itself (size); the building on the site (height, volume, floor space, percent of lot covered, etc.); the activity using the building (number of people, etc.); and the environmental impact of the building and activity (e.g., sound decibels, etc.).

2. There is also a range of means to remedy or prevent a land use deficiency, such as persuasion or compulsion of the owner or user or the employment of social and economic incentives. These constitute classes in an additional field of the prescriptive area which are not represented in the illustrative sentence. For a detailed classification of this field, see Appendix B.

3. Americans took the wrong road in 1966 by arbitrarily restricting the meaning of land use to one of its dimensions—"Man's activities on the land which are directly related to the land"—thereby excluding development status, physical adaptation of the site, and tenure (see Clawson and Stewart 1966).

Reference

Clawson, Marion, and Charles L. Stewart. 1966. *Land Use Information: A Critical Survey of U.S. Statistics Including Possibilities of Greater Uniformity.* Washington, D.C.: Resources for the Future.

What Is a Region?

The term *region* is another name for *unit of land*. So defined, the term can denote anything from a single urban lot to the whole planet, although it is rarely applied to any land unit smaller than a metropolitan area.

Regions are described by drawing lines on maps, a process called regionalization. When a social scientist, a planner, a public administrator, or, indeed, an ordinary citizen delineates a region, this is not an aimless act. He or she has a purpose in doing so. Moreover, not all regions are drawn for the same purpose. The classification of regions, therefore, must begin with the classification of purposes. The essay that follows identifies four purposes and their corresponding types of region: scientific description, environmental evaluation in terms of human well-being, social control, and the invoking of an ideal societal objective. It is followed by an essay that explores the dynamic relations among these basic motives and the manner in which their interactions structure time and space.

6

Classifying Regions

What is a region? I have had trouble enough with
ecosystems, and I must admit I can't find much of a
definition of regions either. I went back to Richard
Hartshorn [sic] and he tells me that a region is
essentially what you want it to be. You can have
regions of all kinds and for all purposes.

—Edward H. Graham

These are exciting times for regional scholars. The world's spatial order
is breaking up and reforming itself along new lines. Consequently, the
opportunities for observing the processes of region-formation have rarely been so favorable.

The causes of this activity are well known: advances in transportation
and communication technology; the new environmentalism; the emergence of transnational social and economic institutions; and the revival
of political localism. These are but a few of the forces acting to erase old
boundaries and to establish new ones more in keeping with changing
societal goals. Among the most challenging tasks now facing regional
students are to inventory the new regions and to classify them; also, to
understand how they will interact with each other, henceforth, so as to
transform the structure of social, economic, and political space.

The conceptual spadework necessary for these tasks has already been
in progress for some time. Geographers, in particular, have given much
thought to the clarification of the basic language and concepts of regional studies. For a sample, see Bunge (1966), Cohn (1966), Schwartzberg
(1966), and Minshull (1967).

Two areas of inquiry are of central importance to this study. One is the
meaning of "region." Is it a real or an artificial unit? The other is how to
classify regions. From a taxonomist's standpoint, of course, these subjects are intimately connected, since the first requirement of any taxonomy is a clear conception of the taxonomic unit (i.e., the object to be classified). Where this is lacking, the search for order can only be a blind and
fumbling process.[1]

The substance and method of regional classification depends very much, therefore, on the answer to a basic ontological question. Are regions real objects in nature, or are they merely convenient abstractions—artificial entities which originate and disappear with the temporary purposes of the people who invent or use them? Although this question is still a matter of considerable disagreement, the weight of opinion seems to lie on the side of those who hold that "region" denotes primarily a device for the purpose of studying or dealing with some portion of the earth's surface. Let the purpose change, and the region will change with it.

The man who formulated this answer most neatly and most influentially was the geographer Derwent Whittlesey (1954, 30). A region is neither "self-determined nor nature-given. It is . . . an entity for the purposes of thought, created by the selection of certain features that are relevant to an areal interest or problem and by the disregard of all features that are considered irrelevant."[2]

The significance of Whittlesey's definition, if one accepts it, is twofold. First, it resolves the ontological argument in favor of the abstractionists: regions are mental constructs not natural objects. Second, his definition shifts the locus of the taxonomic problem from the natural world to the realm of human purpose. For if regions are products of areal interests, it follows that one approach, perhaps the most profound approach, to a classification of regions, is by way of a classification of the human purposes and areal interests that have produced them. This is not to contend that all or even most scholars have reached Whittlesey's conclusion, only that it is a logical consequence of the proposition that regions are "intellectual concepts."

Whittlesey himself began to identify and relate modes of areal interest to regional studies in a manner suggestive of the regional classification system which constitutes our main subject.

All regional geography appears to reach its objective through one or another of three modes of operations. 1. Academic study, for the sake of understanding the present state of a region and so much of its past as contributes to that understanding. . . . Scientific curiosity prompts such a study, and it may be formalized . . . as follows: where A is found, x, y, and z are also present. . . . 2. Practical study of the present state of a region, with a view to prospects of impending or current change, and possibilities for alteration. . . . The elements are associated in the region according to the formula: if A is wanted, full account must be taken of x, y, and z; change made in A may also alter x, y, and z. The conclusions result in prescription in anticipation of alteration (either prevention or improvement). The findings constitute materials helpful to the engineer or planner. . . . 3. Prejudged study of . . . a region with the avowed intention of altering it along preconceived lines. Reform is the underlying motive of study. . . . The elements formulated run as follows: A ought to be wanted, therefore, x, y, and z must be bent to achieve A. . . . Geopolitik is the best known example of this attitude. Its generalizations have no reliable relation to truth. (57–58)

Curiously, Whittlesey stopped short of deriving types of regions directly from his modes of geographic study. From the above it will be evident that he continued to regard regions as preexistent entities—subject to these study-modes but not produced by them, even though this contradicts his own pronouncement in the same chapter that regions are essentially "intellectual concepts." Others have also noted this inconsistency in Whittlesey's thinking (Minshull 1967, 121–22). Yet, to this writer's knowledge, no one has resolved it satisfactorily.

The intent here, therefore, is to take up the question of the relation of regions to types of human thought and purpose where Whittlesey left it more than twenty years ago. Our argument, briefly, is as follows: 1) the modes of geographic study do not operate on regions, they create regions; and 2) the primary task of regional taxonomy, therefore, is to correlate the diverse spatial entities (regions) found in the literature of regional studies with their generating modes of thought and human purpose.

The argument requires us, first, to demonstrate the existence of a basic set of human functions or purposes (i.e., "areal interests") underlying the processes of regionalization. This is attempted in the following section, with the aid of an elementary model of human behavior and of language as a form of symbolic behavior. Our analysis, if correct, indicates that the act of delineating a region involves the performance of one or more of a group of four symbolic functions. In the third section, four types of regions are identified which correspond to these functions. Our analysis does not rule out the possibility of other symbolic functions—therefore, of other types of regions—but the four identified here appear to be the major ones. Examples of regions of each type are presented and discussed.

Human Behavior, Language, and Regional Studies[3]

Biologists tell us that one of the distinguishing characteristics of life is irritability. Touch an organism and it responds. It finds the stimulus rewarding or threatening and reacts (adapts) accordingly. In the human organism, speech frequently accompanies the response. Later, in order to recall the experience or to communicate it to others, we may speak without acting. Thus speech, which in the first instance accompanied the act, becomes a symbolic substitute for action.

The elemental structure of behavior and its relation to language is further specified in figure 6.1. Corresponding to the two fundamental phases of human behavior—stimulus and response—are four basic behavioral functions.

First is the curiosity-satisfying function of merely exploring the environment (stimulus), with the senses represented by the term *seeing*—although *touching, hearing,* or *tasting* would serve as well. Regardless of the sense modality involved, the relevant question in this phase of the act is simply, What is it? When seized on by the human intellect, this question is capable of elaboration into scientific knowledge.

A second phase of behavior is becoming more than intellectually interested in the environment (i.e., judging its significance for good or harm), represented by the term *caring*. Here the relevant question is, What does it portend for me?

A third phase is taking some appropriate adaptive action. Thus, we attempt to perpetuate the good or, as the case may warrant, to eliminate the danger (*doing*).

A fourth phase of human behavior, perhaps at a higher level, consists of imagining the world (the environment) transformed in accordance with some esthetic, moral, or political ideal.

All of the above may occur simultaneously. Nevertheless, they are conceptually separable.

Human language parallels behavior. Just as the latter is reducible to two fundamental elements, stimulus and response, so a typical human utterance has two components: a reference to an external object or event (pointing) and a symbolic response (valuing and urging action). Pointing, valuing, and urging action are the ultimate bases of three modes of discourse: scientific, normative, and technical.

Ordinarily, one does not think of highly developed pursuits, such as physics, the law, or regional studies, as forms of language. Yet, the learning which constitutes the special expertise of each of these disciplines consists of symbols—words, mathematical notations, lines on maps, and the like—used to describe some aspect of reality or to give directions for changing reality. These different languages, moreover, can be distinguished from each other insofar as they stress one or another of the basic language functions. Thus, the pure sciences (e.g., theoretical physics and theoretical biology) restrict themselves insofar as possible to the referential function. Their objective is simply to comprehend the world, not to evaluate it or change it. The pure sciences are to be contrasted with fields such as ethics or the law, in which the gesturing functions of language predominate (evaluation and prescription).

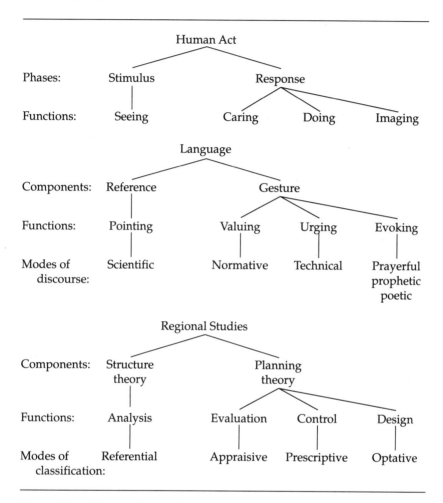

Figure 6.1. Human Action, Language, and Regional Studies: A Structural Comparison

Most fields of human endeavor are not so specialized. They retain all of the functions of language. So it is with regional studies. It endeavors not only to describe and analyze an environment of natural and cultural phenomena with respect to their spatial organization (regional structure theory), but it also evaluates these phenomena and attempts to control them for pragmatic as well as for ideal social purposes (regional planning).

Mode	Relevant Spatial Phenomena	Basis of Regional Definition	Examples
Referential	Past, present, and future natural and cultural features	Disinterested observations	Physiographic regions (e.g., Great Plains) Economic regions (e.g., Cornbelt) Projected urban regions
Appraisive	Territorial quality of life indicators (economic, social, environmental) poverty, pollution, natural hazards	Evaluations	Poor regions (e.g., Appalachia) Polluted regions Regions of seismic or other natural risk (e.g., California)
Prescriptive	Types of territorial control exercised or proposed (e.g., preservation, conservation, reclamation, reservation)	Remedial or preventive rules of action	National forests National parks, and monuments Grazing districts Managed coastal zones Indian reservations
Optative	Types of ideal territorial order envisioned (esthetic, moral, political)	Aspirations	Pearcy's ideal 38-state U.S. The world as "Global Village" and/or "Space-ship Earth"

Table 6.1.   Modal Regions

Modal Regions

The basic language functions are the ultimate sources of the four modes of regional study and of their corresponding types of region, as indicated in the first and last columns of table 6.1. Each mode will be discussed in turn.

Referential Regions

This term denotes those regions that are the products of scientific inquiry. Here *scientific* signifies that the primary object of the inquiry is to discover order in the human and nonhuman environments, as distinguished from attempting to reshape those environments in line with particular values and purposes.

Not surprisingly, many classes in the referential mode reflect the organization of science itself. Corresponding to the division of science into its two great branches, natural science and social science, there are natural regions and sociocultural regions. Natural regions include the physiographic and biotic regions (flora and fauna). Sociocultural regions include the economic, political, and religious regions. *Nodal* and *uniform* are also designations in the referential mode used to characterize certain regions according to their internal composition and structure. These, too, are well known to regional students and need not detain us here.[4]

The idea of a linguistically based classification system suggests the use of tense (i.e., time distinction) as a taxonomic factor. Tense can help dispel the ambiguity that plagues the language of regional studies. For example, the term *past referential* should be used to denote cultural regions that have ceased to exist. These are commonly referred to as historical regions. Past referential is to be preferred, since it places the region totally in the past, whereas *historical* may also imply origin in the past but continuance into the present. The territories once occupied by now extinct or relocated Native American tribes are instances of past referential regions of the cultural variety.

The use of tense can also help distinguish between two other types of regions that are frequently confused: 1) the regions that one day will exist, given the continuance of present trends (e.g., the West Coast megalopolis projected by Pickard and shown in figure 6.2); and 2) the region that some people believe ought to exist because it would embody their vision of the good life. Both are vague, not-yet-existent spatial entities. Yet they differ radically with regard to their sources in language and behavior. The former is a future referential region, while the latter is not a referential region at all. It is a region in quite another mode—the optative mode—which will be discussed later.

Appraisive Regions

In a growing number of studies, the relevant areal interest is not the scientific description and analysis of spatially variable natural and cultural features of the environment, but the evaluation of these features from

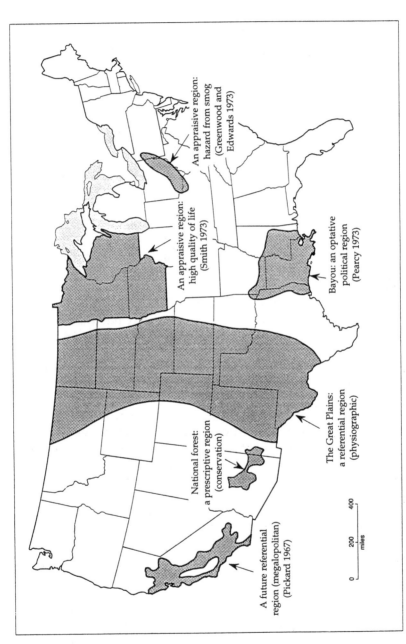

Figure 6.2. Selected U.S. Regions in Various Modes

An appraisive region: hazard from smog (Greenwood and Edwards 1973)

An appraisive region: high quality of life (Smith 1973)

Bayou: an optative political region (Pearcy 1973)

National forest: a prescriptive region (conservation)

The Great Plains: a referential region (physiographic)

A future referential region (megalopolitan) (Pickard 1967)

0   200   400
miles

the standpoint of human welfare. Such studies are in the appraisive mode.

Appraisive studies may yield appraisive regions. One well-known example is the set of economic development areas defined by the U.S. Department of Commerce—New England, the Coastal Plains, Appalachia, the Ozarks, the Upper Great Lakes, the Old West, the Pacific Northwest, and Four Corners. These regions were said to be characterized by "the persistence of gnawing poverty, stubbornly high unemployment rates, inadequate education and skills, racial and ethnic tensions, shabby housing, glaring transportation needs and, in general, wretched misuse of human and natural resource potential" (Levin 1968, 66). The emotive qualifiers—*gnawing, glaring, wretched,* and so on—are sufficient to indicate the appraisive nature of these entities.

With the distinction between referential and appraisive regions, a certain movement and direction in the field of regional studies becomes more apparent. Appraisive regions have not always been in vogue. They owe their current prominence in large part to the social-indicators movement, which is a legacy of the social upheaval of the 1960s. Like other scholars, geographers and regional scientists have been responding to the demand for social sensitivity in their scholarly activities.

Geographer David M. Smith begins his inquiry into territorial social indicators "with the assumption that there is a dimension of human existence called social well-being, and that the people living in a specific area can be meaningfully differentiated from those living in other areas with respect to this dimension." As Smith notes, "the concept of social well-being comes close to that of 'the quality of life'" (1973, 7). One comparatively well-off region, according to Smith, comprises the states of Iowa, Minnesota, and Wisconsin (figure 6.2).

Following hard on the heels of the social-indicators movement came the new environmental awareness. This movement has engendered two types of appraisive region. The first is the natural hazard region, illustrated in the work of the Canadian geographers Kenneth Hewitt and Ian Burton. Starting from the goal of assessing all natural hazards that affect or may affect one place, their studies soon grew into "a more theoretical analysis of . . . hazard problems" (Hewitt and Burton 1971, 3). In the United States other investigators have defined regions of high seismic risk as well as regions that are vulnerable to other natural disasters, such as hurricanes and tornadoes.[5] Such regions of natural hazard can be distinguished from regions of man-made hazard, for example, the smog region identified by Greenwood and Edwards (1973, 147) and shown in figure 6.2.

A tentative general classification of regions in the appraisive mode might run as follows: 1) quality of life regions, comprising regions of socioeconomic well-being and regions of special risk and regions of man-made risk; 2) esthetic quality regions, and 3) moral quality regions.[6]

Prescriptive Regions

Prescriptive regions are the product where the object of regional studies is direct action, as opposed to scientific knowledge or social evaluation. Prescriptive regions may be defined as spatial entities for the purposes of social and environmental control.

Nations, states, and cities are controlled territories. Are they, therefore, prescriptive regions? Clearly, they are cultural regions, the territories of people related by political and other ties. By this criterion they belong in the referential mode. On the other hand, such entities are often used prescriptively by planners, legal officials, and public administrators to stipulate the spatial range of a rule, law, or remedial measure.

The resolution of this seeming paradox lies in the realization that modal regions are abstractions rather than concrete objects. Consequently, they are not subject to the constraint that binds real objects (i.e., that two or more of them cannot occupy the same place at the same time).

Consider, for example, any three regions in different modes, such as a local polity (referential), a health survey area (appraisive), and a mosquito abatement district (prescriptive). When mapped, these regions may be totally discrete, they may overlap, or they may coincide precisely.[7] Whatever the case, considered solely with respect to the type of areal interest they represent, they are three distinct spatial entities. By the same token, any nation or state may at one and the same time be a referential, an appraisive, and a prescriptive region.

In the United States, regions by prescription abound, especially at the local level (e.g., land use regulation zones, soil conservation districts, air pollution-control districts, flood-plain regulation zones, coastal management zones, and the like). Trans-state examples are less common (e.g., national forest conservation regions, and national seashore conservation regions [figure 6.2]). Still rarer are transnational prescriptive regions, such as the Columbia River Treaty Region comprising parts of the United States and Canada.

Theoretically, there is no limit to the number and character of regions by prescription. In practice, however, their appearance and disappearance, as well as their specific functions, are governed largely by the prevailing ideological and constitutional environment—which varies widely on a global scale. A case in point is migration control. Britain, Sweden, and many other countries have established prescriptive regions expressly and explicitly to encourage population and industrial redistribution or to keep existing distributions from changing adversely to a government purpose. In the United States, the mere idea of migration control encounters stiff resistance, owing to the widespread private ownership of land and the constitutional restrictions on interference with freedom of movement. Consequently, although in America prescriptive regions for purposes of migration control exist (e.g., agricultural conservation districts, large-lot residential zones, and wilderness reserves), they tend to be rationalized in ecological terms.

Optative Regions

One classificatory mode remains. Its source is the transcendental element in regional studies, and it corresponds to the creative function of human language—poetry, prophecy, and prayer. Following the terminology of I. A. Richards, I have called it the "optative mode." The term *optative* means expressing or giving voice to a wish or desire. Accordingly, optative regions are spatial entities for hortatory purposes. They exist to invoke an ideal societal objective and to state it persuasively.

G. Etzel Pearcy's proposal for a thirty-eight-state U.S.A. is an example of optative regionalization. Pearcy's principles for revamping the American states and reducing their number include consistency in size, compactness in shape, elimination of river boundaries, and the use of short lines that can change direction as needed to accommodate natural and cultural boundaries (particularly economic). Not least revealing of the optative impulse in Pearcy's proposal are the colorful names for the new states, many of them derived from some feature of the natural environment—Cascade, Bitterroot, Platte, Prairie, Bayou (figure 6.2), and Piedmont.[8]

This notion that the spatial structures of man's devising—his planned administrative and legal units—ought to conform to nature's and culture's own structures is a perennial ideal in American regional planning. In fact, it may be seen as one of the major driving forces in American planning history. No student of the city's history in the first third of the present century can fail to be impressed by one of the enduring purposes of that period—to overthrow the ward as the city's basic political unit and replace it with an idealized cultural unit, the family neighborhood.

A similar venture in optative regionalism can be observed in the western United States. Here the relevant cultural and natural structures were the family farm and the river basin. Beginning with John Wesley Powell, the aim of reformers was to reorganize the West on a hydrographic basis—not only for the purpose of conserving scarce water resources but also to facilitate the creation of institutions of economic cooperation much larger than the family but balanced like the family and retaining its communal sense. When this ideal was carried east it was embodied in one of the nation's most truly optative regional enterprises—the Tennessee Valley Authority.

Notes

This essay is adapted with permission from the *International Regional Science Review* 1 (Fall 1977): 1–13.

1. For a lucid and systematic exposition of the nature and problems of regional classification, see Grigg (1955). An excellent summary of current classification problems and methods in geography can be found in Abler, Adams, and Gould (1971). Geographers, regional scientists, and others have recently been very active in adapting and applying the principles of numerical taxonomy to the identification of spatial entities (Sokal and Sneath 1963; Lankford and Semple 1973).

2. The chapter in which this definition appears is presented by Whittlesey in the form of a report of the Committee on Regional Geography of the American Association of Geographers, but the definition, as well as the modes of regional study discussed, are associated with Whittlesey, himself (see, for example, Minshull 1967).

3. Because of space limitations, this exposition is necessarily highly compressed. The basis of the analysis of the functions of language can be found in numerous publications on linguistic theory and literary criticism, but I have drawn most heavily here from the seminal work of Ogden and Richards (1946) and Morris (1955). I take full responsibility, of course, for this modification, elaboration, and extension of their analyses, and for applying it to regional classification. A similar framework was used previously by this author in classifying land use.

4. The varieties of classification in the referential mode are too numerous to review here. Throughout this discussion reference to the actual or possible classifications in each mode are intended to be illustrative, not exhaustive.

5. For a review and assessment of this research, see White and Haas (1975).

6. No one, to this writer's knowledge, has yet made explicit regional comparisons and classifications in terms of esthetic or moral qualities of the environment.

7. For obvious reasons, appraisive and prescriptive regions frequently coincide.

8. Pearcy also recommends his proposals on pragmatic grounds. Supposedly, his thirty-eight states would incur less governmental costs than the present fifty-state system. Perhaps, but nowhere does he provide convincing support for this assertion.

References

Abler, R., J. Adams, and P. Gould. 1971. *Spatial Organization: The Geographer's View of the World*. New York: Prentice-Hall.

Bunge, W. 1966. *Theoretical Geography*. Lund, Sweden: Department of Geography, Royal University of Lund.

Cohn, B. S. 1966. "Regions Subjective and Objective: Their Relation to the Study of Modern History and Society." *Regions and Regionalism in South Asian Studies*. Program in Comparative Studies on Southern Asia, Duke University.

Graham, Edward H. 1966. *Future Environments of North America*. Edited by F. Fraser Darling and John P. Milton. Garden City: Natural History Press. Epigraph appears on 133.

Greenwood, N., and J. Edwards. 1973. *Human Environments and Natural Systems*. Belmont, Calif.: Wadsworth Publishing.

Grigg, D. 1955. "The Logic of Regional Systems." In *Annals of the Association of American Geographers 55*, no. 3 (Sept.): 465–91.

Hewitt, Kenneth, and Ian Burton. 1971. *The Hazardousness of a Place: A Regional Ecology of Damaging Events*. Toronto: University of Toronto Press.

Lankford, Philip M., and R. Keith Semple. 1973. "Classification and Geography." In *Geographia Polonica 25* [publication of the Polish Academy of Sciences, Institute of Geography]. Warsaw: Polish Scientific Publishers.

Levin, Melvin. 1968. "The Big Regions." *Journal of the American Institute of Planners 34* (March): 66–79 .

Minshull, Roger M. 1967. *Regional Geography*. Chicago: Aldine Publishing.

Morris, Charles. 1955. *Signs, Language, and Behavior*. New York: George Braziller.

Ogden, C. K., and I. A. Richards. 1946. *The Meaning of Meaning*. New York: Harcourt, Brace.

Pearcy, G. Etzel. 1973. *A 38-State U.S.A.* Stockton: Plycon Press.

Pickard, Jerome P. 1967. *Dimensions of Metropolitanism*. Research Monograph 14. Washington, D.C.: Urban Land Institute.

Schwartzberg, J. 1966. "Prolegomena to the Study of South Asian Regions and Regionalism." *Regions and Regionalism in South Asian Studies*. Program in Comparative Studies on Southern Asia, Duke University, 1966.

Smith, David M. 1973. *The Geography of Social Well-Being in the United States*. New York: McGraw Hill.

Sokal, R., and P. Sneath. 1963. *Principles of Numerical Taxonomy*. San Francisco: W. H. Freeman.

White, Gilbert F., and John E. Haas. 1975. *Assessment of Research on Natural Hazards*. Cambridge: MIT Press.

Whittlesey, Derwent. 1954. "The Regional Concept and the Regional Method." In *American Geography: Inventory and Prospect*, ed. Preston E. James and Clarence F. Jones. Syracuse: Syracuse University Press.

7

Regionalization as
a Symbolic Process

Anyone who has looked for stable meanings in the language of regional studies must agree that it is a bit like trying to pin down the "colers," "vapors," "humors," and "biles" of medieval physiology. I have in mind such terms as *regionalism, regionalization, regional planning,* and *regional science.* In 1938 the sociologist Howard Odum identified no less than forty-one concepts of "regionalism" and if the range of meaning has narrowed since his day, I am not aware of it.

The prime example of ambiguity is *region* itself. What is a region? This is the perennial question that thus far has resisted all attempts to deal with it adequately. Regional scholars have responded in diverse ways. On the one side are those who appear satisfied with a single or a few meanings of *region* appropriate to their purposes. On the other side are the pluralists who, although they are alive to the variety of meanings inherent in *region,* are content simply to refer to that variety without any great concern about their apparent miscellany. There is a third approach. Rather than foundering on the Scylla of the one meaning or the Charybdis of the many meanings, it seeks, like Ulysses, to steer a middle course through the dilemma. This is the definitional strategy followed here. It consists in uncovering the hidden system of related functions that underlie this single word *region* and that account for the observed semantic variability of the term. Thus, the unity of the concept *region* is saved without the sacrifice of its multiple meanings.

How to demonstrate the hidden order in the multiple meanings of *region?* [In the preceding essay it was shown] that the act of delineating regions on a map as practiced by geographers, planners, regional scientists, and others involves a variety of linguistic modes or language functions and that these modes correspond to identifiable spatial entities or "modal regions." Here, we carry the analysis further.

Mechanism	Interregional Spatial Relationship	Examples
Verbalism: positive and negative	Contiguity	Rest of the world, "treeless regions," "Outback," "Down Under"
Optative projection	Hierarchy	Europe and the local communities
Inversion	Congruency and hierarchy	Unigov and Minigov
Hypostasis	Congruency	Samaria and Judea
Paradigmatic change	Congruency	Region as a great neighborhood; region as a great family

Table 7.1. Region-Generating Mechanisms

Region-Generating Mechanisms

The mere act of delineating a region in one mode often gives rise to another region of the same mode or of a different mode. Five processes whereby the delineation of a region generates one or more additional regions are listed in table 7.1. These are: verbalism, optative projection, inversion, hypostasis, and paradigmatic change. Each process, moreover, results in a definite type of spatial relationship between the original and the generated regions. In the case of verbalism, the relationship is contiguity. In the case of projection, the relationship is treelike or hierarchical. In the case of inversion, it is congruency. Region formation is often a compound process linking several of the individual mechanisms in a series of distinct phases.

Verbalism

Consider a territory of any size. A region carved out of that territory will always result in a complementary region of the same mode. If Illinois is the territory, then the delineation of the referential region "Chicago" will automatically produce a complementary referential region "rest of Illinois." The complementary region is positive when it is regarded as a

spatial entity in its own right with its own name. It is negative when it
is viewed as a mere residual, a leftover without any identity of its own.
An example is Australia's "Outback." The colloquial epithet for Australia, "Down Under," is, itself, an instance of negative dichotomization.

This propensity to name one region in terms of another is called "verbalism" by the historian-ecologist James Malin. He notes that "because
the civilization of Western Europe and eastern America developed in a
predominantly forest environment, the prevailing geographical terminology is that of the forest or high-rainfall climate." "Forest man," moving from Pennsylvania onto the plains and prairies, called them "tree-
less and subhumid," names which have stuck although they hardly do
justice to the ecological nature of this great region (1984, 22). Malin de-
plores verbalism as a distorting factor in regional geography (30).

Optative Projection

To explain the mechanism of optative projection one must begin with
prescriptive regions. Prescriptive regions are spatial entities for control
purposes. There are two kinds of prescriptive regions. Unifunctional
regions are one-function regions such as land use zones, soil conservation districts, drainage districts, sanitary districts, mosquito abatement
districts, and coastal management zones. A multifunctional region is a
prescriptive entity whose reason for being is to contain and regulate the
relations of the one-function regions. It is a region of regions. An example is the Reedy Creek Improvement District in Florida (otherwise
known as Disney World) which has the following functions: drainage
control, "reclamation, irrigation, water and sewers, waste disposal, mosquito abatement, airport and highway construction, parking, recreation,
fire protection, utilities, mass transit and land use," and in addition has
the powers of owning and leasing property and of eminent domain
(McClaughry 1980, 376–77). Only police protection is lacking. But this
type of region which stops just short of being a full fledged polity is exceptional. The typical multifunctional regions in the United States are
the city, the state, and the nation—full-fledged legal-political units.

By optative projection I mean the propensity of each type of legal-
political region to give rise to two ideal (i.e., optative) regions, one
smaller than itself and which it wholly contains (a micro-region) and
the other larger than itself and by which it is wholly contained (a
macro-region). The force behind the projection is the persistent notion
that a nation's official and duly constituted political subdivisions, as
well as the nation itself, are arbitrary and artificial units that need to
be supplanted by entities that are whole and natural. It is their puta-
tive naturalness and wholeness that constitutes the ideality of the new
projected units.

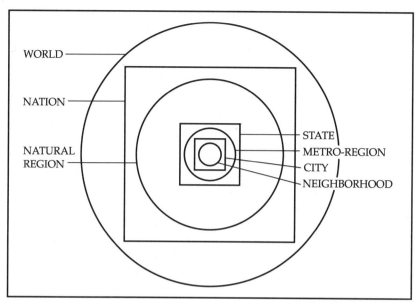

Figure 7.1.   Optative Projection

Optative projection from a North American perspective is diagramed in figure 7.1, where squares represent prescriptive (i.e., established legal-political) regions and circles optative regions. The city projects two types of optative region: the neighborhood, a micro-region admired for its supposed [social] basicness and simplicity, and the metro-region, a macro-region whose ideal feature is its functional wholeness. The American state or Canadian province, the next higher prescriptive region, also projects two optative regions: the metro-region, a fundamental and unitary constituent of the state, and the river basin or some other natural region of which the state or province may be only an arbitrary fragment. Finally, there is the nation, the highest order prescriptive region which stands between two natural regions, the river basin and the planet itself. Thus, the whole earth is organized as a hierarchy of alternating prescriptive and optative units (figure 7.1). The macro-region at one scale is the micro-region at the next higher scale.

In the United States, corresponding to the hierarchical spatial ordering of the two types of region, there has also been a temporal or historical ordering consisting of alternating prescriptive and optative regions, reflecting prevailing social and economic conditions. In the depression decade of the 1930s, it was the city, state, and nation which were the ascendant entities. In the 1960s, by contrast, what counted was the neighborhood and the planet, while the official units and their boundaries seemed to blur. When times are hard, society falls back on its "real" tools, its duly constituted and legal regions to implement remedial measures. In good times, the human imagination is free to imagine better worlds.

Among the American established legal-political entities—city, state, nation—the city has been the most prolific projector of idealized (i.e., optative) entities. This is the result of the low esteem in which American intellectuals have traditionally held the city (White and White 1962). In the realm of politics the anti-city ideology has generated both a neighborhood government movement and a metropolitan region movement. Despite their different spatial scales, the two movements are twins and often allies. Both seek to supplant the city as the prime local political territory with other spatial constructs. The objectives of the neighborhood movement are to restore the presumed benefits of pre-urban and pre-industrial organization: nearness of nature, opportunity for neighborly association, and protection of the home from the intrusion of alien values. The objectives of the metropolitan region movement are to promote efficiency and equity by gathering all local urban functions and problems within the reach of a single jurisdiction.

In Europe, by contrast, the leading generator of ideal regions is the nation. The opposition to the nation has been well described by Carl Friederich, as evident in an institution called in France the *jumelage* (*gemallagio* in Italian, *Verschwisterungen* in German). The *jumelage* is an elective pairing of two or more towns, cities, or communes in different countries. Lyons and Frankfurt comprise a *jumelage*, as do Aubenas in Switzerland, Zelzate in Belgium, and Swarzenbach in West Germany (Friederich 1963, 36).

On the face of it, the purpose of a *jumelage* is quite practical—the exchange of products, personnel, and experience among local communities with similar problems. Actually, the *jumelage* has symbolic functions as well. One is to celebrate the principle of local self-determination. The other is to assert the ideal of European unity. Both purposes are evident in the following oath sworn to by the mayors of the twin towns on the occasion of the formation of a *jumelage:* "On this day, we take the solemn oath of maintaining permanent ties between our cities, of encouraging in all spheres the transactions between their citizens for the purpose of developing by means of a better mutual understanding the living sentiment of European fraternity, of combining our efforts in order to contribute with all our means to the success of that necessary enterprise of peace and prosperity: The Union of European Peoples" (Friederich 1963, 36).

Local self-determination and European unity? The contradiction is

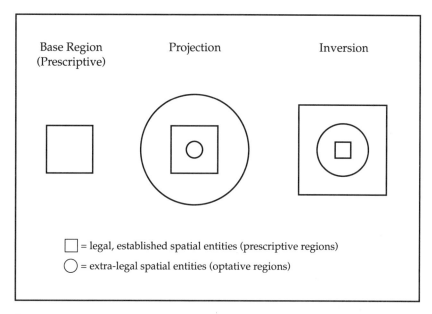

Figure 7.2.   Projection-Inversion Sequence

only apparent. The principle which reconciles the two purposes is anti-nationalism. Just as the nation is seen as stifling the towns, so, too, it is regarded by some as blocking the path to the peaceful repossession of the common European heritage which includes local autonomy. The towns and Europe are allies, optative regions against the nation.

Inversion

Inversion is the two-phase process whereby erstwhile optative regions become established legal-political units and the former legal-political units, now surpassed, are converted into optative regions, that is, they are romanticized, a form of idealization.[1] Using our geometric symbols in figure 7.1, one might say that the circles are squared and the squares circled (figure 7.2).

Marion County, Indiana, is a place where both optative projection and the inversion process went a certain distance before they stalled. For many years there had been a growing conviction on the part of some that the "problems and concerns" of Indianapolis "were not confined by city limits" (Willburn 1976): Indianapolis was only one piece of an ideal functional whole, the metropolitan county. On the other side were those who believed that what was required was a devolution of power in favor of the city's neighborhoods. These two movements represented the optative projection phase of the cycle. It was followed in the 1970s by an inversion phase. Under a Republican administration the corporate limits of Indianapolis were expanded to include the whole of Marion County, creating a new congruent prescriptive entity called Unigov. Unigov had its counterpart in a plan to create fifty-four community council areas ("Minigovs"), each with a modicum of self-government. What Unigov was to the metropolitan community, these Minigovs were to be to the city's "natural neighborhoods," realizations of an ideal—the conversion of optative regions into official legal-political entities. A Minigov bill passed into law in 1971 in the Indiana General Assembly. Eventually, the idea petered out. Resistance came from many Indianapolis councilmen who feared the scheme was a threat to their established councilmanic districts.[2] The legal creation of Unigov (and the establishment of Minigovs, if it had actually taken place) is what I have called the squaring of the circles—the superimposing of a congruent prescriptive region on an optative region.

Inversion includes the circling of the squares. When a prescriptive region is supplanted by another larger prescriptive region (as Indianapolis was by Unigov), it may become an idealized object of nostalgia. "If I forget thee Oh Jerusalem!" and "Oh Rome!, My Country! City of the Soul!" are some poetic examples. Think also of the antebellum South, the Confederacy, and the romance that has been made of them. But one need not go so far in time or so far from home to observe the importance of nostalgia as a factor in the organization of space. With the expansion of American cities, a myriad of surpassed old towns have been romanticized: Vieux Carré, Old San Juan, Georgetown in Washington, D.C., and Pullman, Illinois, are some far-flung instances. But even this does not constitute the last step in a process of symbolic regionalization. Such entities soon give rise to the "historic district," a special type of prescriptive region:

> Be it ordained by the City Council of the City of Galena, Jo Davies County, Illinois, as follows, to wit:
>
> Section 1: All areas, place buildings, structures, works of art and other objects individually and collectively, whether owned or privately controlled or by any public body located within the part of the City of Galena commonly described as "the original city" and recorded as the city limits in the Court House of Jo Davies, State of Illinois, on the 28th of March, 1838, and all subdivisions added to the city prior to the 31st day of December 1859, are hereby designated as areas, places, buildings, structures, works of art or other objects having a special architectural, community, or aesthetic interest and value. (City Council of Galena, Illinois 1965, 1)

Thus, many surpassed regions end up mummified or as prized antiques. To summarize, region formation in the United States is often an automatic process linking several of the individual region-generating mechanisms in a kind of chain reaction. A prescriptive region, usually a city, projects two types of optative region: a metro-region and a set of neighborhood regions. All regions are then inverted. The optative regions are legitimized to become duly constituted government units (prescriptive regions), while the former prescriptive region, or part of it, is romanticized or otherwise idealized. A final step occurs when the now idealized city undergoes a further metamorphosis as a special historic district. Thus, in the temporal dimension, as in the spatial, the process of region formation consists of a series of alternating prescriptive and optative regions. As seen in the case of Indianapolis, actual events or particular circumstances may intervene to prevent the full working out of these processes, but they are nonetheless present as powerful region-generating tendencies within the North American metropolitan system.

Hypostasis and the Reverse Logic of Planning

A region, most briefly defined, is any quantity of space or time treated as a unit (Boulding 1985). The term *referential region* denotes those spatial units that are mainly the results of scientific inquiry. Here "scientific" signifies that the relevant areal interest is to discover nonhuman order in the environment, as distinguished from attempting to reshape the environment in line with human values. The idea of scientific truth implies faith in the existence of an objective world totally independent of man but knowable by him. And among the products of this faith are regions which are regarded as true nature-given regions, not mere abstractions.

Scientific inquiry is not the exclusive producer of referential regions, however. Certain other regions in the same mode have their source in one of the other grand motifs of regionalization—valuing and acting. For lack of a better term I have given them the name *hypostatic* regions. They are noteworthy because they help answer the questions, Where do regions come from? What are the forces behind their generation and proliferation? and What symbolic functions do they serve?

Hypostasis is the noun form of a Greek word whose verbal form in English is *hypostatize*. This verb means "to make into, or regard as a separate and distinct substance; also to assume as a reality." As used here, hypostasis denotes a process whereby an appraisive region indirectly generates what is assumed to be a "real" region, that is, a referential region either of the natural or of the cultural variety.

To explain hypostasis and how it becomes a phenomenon frequently observed in planning and politics, we must now add two more terms to our graphic vocabulary. In figure 7.3, the irregular polygon represents any referential region, and the shaded patch an appraisive region. The square, as previously defined, stands for a prescriptive region. In what manner do planners relate these spatial entities? In what sequence? There are two answers to these questions corresponding to two radically different models of planning. The first is represented by the following sentence: "Something is wrong, let us correct it." Here, "something" corresponds to reference, "wrong" to appraisal, and "correct" to prescription. According to this model the planner begins with a "something," an object assumed to be given by nature or history. He or she evaluates it (it is "wrong") and acts ("corrects"). Expressed in spatial terms, a referential region leads to an appraisive region, which in turn leads to a prescriptive region (figure 7.3a).

This is the classic model. It follows the stepwise course laid down by Patrick Geddes: first a regional survey to get the facts, then a regional plan comprising the functions of appraisal and prescription. This model is based on the idea of the primacy of an a priori objective world, a created world, independent of human interest, whose structure is open to human discovery, description, and action.

But planners and politicians are not primarily scientists or historians. They do not necessarily begin with given natural or historical objects. Typically, their first impulse is to do, to act, to change, not to know. Therefore, they often start at the other end of the chain. Just as science begins with nature, and planning with human action, so the logic of this kind of planning is the reverse of the logic of science. Correspondingly, an alternative model of the planning process might read: "Since we are correctors correcting, something must be wrong," or (giving it an ethical twist), "something is being wronged. What is it? Where is it?" Once posed, these questions are not long in discovering or inventing a corresponding object. Here, action precedes reference. Absurd? No more so than the existentialist proposition that existence precedes essence. In this model regional planning is man-centered. Its referential regions are products of politics not of scientific inquiry. Planners use them to justify their interventions. They bank upon the pious public sentiment that what nature or history has created must be respected and deserves support. It is for this reason that the route from an appraisive to a prescriptive region often passes through an invented or invoked referential region, whose function is mainly if not totally tactical (figure 7.3b). For example, the "discovery" of a cultural fossil, a piece of old British America, lent the force of sentiment to the establishment of the Appalachia Regional Commission in the 1960s. The rediscovery of Appalacia owes

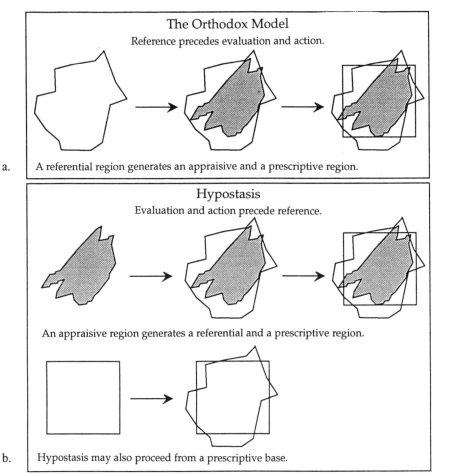

The Orthodox Model
Reference precedes evaluation and action.

a. | A referential region generates an appraisive and a prescriptive region.

Hypostasis
Evaluation and action precede reference.

An appraisive region generates a referential and a prescriptive region.

b. | Hypostasis may also proceed from a prescriptive base.

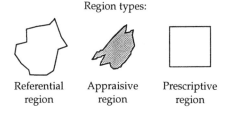

Region types:

Referential   Appraisive   Prescriptive
region   region   region

Figure 7.3.   Two Models of Planning

more to the reformist energies of the New Deal and the Great Society than it does to cultural geography. But the sword cuts two ways. Hypostasis can be used to block action as well as to stimulate it. In the same decade, while urban renewal planners were busy characterizing certain city areas as slums so as to justify tearing them down, their opponents were countering with appraisals and prescriptions of their own which led them to discover "ethnic villages" and other not-to-be-meddled-with cultural regions underlying these areas.

Past or suppressed referential regions of the cultural variety lend themselves very well to resuscitation by means of hypostatic projection and are used by contending parties to gain or retain a diplomatic or military edge. Consider the case of modern Israel. It began as an optative region, partly of the prophetic, partly of the romantic, variety. In 1948, a congruent prescriptive region was added, the State of Israel (inversion). Recently, in part for political reasons, two biblical subregions were hypostatized: Samaria and Judea. Meanwhile, Israel's arch-enemy Assad has been doing some hypostatic maneuvering of his own, viewing Lebanon and, one must presume, Israel itself, as two provinces of "Greater Syria," the heir of the ancient Assyrian empire. Thus, as symbolized by figure 7.3, hypostasis may proceed from a prescriptive base. Hypostasis can also be used to exploit a potential economic advantage. Scottish nationalism, for example, has never been extinct, but it experienced a strong resurgence several years ago with the discovery of the North Sea oil, much of which, if Scotland were an independent nation, would have been within her territorial waters. Dead natural regions are also revived, often with political programs behind them, the "prairie," for example.

Paradigmatic Change

As noted, optative regionalization denotes the delineation of a spatial entity considered to be naturally or culturally whole, such as a river basin, a linguistic region, etc. It often includes the envisioning for that entity of some type of ideal ecological, political, functional, or social order.

Paradigmatic change occurs when one ideal model replaces another as the organizing principle for a territory as a result of some all-encompassing global event, usually cataclysmic such as war or depression. In addition to the exogenous influences leading to paradigmatic change, there are those stemming from the models themselves. By this I mean the tendency of one type of model to generate a model of another type. The model may suggest a related but in some respects a subtly different model, or it may even suggest its opposite. Thus, the idea of the region as an impersonal, urbanized metropolis may call forth the counter-ideal of the region as an intimate neighborhood. From the neighborhood ideal, it is but a short step to the image of the region as a great family. "City," "neighborhood," and "family" are, in this context, metaphors, but that does not mean that they are devoid of practical force. The energies of statesmen, politicians, and administrators and the budgets of governments have frequently been engaged in the fashioning of regions based on these metaphors. [Several of the the essays in Part 2 of this volume are interpretations of American social history as the play and the interplay of metaphorical optative regions.]

Summary and Conclusion

What is a region? Geographers, regional scientists, planners, and social scientists of every stripe have argued the question for decades (Gore 1984, 1–11). One of the motors that keeps the debate going is the perception, a correct one, that a phenomenon belongs to (is the intellectual property of) that science or discipline which can impose its definition on all the rest, with all that implies for material and non-material rewards. In other words, there are "turf" issues involved in phenomenon definition, a fact which doesn't make "What is a region?" as a scientific question any easier to handle.

Interdisciplinary politics aside, it makes little sense to argue for the correctness of one definition vis-à-vis all the others. For what the parties to the dispute often overlook is that *region* is first of all a word, and that words are variables whose precise values are very much a matter of the systems of thought that employ them. To put the same idea in a slightly different way, words are points where diverse systems of thought intersect, a fact which explains their ambiguity.[3] The greater the number of systems of thought that crowd through them, the more ambiguous they become. To extend the metaphor, comprehending these words, managing these complex nodes of meaning, is a bit like directing a number of different parades through a busy traffic circle. It comes down to moving, while keeping integral and distinct, the several cross-cutting and opposing flows from one side of the intersection to the other where they can then push on to the next crossroads, that is to say, to the next ambiguous term. The characteristic of the approach taken in this essay and the earlier one of which it is an extension is that it is an exercise in comprehension of the many senses of the term *region* rather than of its definition, which connotes a narrowing down of meaning. Needless to say, this approach has generated its own distinctive view of what regions are and how they are related to each other. In this concluding section I will recapitulate the major findings.

A region is essentially a behavioral phenomenon. Modal regions represent different facets of the adaptive human act, of man adapting to his environment. They are the spatial correlates or projection of that act in its various phases: referring, valuing, prescribing, etc. Accordingly, modal regions are related to one another as the different phases of behavior are related.

First, they occur in sets, each set actually or potentially composed of a referential, evaluative, prescriptive, and optative region. Together, these regions constitute a behavioral whole composed of complementary parts.

Temporality is a second characteristic of modal regions. The different members of the set tend to appear sequentially in time, although they may also appear simultaneously. Also variable is the order of appearance. A prescriptive region, for example, often follows an evaluative region, but sometimes the reverse is true.

A third distinctive feature is the source (not the character) of their spatial relationships. Modal regions in a set owe their spatial patterns to the mechanisms that produce them. Verbalism always produces contiguous regions, optative projection always results in a hierarchical pattern, an appraisive and a prescriptive region of the same set either overlap or they are totally congruent, etc.

Fourth, the relations that obtain among modal regions of the same set are to some extent automatic. That is to say, a region in one mode tends to evoke or call into existence its complementary regions in the same or other modes, a result which follows from the organic nature of modal regionalization. The following is a list of some of the region-generating automatisms.

Delineating and characterizing a region (e.g., as arid, humid, good, bad, rich, or poor) automatically creates a contiguous region of opposite character. For example, when a region composed of a group of U.S. southern and western states was dubbed "The Sunbelt," it was all but inevitable that a complementary region, "The Frostbelt," should automatically come into existence.

Political regions—wards, cities, states or provinces, and nations—automatically generate idealized shadow polities at a scale both larger and smaller than themselves. This effect contributes to societal dynamism. The shadow polities press for legitimation. Superseded official regions repackage themselves as museum pieces.

Appraisive regions frequently lead to prescriptive regions. Sometimes they trigger the discovery or invention of natural and cultural (i.e, referential) regions to support a reform agenda and to induce policy movement.

Metaphors (e.g., global village, spaceship earth) shape spatial relations by construing those relations in terms of familiar, easily grasped images with behavioral and policy implications. When metaphors change (paradigm shift), spatial relations change. Metaphors are subject to sudden change due to catastrophic events, such as depression or war. But there is a subtle dynamic at work independent of external events and stemming from the metaphors themselves [as demonstrated in Part 2 of this volume].

This analysis, if correct, is also useful. Modal regionalization is a reflection of intelligent adaptive behavior. At the same time, as a result of the automatisms involved in this form of regionalization, unintended consequences often occur along the way. To the extent that we can identify such mechanisms, what was formerly mechanical becomes conscious and amenable to control. By learning how regionalization takes place, we need no longer be totally at the mercy of automatic regionalization.

A final conclusion pertains to the policy of the discipline. Regional science is obviously a house with many mansions. Therefore, no one view of what regions are ever can, ever should, prevail, which is to say that inclusiveness, not exclusiveness, ought to be the principle that guides the search for understanding. Each mansion must be explored. Beyond that, there is the question of how the mansions are related to each other, the architecture of the structure. The present essay is one attempt to describe that architecture.

Notes

This essay is adapted with permission from *Canadian Journal of Regional Science* 11 (Fall 1988): 1–17.

1. I use the verbs "become" and "are converted into" to avoid an awkward but more precise formulation. The logic of this analysis should require us to say that an optative region generates a congruent prescriptive region of the legal-political type and that a surpassed legal-political region generates a congruent optative region.

2. Telephone conversation with Michael Carroll, former deputy mayor of Indianapolis, Sept. 12, 1984.

3. I first encountered these views on the nature of meaning and its relation to words in the teachings of Ivor A. Richards.

References

Boulding, Kenneth E. 1985. "Regions of Time." *Papers of the Regional Science Association 57*, 19–32.

City Council of Galena, Illinois. 1965. "Historical and Preservation Ordinance," Aug. 25.

Friederich, Carl. 1963. "The Grassroots Base of European Unification." *Public Policy* (12): 24–40.

Geddes, Patrick. 1949. *Cities in Evolution*. London: Williams and Norgate.

Gore, Charles. 1984. *Regions in Question*. New York: Methuen.

Malin, James C. 1984. *History and Ecology*. Edited by Robert P. Swierenga. Lincoln: University of Nebraska Press.

McClaughry, John. 1980. "Neighborhood Revitalization," in *The United States in the 1980's*, ed. Peter Duignan and Alvin Rabushka. Stanford: Hoover Institution, Stanford University.

Odum, Howard W., and Harry Estill Moore. 1938. *American Regionalism: A Cultural-Historical Approach to National Integration*. New York: Henry Holt.

White, Morton, and Lucia White. 1962. *The Intellectual versus the City*. Cambridge: Harvard University Press.

Willburn, York. 1976. "Indianapolis: City and County Together." *New York Affairs* 3 (Spring): 34–44.

PART 2

Planning as Social Invention

The two master themes that inform this work are planning as language and planning as social invention. The two themes are not unrelated. They are linked through the optative mode, that language mode that corresponds to human aspiration, to the call to go beyond mere betterment to an ideal state of human affairs, to what Shelley called "the devotion to something afar."

Every profession, if it is truly a profession and not just a trade, aims at a distant goal beyond its everyday concerns. The planner's devotion to something afar is sometimes represented by the concept "urban design." Typically, this phrase connotes the search for excellence in the built environment, for a whole harmonious urban structure in which the beautiful is useful and the useful beautiful. But beyond its esthetic-utilitarian function, design also entails vital cultural work—the creation or invention of stable new forms by combining into spatial and institutional relationships qualities that, up to the point of their being joined, have seemed logically or practically unrelatable, or even downright inimical to each other.

Social inventions have to undergo the test of reality; they have to prove themselves in a world of voters and consumers. Not all pass that test, some because they are anachronistic and no longer meet the real needs of the people for whom they are intended. Others fail because their inventors or implementers may be heedless or oblivious of the limitations imposed by the constitutional environment in which they are produced. There is no more bitter or cynical human being than the planner who, after a lifetime of effort in vain, despairs and proclaims that, in America, planning is impossible. The problem may, in large part, stem from a misunderstanding of the special character of American planning. Lacking the power to command, the American planner has to resort to indirection and persuasion. Both methods presuppose a considerable knowledge of social dynamics. How is society constructed? What causes change? How can change be induced? It is no coincidence, therefore, that the United States is one of the countries in which the search for strategic control variables through mathematical modelling has proceeded the farthest. The other major control mode of American planning, persuasion, has its roots in the same condition of relative powerlessness. If people cannot be forced to move, they may, through the medium of symbols, be induced to move themselves. This is one of the functions of social inventions, to move people, to prefigure a possible future. Thus, even social inventions that have been tried and have failed may nevertheless continue to make their influence felt as moving symbols. An example discussed in the final essay of this volume is the Cincinnati Social Unit, a symbol of the deep cultural need to reconcile the democratic and the technocratic elements in American society. The particular form in which the uniting of these two types of governance is envisioned may have been unworkable, but the concept itself was valid and remains so.

Regions of the Heart

The regions in several of the following essays, realized or just dreamed of, exemplify the inventive function of planning: the rural West as a social invention joining the values of family farming with the opportunities of commercial agriculture; the eastern urban region as a "marriage of town and country"; the United States as a "family" combining the advantages of a market economy with those of a welfare state; the Dutch city, reconciling the desire for access to the world with "social protection of the home," and the world itself as a transnational region restoring the myriad ties between people and places that political boundaries have sundered. What all these invented regions have in common is that they evince a deep-seated yearning to overcome some barrier to human wholeness, a barrier imposed by society or even by nature herself. They are regions of the heart.

8

City Encounter and Desert Encounter: Two Sources of American Regional Planning Thought

Referring to the American experience, the historian Richard Hofstadter wrote, "The United States was born in the country and has moved to the city" (1955, 23). This is a nice opening phrase, but it tells only part of the story. At the turn of the century while some Americans were moving to the city others were moving to the arid West. As different as they were in many respects, the city encounter and the desert encounter were alike in that both resulted in planned attempts to establish rural institutions in inhospitable environments. In the urban East, the basis for regional planning was the neighborhood concept. In the West, it was the cooperative colony and the scientific family farm.

While both of these movements are well known, the original connection between them has long been obscured by the diverse outward forms in which the attempted solutions to the problems of the city and the desert necessarily manifested themselves.[1]

The present essay is a study of this similarity-in-diversity and of the geographical symmetry which characterized the American planning movement in its original phase. The first section is an account of the rise and enlargement to regional and even national proportions of the family neighborhood idea in the urban East. The second part deals with the career of the family farm idea in the arid West. The concluding section is a brief commentary on the continuing influence of these concepts in contemporary planning.

The Region as Neighborhood

Contrary to widely held views, there was never a time when American urban planning was concerned only with the "physical city," nor, except in certain professional aspects, is it descended from the City Beautiful movement. Spiritually, it stems rather from the deep critique of urbaniza-

tion and industrialization conducted by social scientists and social reformers in the first two decades of the twentieth century. In the name of
community these critics directed a tireless diatribe against the industrial
city and with such eloquence that in time their voices came to be heard (if
not heeded) above all others in the budding planning movement.[2]

It would be difficult to name a single progressive reformer who did
not believe that one of the worst features of the industrial city was its
effect on family life, but certainly a key figure, in that his ideas provided
a theoretical grounding for this belief, was the pioneer social-psycholo-
gist Charles Horton Cooley (1864–1929). Cooley spent most of his life as
a student and teacher at the University of Michigan in Ann Arbor. Originally an economist, he turned while still a young man to the teaching
and study of sociology. In 1902 he published his most influential work,
Human Nature and the Social Order. The two ideas for which he is best
known are "the looking-glass self" and "the primary group," concepts
which stressed the social as opposed to the biological origins of the individual human personality.

In his theory of the primary social group, Cooley taught that personality and society are inseparable. The healthy personality with its attributes of ambition and affection is not an inborn quality of the individual. It cannot be acquired "except through fellowship, and it decays in
isolation" (1909, 30). The family and the neighborhood are the main
nurseries of the healthy personality and the healthy society. Where these
primary groups are absent, or where their functioning is impaired, personal and social derangement are sure to follow.

Cooley believed that "the organization of society may not only fail to
give human nature the moral support it needs, but may be of such a
kind as actively to promote degeneration" (1918, 192). This was a theme
developed at some length by the Chicago sociologist Robert E. Park. In
the city, "population tends to segregate itself, not merely in accordance
with its interests, but in accordance with its tastes or its temperaments."
Particular impulses rooted "directly in the original nature of the individual" held sway over wide areas. Park termed such areas "moral regions," and he believed that they provided the place of abode as well as
the chief training grounds of the aberrant or eccentric personality (Park,
Burgess, and MacKenzie 1925, 43, 45). He thus discerned the source of
personal and social disorder in the very spatial structure of the city. It
remained only for Louis Wirth to stigmatize urbanism as a way of life
"consisting of the substitution of secondary for primary contacts, the
weakening of bonds of kinship, and the declining social significance of
the family, the disappearance of the neighborhood, and the undermining of the traditional basis of social solidarity" (1938, 20–21).

With learned treatises such as those of Cooley, Park, and Wirth to support them, urban reformers regarded the ordinary family neighborhood as the seed of social regeneration. Structurally, the family neighborhood was part of the city. Morally, it was the very antithesis of the city. The task was to rescue this good seed from the surrounding city and use it to rear a new and healthy social order. Thus Mary Parker Follett made the neighborhood the basis of her *New State* (1926). The neighborhood, she thought, is par excellence the place where all of a person's selves meet on the most intimate basis for reconcilement. As the fundamental political unit, it was to be preferred above all other human groupings.

The neighborhood was also the basis of projects hatching in the minds of urban and regional planners. Creating or preserving the family neighborhood within the city was the immediate task. Ultimately, however, the city, that false community, would have to be replaced by the regional neighborhood. Thus, the basis was laid for a division of labor between those who worked to transmute the city from within and those who addressed themselves directly to geographically broader tasks of environmental reconstruction—between neighborhood planners and regional planners.

Neighborhoods, Garden Cities, and Regions to Live In

Wresting the city from the grip of the established industrial order and reclaiming it for community uses began modestly as a process of adaptation. The "movement for the wider use of public property" was their prosaic name for it, but the reformers were enthralled with their new vision. Where before they had seen only a wasteland, they now espied a new world of opportunity. Schools might become civic centers. Daytime arsenals and armories could double as evening dance halls and sports arenas. Even roofs, docks, and piers could be reclaimed and made to serve the human uses of the good community.

To assert the right to a wider (i.e., to a communal) use of public property was one thing. It was quite another to make this claim stick. In the beginning the main action focused on the neighborhood school as an adult social center. Although in many cities the adult use of schools was common enough, this practice was countenanced as a privilege rather than conceded as a political right. The leading proponent of the people's right to use the neighborhood school was Edward J. Ward, a Presbyterian minister from Silver Creek, New York, who had succeeded in uniting its citizenry around a town clubhouse. Ward blasted the school authorities for failing to distinguish between its relation to adult citizens and its relation to the children of the citizens in the administration of public property: they assumed that their authority to regulate the use of the schools extended to children and adults alike. While Ward (1915) conceded the board's authority over the children in regular class hours, he hotly disputed their authority over the adult citizenry, on grounds that the board was subordinate to the citizenry.

Ward's ambition was to convert neighborhood schools into adult social and civic centers. His chance came in 1907 when he was chosen to supervise the wider use of the public school plant by the board of education of Rochester, New York. With a budget of $5,000 for the year and the support of eleven local organizations, a middle-class school located in the center of the city was selected for trial. Larger appropriations and the opening of additional centers followed until the experiment ran into political opposition, but not before the feasibility of the neighborhood school center idea had been demonstrated to a national audience of professional organizations.[3]

The connection between the schoolhouse, the social center movement, and the movement for the wider use of public property was spelled out by George M. Forbes, an associate of Ward and president of the Rochester Board of Education. The social center, he explained to the National Conference of Civic and Social Center Development, was not a building nor was it a school in the ordinary sense of that term. The school is "an absolute monarchy," while the social center was the distinctively democratic institution, whose aim was "to make each neighborhood conscious of its civic functions and power," to "make real democracy conscious and bring it into action." The special value of the schoolhouse for this purpose was that it was "consecrated to education" and therefore suitable to be the instrument of that deepest and most fundamental education "upon which the very existence of democracy depends," the exercise of the community spirit (1916, 54–56). Ward himself insisted on the schoolhouse. Not only was it neutral ground, a place to which all might repair regardless of family, church, or national identity. It was also common ground, for no other building could symbolize as well "the common obligation for the future" (1915, 11).

The significance of the schoolhouse is further revealed in the varied metaphors used to characterize it. As "the neighborhood capital" it stood opposed to city hall. William Allen White compared the schoolhouse to the New England town hall which had proven stronger than King George and his armies. It had "shattered caste based upon birth," but now the old town hall was gone and the times demanded a new town hall. The schoolhouse was to be the new town hall (quoted in Ward 1915, 14).

Clearly, the neighborhood idea was a political concept before it became a planning concept. And yet what the reformers had in mind was more than a political entity. Clarence Perry later amplified the image in social and cultural terms. "It would be a place where people would meet regularly to discuss their common affairs, sing together, dance and play, . . . where the jobless would find employment, where the wealthy would occasionally put their art treasures on exhibition for the benefit of all" (1921, 4). Nor were the esthetic possibilities in the concept neglected. The movement aimed at making "the common interest interesting" (Ward 1915, 11). The time was at hand when it would be possible to "draw illustrations of 'children playing in the market place' from modern cities as well as from Jerusalem of old" (Ward n.d., 7).

Reclaiming the impersonal city and its physical structures for communal uses began on an ad hoc basis, but the urge to give the social center concept a distinctive architectural expression was not to be thwarted forever. Dwight Perkins, an architect, addressing the National Educational Association in 1912, noted that the most obvious result of the social center movement to date was that the front door of the schoolhouse was left unlocked for a few days each week. Nevertheless, structural adaptation to "the social awakening" could be observed in the tendency to equip new high schools with swimming pools and gymnasiums and to provide them not only with large assembly halls but also with lecture and meeting rooms for evening use. Even shops and lunchrooms were becoming common.

Moreover, the movement for the communal use of public property was coming to involve many more institutions than the school. It encompassed also parks, playgrounds, libraries, settlement houses, and even some private and commercial buildings. "Why," Perkins asked, "should one of my dollars be spent by a park board, another by a library board, still another by a school board and a fourth contributed more or less understandingly to be spent by a settlement board, when all four are for the same essential purpose and could be administered . . . by one agency, according to one plan in one group of buildings arranged to avoid wasteful duplication of construction and maintenance?" (1912, 237).

The following year the City Club of Chicago sponsored a competition for the design of a quarter-section (640 acres) on the outskirts of the city, where land was under rapid development "without that intelligent direction which is necessary for the good of the city and its population" and without recognition of the need for parks, recreation centers, and neighborhood institutions (Yeomans 1916, 1). Of particular interest was the design submitted by William Drummond. "Order," he wrote, "is the keynote of our plan." Drummond's intention was to design an area which would serve permanently "as a neighborhood or primary social circle" (quoted in Yeomans 1916, 39–40). The basic "intellectual, recreational, and civic requirements" would be at the center, while local business would be housed at the corners. Moreover, "in a series of such units" there would be a specialization of neighborhood centers by type to achieve adequate spacing between like centers. Drummond's plan thus appeared to reconcile neighborhood with urban functional specialization.

Perkins had urged the freeing of the social center idea from its dependency on the use of existing public property. The contribution of Drummond and of Clarence Perry was to include the residential environs in the planning, and thus both men arrived at the idea of the complete residential module or "neighborhood unit." As a young staff member of the Russell Sage Foundation, Perry's first job had been to investigate the extracurricular use of public schools in the New York area. He soon found the evening use of public schools for recreational, cultural, and social work to be a widespread practice in most of the nation. And yet the neighborhood idea had nowhere fully succeeded. "Why was the ideal praised by Woodrow Wilson and Charles E. Hughes, and preached by the leaders in social progress, not being realized?" (Perry 1939, 208).

This question was transformed into a matter of immediate import in 1922 when the Sage Foundation announced its intention to finance and direct the making of a plan for metropolitan New York. One of the plan's stated priorities was to bring both work and recreational opportunities within the ambit of the residential neighborhood. This clear purpose set Perry thinking about the design requirements for a safe and convenient neighborhood life. If a playground were located along an arterial street which children had to cross, they would be risking their lives. Or, if it were located at the boundary of a residential and a nonresidential area, then the play service district would be lopsided. He concluded that a "neighborhood playground could not be treated by itself" (Perry 1939, 209). Consideration must be given not only to other public elements, but to private dwellings as well. It was a question of their overall location and arrangement. How to build an urban neighborhood?

Perry found the answer in his own neighborhood of Forest Hills in Queens, New York, built by the Sage Foundation and designed by Frederick Law Olmsted and Grosvenor Atterbury. [It appeared to him to have what the average neighborhood lacked—distinguishing physical features, neighborhood services, a homogeneous population, and effective neighborhood oganization.]

It was by perfecting the design of Forest Hills that Perry arrived at his social invention which, like Drummond before him, he called the "Neighborhood Unit." Its purpose was twofold: to lay "the physical basis for that kind of face-to-face association which characterized the old village community" and to hold the anomic city at bay (*Regional Survey of New York and Its Environs* 1929, 23). In size, it would be just large enough to accommodate the population of one elementary school. All community institutions would be protectively grouped at the center, with commercial facilities relegated to the bounding arterial streets, which were to serve as channels for diverting the flow of traffic around rather than allowing it to pass through the neighborhood.

The neighborhood unit was a design destined for repetition on a larger scale. In the same decade that Perry's work was published, the architects Clarence Stein and Henry Wright were endeavoring to create new physical forms for neighborly life beyond the crowded inner city. The outcomes were Sunnyside Gardens, New York, and Radburn, New Jersey. Routing the highway around the town, reducing the area in streets, turning the houses away from the street to form a superhouse, separating foot and wheel traffic—these were the hallmarks of Radburn, and all were part of the neighborhood idea in planning.

Lewis Mumford projected the image of the neighborhood on an even larger screen, the region.[4] Mumford's regionalism was partially inspired by Ebenezer Howard. He honored the English planner's contribution which was "to outline the nature of a balanced community and to show what steps were necessary . . . to bring it into existence" (1965, 33). Even so, Mumford came to doubt the sufficiency of individual garden cities as a reform measure. By themselves, they could hardly be expected to make headway against "all our dominant institutions," whose effects "ramify in all directions—into the law courts and the constitution, into the educational system and its program, into the road engineer's shack and the tax-assessor's office." Garden cities were but "drops in a bucket," whereas what was needed was "to change the shape of the bucket itself, that is to say, the frame of our civilization" (1927). The region was to be the new framework. Without abandoning the garden city idea, Mumford placed his faith in regional planning, which he took great pains to distinguish from city planning. Unlike city planning, regional planning "asks not how wide an area can be brought under the aegis of the metropolis, but how the population and civic facilities can be distributed so as to promote and stimulate a vivid, creative life throughout a whole region." It promised "a new environment . . . in which the school may work intimately in touch with the home and with industry and with the surrounding world of nature" (1925b, 151–52).

The neighborhood unit, Sunnyside, Radburn, and Mumford's regionalism were the products of a single school of thought. Perry and Drummond provided the basic model, Stein and Wright enlarged it to town scale, while Lewis Mumford and Benton MacKaye magnified it still further to regional scale.

Western Influences: Conservation and Community

Although in the 1920s the neighborhood was well on its way to becoming a model for regional and national planning, its career was suddenly complicated by an encounter with another major force in American planning thought, this one emanating essentially from the West. While much has been made of the attempt to establish eastern values and institutions in the West, less attention has been paid to the opposite tendency—the counterflow of western influences eastward.[5]

One of the major influences of the western experience was that it provided urban reformers with powerful new metaphors for pushing their attack on the city. As proponents of community touting rural values, they saw the city as a region devoid of human fellowship and moral direction. From here, in the age of western settlement, it was but a short step to the notion of the city as a desert, a wasteland. A passage from Lewis Mumford epitomizes this peculiar conjunction of the urban, the rural, and the western: "[Regional planning] does not aim at urbanizing automatically the whole available country-side; it aims equally at ruralizing the stony wastes of our cities" (1925, 151). Besides the desert, other western images such as conservation and flood control found their way into the urban reformer's vocabulary. These did not remain mere figures of speech. Their effect was to shape a conception of regional structure and a strategy of regional planning which, in certain respects, ultimately came to conflict with the ideal of regional community.

Edward Ward occasionally resorted to conservationist imagery. Public property unused for community purposes was considered a wasted resource (Ward n.d., 15). The real wasted resource, however, was the neighborhood energies which gushed forth, workless and destructive. But that same "water pressure which might mean the devastation of the valley, converted into directed power . . . means its life" (Ward 1915, 9). There is no evidence that Ward was troubled by the contradiction between the democratic neighborhood and the directed neighborhood. A contemporary of Gifford Pinchot and Frederick Newell, he took it for granted that community conservation was not to be accomplished without expert guidance: "Social Center development is the construction of the necessary machinery whereby hitherto wasted civic and social forces may be coordinated to develop for all . . . benefits in light and power. The first thing that is necessary in any city . . . is the engagement of a man who . . . is technically qualified . . . to assume direct responsibility for the wider use of school property from the beginning" and "to cooperate efficiently with school principals in the service of the various neighborhoods" (1915, 34–35). This "social engineer" was the counterpart of the irrigation engineer.

For Lewis Mumford, the settlement of America has been a story of vast population migrations, ravaged resources, and belated conservation missions. The original conservation movement was an attempt to rescue the land from the damage left by a first migration—the opening of the West to the "land-hungry European." Its counterpart in the city was the housing reform movement, a "special kind of 'conservation,'" instituted to save "human resources" left stranded by the "westward march of men and manufactures" to the nation's chief power and mineral centers (Mumford 1968, xiii). Regional planning is the newest conservation, aiming to conserve both human values and natural resources. Its special object is to control the latest disorderly migration to the suburbs and to impart to it a more humane shape.

With Benton MacKaye, yet a different facet of conservation comes to the fore. Like Ward, he used water imagery, but where Ward saw gushing civic and social energies, MacKaye saw the menacing aspect of water. For him, regional planning was a problem in flood control.

As a young man in the U.S. Forest Service, MacKaye had ample exposure to watershed problems and water engineers. Later he worked for the single-taxer Louis F. Post when Post was assistant secretary of the interior in the Wilson administration. In 1916 Post and MacKaye prepared a bill for national colonization for Representative Robert Crosser of Ohio to create small farms with public funds to be retained in public ownership as an antispeculative measure. The ground rents would be plowed back into services and facilities for the settlers and would help to defray state and local taxes. The bill died in the House Labor Committee, but it was nonetheless a significant step forward in the development of community planning thought in this country. Its immediate targets were the lumber and mining industries, whose operations were a paradigm case of what conservationists had been decrying for years— the simultaneous ruin of human and natural resources. Timber mining, being a tramp industry, is a breeder of tramps is the way MacKaye put it (1919). With the Crosser bill, Post and MacKaye hoped to make of the lumber industry an object lesson in multiple reform. "Do not forget," Post told the Labor Committee, "that this is not merely a farm proposition, a grazing proposition, or a forestry proposition, but it is all of these added to a community proposition" (U.S. House 1917, 28, 80).

In the 1920s, as a member of the Regional Planning Association of America, MacKaye gave voice to a philosophy of regional planning that was both conservationist and, in a sense, conservative. That is, it envisaged not only the protection of natural and human resources, but also the salvaging of what remained of those cultural arrangements which had flourished in all countries prior to the coming of industrialism. Wherever he looked—in China, in India, in Europe—he saw a standardized metropolitanism "which forms itself around the traffic stream of modern industry and commerce" threatening to wash away the vestiges of a preindustrial "indigenous world." It was the contact of these two worlds on the eastern seaboard which constituted "the basic problem" of American regional planning, a problem which MacKaye, true to his conservationist background, conceptualized in water-engineering terms (1962, 45, 55).

In New England, the indigenous world was a fine old blend of the primeval environment and the remains of the colonial civilization. MacKaye surveyed the scene and asked the "rock-bottom question" of how to keep the rising metropolitan tide from bursting its dams at Boston, Springfield, Worcester, New London, and New Haven and drowning the downstream "indigenous" communities. This question marks a turning point in regional planning thought. Far from irrigating the urban desert with a spirit of community—the aim of earlier metropolitan reformers—it implied the sealing off of the metropolitanized sector of the region from the indigenous sectors. It signaled the abandonment of the city.

MacKaye's plan rested on two key structural elements: the "open way" comprising the natural space between indigenous towns and villages—wild lands, wastelands, ravines, hills, and mountain ridges—and the motorways which constituted the main channel for the controlled flow of metropolitanism. Placed athwart the motorway, the open way should be a dam to metropolitan sprawl. A well-designed network of such dams would divide the flood waters of metropolitanism into separate "basins," averting "their complete and total confluence." Within each basin the motorway would be contained by open zones guarding it on each side. These were the "levees" through which would pass the flow of traffic "but not the flow of metropolitanism." For "the motor truck is one thing, while the factory is quite another; the family sedan is one thing, while the apartment house is something else" (1962, 179–82). A few years later [1931] he added to his advice for canalizing "the Flood" by proposing the townless highway: "establish stations for entrance and departure where gas and food and every traveler's whim is to be served, then close the road *between* the stations to entrance, parking, exit. . . . The essence of the pattern is *inaccessibility*" (1968, 143–44). It was with reference to this scheme that Mumford later credited MacKaye with having anticipated the modern limited access expressway (1968, 213).

Mackaye's solution prefigures the contemporary metro-regional plan with its pictures of protected suburban enclaves, its limited access highways for providing suburbanites with access to their central economic and cultural institutions, and its wedges of open space flanking the transportation corridors. To say that Mackaye's concepts were more than anticipatory is perhaps to credit metaphors with greater power than they possess; nevertheless, it is difficult not to see in the flood management metaphor a formative influence. With this metaphor the image of the region ceases to be "a framework for neighborly association" (Mumford's phrase)[6] and becomes a tense structure for channeling population flows, for regulating the spatial relations of diverse cultures and populations. Most recently, in the name of environmental conservation, it has become a structure for regulating race relations.[7]

The Region as Family Farm

Despite their many differences, eastern and western planning were related at birth and showed the marks of their common origin. Family and community were shared themes. Just as the aim of eastern planning was to establish a haven for family life in the anomic city, so the purpose of western planning was to make the drylands safe for family farming. In the arid West men faced and attempted to "reclaim" external nature for its accustomed uses. What the eastern reformers confronted in the city, what they wished to reclaim, was their own cultural nature, fragmented and distorted by industrialism and urbanization—an incomparably more difficult task. In both cases the result was cultural conflict. In the East, a retreating "older America" attempted by means of regional planning to stave off an alien metropolitanism whose land use symbols were the skyscraper, the tenement house, and the motorway. In the West, the threat was from an alien system of land tenure. Not even water management was an exclusive western concern, although as we have seen, its eastern uses were derivative and metaphorical.

The connection between the family, the farm, and the western region was dramatized one blustery May day in 1952 on a site three miles north of Moses Lake, Washington, a community about a hundred miles east of Seattle. "Farm-in-a-Day" was part of a larger ceremony, the Columbia Basin Water Festival celebrating the beginning of the delivery of irrigation water to the million-acre Columbia Basin project.

The aim was to create in one day, from sage brush and native cover, a completely developed, eighty-acre, irrigated farm valued at $50,000, with farm machinery, home furnishings, and other fixtures, all to be presented to "the nation's most worthy veteran." To witness this event, thousands of people assembled on farm unit 167, block 40, on the official project plan. The women present were most interested in the farmstead, a three-bedroom, ranch-style, custom-built house of 1,500 square feet on a concrete floor. The house, provided with all modern conveniences, had been designed by five Seattle architects representing the Washington chapter of the American Institute of Architects. Sprinkler-irrigated pasture and alfalfa would comprise about one-quarter of the irrigated acreage. The remainder was to be surface-irrigated (Columbia Basin Celebration, Inc. 1952). At midnight, at the signal of exploding bombs, fifty tractors went into action, leveling, grading, seeding, fertilizing, corrugating, and irrigating. They worked all night, and by afternoon all phases of land preparation had been completed (*Columbia Basin Herald*, March 8, 1955).

The object of this public largess was Donald R. Dunn, a thirty-year-old World War II veteran and recent Kansas flood victim chosen in a search conducted by the Veterans of Foreign Wars. The big search had been a national affair. State winners were selected from thousands of applicants. A final winner was selected by a national board of judges. Two years before, the veteran and his family had been well established on four hundred acres by the Cottonwood River near Marin, Kansas, hoping for a bumper crop to help him pay off his loans for heavy stock and equipment. But on July 8, 1950, heavy rains caused the Cottonwood to rise, forcing the Dunns to flee Marin. By the time they returned several days later, the river had swept away years of hard work along with their crops and equipment. On borrowed funds, Dunn took his family to Yakima, Washington, where he found a job selling farm equipment. It was here that the "Big Search" found him (Columbia Basin Celebration, Inc. 1952).

The local residents, landowners, and businessmen who promoted Farm-in-a-Day required that the winning veteran should have a farm background, be earnestly interested in farming, and have personal attributes which would ensure that he would be a good citizen, a permanent asset to the "homeland of modern pioneers." An honorable discharge was taken for granted, war-time valor was to be hoped for, actual present need was to be duly weighed, but character, farm knowledge, integrity, and convincing love of the soil were essential (*Columbia Basin Herald*, March 8, 1955). The record showed that Dunn had all of these traits, and he was a disaster victim to boot. He thus appeared to conform in every respect to the traditional model of the perfect settler.

The events of May 29, 1952, were more than a publicity stunt. Farm-in-a-Day was the ceremonial enactment of an old folk dream—the establishment of the family farm in the drylands. The man who first attempted to put this dream on a scientific footing was John Wesley Powell. Powell explored the Great Plains, but, more important, he was the first to try to bring settlement policy beyond the 100th meridian into line with the climatic realities of the arid regions: "The physical conditions which exist in that land, and which inexorably control the operations of men, are such that the industries of the West are necessarily unlike those of the East, and their institutions must be adapted to their industrial wants" (Powell quoted in Webb 1931, 2).

The readaptation of man and environment in the arid West was to be a reciprocal process. Irrigation must replace dry farming, and cooperative colonies must replace the solitary homesteader. Powell proposed two pieces of legislation, one to govern the irrigable portion of the Great Plains and the other for the nonirrigable portion. Irrigation and pasturage districts of at least nine settlers each would be set up, with a limitation of eighty acres per person in the case of the irrigation districts and of 2,560 acres in the case of pasturage (Powell 1879). Powell saw quite clearly the relationship between types of land use and possible forms of community life. In pasture lands, settlement, in the nature of things, must be scattered. Therefore, if settlers were to "have the benefits of the local social organizations of civilization—as schools, churches, etc. and the benefits of cooperation in the construction of roads, bridges and other local improvements—" it was "essential that the residences should be grouped to the greatest possible extent," an arrangement that might be facilitated "by making the pasturage farms conform to topographic features in such manner as to give the greatest possible number of water fronts" (1879, 22–23).

The homestead laws had been enacted to ensure equality of opportunity in the development of the West, but Powell (1889) saw that equality would require the revision of these laws, for setting equal men on unequal land could only result in the ruin and dependency of thousands. To prevent the monopolization of agricultural resources by a few, water and land law would have to be revised. Above all, the right to the water should be made to inhere in the land for "the land without water is without value. . . . If one man holds that water he practically owns the land" (1890, 112). Powell proposed to organize the entire arid region into hydrographic basins, each a self-governing commonwealth.

Cooperative Colonies

Powell's successors, in the sense that they labored to transpose a vision of the good rural society to the West, were Elwood Mead and M. L. Wilson. He stood in the same relationship to these innovators as Edward Ward to Perry, Wright, Stein, and Mumford. A native of Indiana, Elwood

Mead began his career as professor of irrigation engineering at Colorado Agricultural College. In 1888 he moved to Wyoming and, when that territory achieved statehood, became its first state engineer, a post held for eleven years. In knowledge of the arid region, Mead was the reputed equal of any man in the West. With Buffalo Bill Cody he had explored the far reaches of Wyoming rivers. It was in Wyoming, also, that he attained worldwide renown with his plan for retaining public ownership over all state water resources for the benefit of settlers. Mead was in California as chief of the irrigation and drainage section of the U.S. Department of Agriculture when, in 1907, he was invited to serve as chairman of the State Rivers and Water Supply Commission in Victoria, Australia (*Reclamation Era* 1936, 33–34).

The American state of California and the Australian state of Victoria had much in common. Their shores were washed by the same ocean; the people spoke the same language and shared the British political tradition; and both struggled to adapt their culture and institutions to an arid environment. The Australians had been disappointed when irrigation works constructed several years earlier failed to produce an income commensurate with their cost. An investigation revealed that the fault lay not in the irrigation works but in the prevailing ownership pattern. The land was held in blocks too large for the intensive cultivation required by irrigation. The choice was between more intensive farming through a tenancy system and the breaking up of the larger holdings for sale to settlers. In deciding upon the latter course, the Victoria government committed itself to a system of state support that became a model for other countries to follow. To Mead, who had helped devise and administer the system, it was clear that the same approach must be applied at home.

In 1915 Mead returned to California and became the leading spirit there of land reform, Australian style. With the support of the administration, he succeeded in establishing the State Commission on Colonization, with himself as chairman. Mead and the commission conceived of their task as primarily educational. Believing that the general public was not yet ready for so radical and extensive a change as had occurred in Australia, the commission called for a demonstration of planned rural development under state auspices at a scale not larger than ten thousand acres of land. In 1917 a bill to that effect was introduced into the California legislature and adopted (Mead 1920).

The bill's provisions were embodied in the California State Land Settlement Act of 1917. The social ideal behind the law is indicated in a saying which was widely current at that time: "it takes three crops of settlers to put a farm on its feet." Essentially, it was a problem in conservation—how to keep that first settler from going broke. Colonization might succeed on the first try if the high cost of improving raw land could be balanced by government aid. A first requirement was large-scale land preparation—clearing, grading, irrigating. Second, was the scientific sizing and pricing of the farm units. Once on the farm, the settlers would need expert instruction and supervision to see them through the first difficult years. Planned social centers would fend off desert and mountain loneliness, but the critical requirement was economic cooperation. To reduce operating costs, the families must band together for cooperative buying and selling, animal breeding, and the use of heavy equipment. Most important was the human factor, for in the end the safety of government credit, and therefore the success of the whole venture, would depend on the selection of families qualified by experience, temperament, intelligence, and current assets. In a contemporary article prophetic of the Moses Lake affair thirty-three years later, Mead (1919, 37) translated all of this into the most direct human terms: "A farmer buys a farm worth $15,000 for $1500 down and pays the rest on long-time payments at a low rate of interest. The State is back of him. An expert farmer is there to guide him as to what to grow and how to take care of his land. His house is built for him by an expert architect, electricity, running water, sewers—all are his. The result is he lives in a better house, wears better clothes, uses better tools, has better livestock, raises better crops, makes more money, and his wife and family enjoy a social life unknown in the average farm neighborhood."

Although Mead was a forward-looking man, one of the most progressive-minded of his generation, his writings of the period are studded with dark references to Mexicans, Eastern Europeans, and Orientals. He deplored the practice which allowed "the creation of an alien oriental tenantry in the country." He found them "in sorry contrast to the State's first settlers, who were the finest type of American citizen" (1920, 2, 5). The threat of this alien tenancy system seemed all the more sinister that it was scarcely visible from the outside. Without an appreciation of the dilemmas of California society it would be easy to regard such utterances as plain bigotry. Paul Taylor (1945) has argued, however, that, more than the people, it was the emerging social and economic system which were condemned.

In California, the race problem was part of the labor problem. The day was long past when the hired hand had been a valued and respected member of the farmer's own household. The growth of large, landed estates with their requirement for a large supply of cheap labor had degraded farm labor. It created a rift between the farmer and his American helpers increasingly filled by Chinese, Japanese, Hindus, and Mex-

icans. The trend toward absentee landlordism and an abject Oriental
and Mexican underclass was noted by the Public Land Commission in
1905: "there exists and is spreading in the West a tenant or hired labor
system which not only represents a relatively low industrial development, but whose further development carries with it a most serious
threat. Politically, socially and economically, this system is indefensible"
(Pease 1962, 166). Three years earlier, the Federal Industrial Commission
had elaborated on the human costs of the system: "The renters rarely
ever succeed in laying by a surplus. On the contrary, their experiences
are so discouraging that they seldom remain on the same farm for more
than a year. They are not only unable to lay by any money, but their children remain uneducated and half-clothed. The system is apparently one
of the most undesirable, so far as the effect on the community is concerned" (Pease 1962, 166).

Should this alien system go unopposed in the name of progress? The
question, a perennial one in California politics, had risen twice before—
first with the slavery issue and again with respect to Oriental immigra-
tion (Taylor 1945). Mead was posing it once more with regard to land
settlement policy. Behind the 1917 law was the firm intention that midwestern institutions should prevail in the organization of California rural society. Good land use in midwestern terms meant land use by families, hence the provision to restore the disappearing American farm
worker by aids and benefits as substantial as those extended to farm
owners. There were to be allotments of about two acres each, large
enough for a house and a garden, sold on the same terms as land sold to
the farmers. In this way, it was hoped, city-drift would be checked, the
country would retain its good citizens, people who wanted "good roads,
good schools, and good government" (Mead 1920, 134).[8]

Such were the varied motives behind the 1917 law. To implement the
law, the State Settlement Board was established, with Mead as chairman.[9] The board was authorized to establish agricultural colonies, to
oversee all phases of land preparation including the construction of
buildings, and "to render the allotments habitable and productive in
advance of or after settlement" (California Statutes 1917, 1919). Theoretically, no subsidy was involved, land prices being set to recoup the entire cost of the project, including its reclamation. Provision, however,
was made for limited loans on stock and equipment, and settlers were
allowed forty years to amortize their debts on the land, twenty years for
the structural improvements, and five years for equipment and livestock. These liberal arrangements were the heart of the experiment inasmuch as settlement failure on ordinary reclamation land was attributed to the capital shortage which ruined the settler before he could make
his land productive (Teele 1923).

The immediate fruit of the law was the establishment of two cooperative agricultural colonies. Durham, in the Sacramento Valley, was the more successful of the two, having been founded and settled in 1917 when reclamation costs were low and becoming productive when farm commodity prices were at the their peak owing to the war. Delhi, in the San Joaquin Valley, was less fortunate. In 1919, the date of founding, construction costs were still high, but by the time the land went into production the country was in the midst of the postwar agricultural recession (Teele 1923). Payments in both colonies quickly fell into arrears, and only government leniency kept the settlers going.

In Mead, the western imagination was at work on a larger design for which Durham and Delhi were but the miniature prototypes. "The Arid Region," Mead had written almost two decades earlier, "is the nation's farm, . . . the chief hope of those who dream of landed independency." "Looking down the vista of the future," Mead espied "the dim outlines of a mighty civilization." In western America there was plenty of gold and silver to support it—also "immense deposits of copper, coal, oil and iron." Here "there would be no one-sided development . . . exclusively devoted to the production of corn, wheat or cotton, to manufacturing or to commerce." "The farm, the stock ranch, the lumber camp, the mine, the factory and the store are destined to grow up and flourish side by side, each drawing support from and furnishing sustenance to others" (Mead 1903, 3, 10–11). Regional community was the core of the design, just as community was the aim of the individual cooperative colony.

The Scientific Family Farm

Delhi and Durham demonstrated a certain capacity to control the natural environment, but they also exposed the Achilles heel of the California plan—helplessness in the face of the world economic environment. This was the specific problem addressed by another experiment to construct the good rural western region, Fairway Farms of Montana.

For Mead's region the model was the irrigated cooperative colony. The paradigm for the Montana region was the single family agricultural production unit adapted to a particular regional natural resource base. Through mechanization and the use of the latest scientific management techniques, this specialized economic unit was intended to hold its own with any other wheat-producing enterprise in the nation. Wholeness and balance were not relinquished, however, for these scientific farms were to be family farms, and the region they composed was to be a self-governing "little agricultural country in itself," with its own planning board adapting its production schedules to world market conditions. In this way the advantages of economic specialism would be combined with the benefits of social and political community.

Fairway Farms was the brainchild of Henry C. Taylor, first chief of the Bureau of Agricultural Economics, U.S. Department of Agriculture, and Milburn Lincoln Wilson, promoter of the domestic allotment plan and future chief of the Subsistence Homestead Division of the Public Works Administration. Indeed, his later ventures into national land use planning were the logical outcome of Wilson's Fairway Farms experiment.

"M. L." was born on a half-acre homestead in Iowa in 1885. He liked to stress his farm background, although he was far removed from the stereotype of the horny-handed son of the soil. Paul Johnstone has described him as a philosopher of agricultural life, an immensely cultivated man who liked to gather about him men of ideas.[10] After graduating from Iowa State College in 1907, Wilson went homesteading, first in Nebraska and then in Montana, where he learned at first hand the frustrations of farming in dry country. In time he became Montana's first county agent and the state's first extension leader. At the age of thirty-five, he left to study economics at the University of Wisconsin under John R. Common and Richard T. Ely. It was from these men that he absorbed that institutionalism in his approach to farm problems for which he was well known. Believing that all the farmer's problems were at heart cultural—a world of thought out of tune with a world of things—he saw them yielding only to a patient understanding and treatment of their cultural causes.

No place better exemplified a world of thought out of tune with a world of things than Montana in the 1920s. Billed by the state's promoters as "the last great West," it had been settled by midwesterners under the Homestead Laws of 1862. The most intense settlement occurred between 1908 and 1919, a period of unusually good weather conditions and favorable prices. Following the example of earlier settlers they brought with them their Missouri Valley agricultural subsistence farming and, as a hedge against price variations, a diversified crop of corn, oats, and barley. The system worked well enough while the good weather lasted, but after 1919, when the market failed and a period of severe drought set in, large numbers were forced to flee the state. In the early 1920s the Montana picture was the too familiar one of overdeveloped community facilities, large farm debts, abandoned farms, tax delinquency, and rising tenancy (Renne 1935).

The Fairway Farms project grew out of a meeting of Wilson and Taylor in Montana when the BAE chief was on a western tour inspecting the damages caused by the agricultural recession. He found there not only ruined farmers but also many distressed banks as receptive as the farmers to rehabilitation schemes. Recalling his own experiments in tenant rehabilitation on two Wisconsin farms, Taylor suggested a similar ap-

proach in Montana. Application was made to the Laura Spellman Foundation and a loan secured, supplemented by a grant from the Montana
State College Parnell fund. With this support nine experimental farms
were purchased in 1924. The questions to be answered by the Fairway
Farms project were, How large a land unit is required for successful
farming in various types of Montana land? What size family farm could
operate most efficiently? What low-cost production methods could off-
set Montana's climatic and geographic conditions? What type and how
much equipment would be required for each farm? What mix of land,
labor, and machinery promised the greatest economy? and How could
each farm job be performed with the greatest efficiency? (Starch 1933).

By 1925 most of the farms were equipped and operating with the ten-
ant-purchasers contracted for whole farms. Farm sizes were based on
their capabilities to support a family at an adequate living standard.
Annual amortization rates were pegged to the tenant's yearly income.
Thus, he might be able to survive for years in the face of drought or price
failure. Nevertheless, the same fate befell Fairway Farms as befell
Durham and Delhi. Even the most careful technical measures and institutional arrangements were no match for the general depression that
engulfed the nation in 1929. "Costs could be brought in line with eighty-
cent wheat or even sixty-cent wheat, but when the local price was down
to thirty cents (one day less than twenty cents) all the low-cost achievements went down the drain."[11]

The Fairway Farms project has been called "our first definite experiment in regional land use" (Lord 1947, 302). More accurately, it was a
cultural exploit in the form of a scientific experiment. Like Durham and
Delhi, its purpose was to demonstrate the validity of the folk belief that
good land use in the arid West is land use by families.[12] It was the precise counterpart of those other, eastern, cultural exploits—the building
of Sunnyside and Radburn undertaken to demonstrate the viability of
the family-life neighborhood in the "urban desert."

Conclusion

After fifty years it is not too early to ask what became of these planning
movements. Did they accomplish their ends? Do they survive today?

These are questions that have to be addressed at two levels. At the
mythic level there can be no doubt that the family and neighborhood
ideals are as robust as ever. To trace their history since the 1920s is beyond the scope of this study, but as evidence of their survival one need
only allude to contemporary phenomena as diverse as the commune
movement, the neighborhood government movement, the "global vil-

lage" idea, the "small is beautiful" idea, family farm sentiment, and the current attempt in California to enforce the terms of the 1902 Reclamation Act—all of which reflect in some degree the persistence of the dream of maintaining or restructuring urban and rural society along family or neighborhood lines. Over the years this purpose has been subject to occasional sharp attacks, but the voices raised against it—such as those of Isaacs (1948), Sennett (1970), and perhaps Jacobs (1961) and Alexander (1965)—have attracted attention more by their heterodoxy than by reflecting a real change in social philosophy.

The actual accomplishments of the movements reviewed in this study are another matter. Here it is not conclusive to point out that the achievements of the New Town movement in New Deal days and our own have been quite limited, or that Mead's efforts to establish cooperative colonies in California were failures. When did any ideal ever take on flesh in its entirety or without distortion? More enlightening is to ask what real differences have the ideals of family and neighborhood made in the planning of American cities and regions.

The evidence of real impact seems considerable, and much of it has to do with the effects of attitudes which are now so ingrained that they hardly seem remarkable. The ideal demonstrations, the "experiments," were often failures, but the principles they were intended to demonstrate didn't die. These entered the mainstream of general society and worked there silently. Associated with the resolve to fight free of the prevailing industrial and political order and to reorder society along family and neighborhood lines were three other principles which continue to modify urban and regional structure. They can be called "putting the highway in its place," "putting the experts in their place," and "changing the political map."

The early community planners were not blind opponents of the highway. They knew its benefits, but they also were quick to recognize that the modern highway is not just a road. It links the two sides of the human personality riven by the industrial order—the work side and the home side. Thereby it sustains and symbolizes that schizophrenic order. To planners of the neighborhood school of thought, therefore, street and highway planning is more than an engineering matter or a matter for transportation engineers only. It is an act of social reform. The reduction of the area devoted to streets, the separation of foot and wheel traffic, and the superblock are now common-place transportation planning measures that have their source in the family neighborhood idea. To these can be added zoning. No one would contend that zoning has only one purpose, but certainly one of its main purposes is to protect the home side of life from commercial and industrial traffic.

The progressives were always "fighting city hall," that is to say the "bosses," but to the extent that they were grass-roots democrats [not all were], they also eyed the expert city managers and planners and, indeed, expertise in general, with suspicion. They were not totally opposed to experts. As with highways, they wanted to put them in their place, which meant to subordinate them to the control of the general citizenry. It would be impossible to measure the precise effect of the insistence on citizen control, but wherever a highway is blocked or diverted, a tree or pond saved in the name of environmentalism, or the investment practices of a local bank questioned, there the neighborhood principle is alive and at work. Closely related to this political and intellectual insubordinacy was the reformers' penchant for proposing new political entities coextensive with the new types of community they were inventing. Western examples are Powell's self-governing river basin commonwealths and Wilson's little agricultural countries. In the urban East, it is clearly seen in the desire to erase the ward as the city's basic political unit and replace it with the family neighborhood. In metropolitanism, the neighborhood movement had a counterpart whose purpose was to supplant the corporate city itself. In the 1920s, Charles Merriam and others were already calling for statehood for "Greater Chicago" (Merriam, Parratt, and Lepawsky 1933). The cynical explanation is that these movements for metropolitan planning or consolidation were no more than gerrymandering on a grand scale. That is, as the "old stock" retreated to the suburbs, pressed by the immigrant tide, they intended to protect their stake in the city by absorbing it into a bigger structure (Hays 1964). Perhaps, but even while creating a broader framework for political control they were also discovering a wider field for "the exercise of the community spirit." Whatever the case, both urban movements have survived, with the result that the present-day city is beleaguered on two fronts—from within and below by a resurgent demand for neighborhood government and from above and beyond by the metropolitan government idea. It would be ignoring the facts to pretend that the drawing away of citizen loyalties toward these two idealized communities—the neighborhood unit and the metropolitan unit—has not affected the recent social, economic, and political fortunes of American cities, or that it will soon cease to do so (Kotler 1969).

Notes

This essay is adapted, with permission, from the *Journal of the American Institute of Planners* 44 (Oct. 1978): 399–411. It is based on research conducted primarily under a Guggenheim Fellowship in 1970–71. My special thanks to Andrew M.

Isserman, whose lively interest in this personal synthesis of the social visions of earlier generations of planners encouraged me to believe that others would share his interest. I am indebted to him and to Anthony Sutcliffe, Donald A. Krueckeberg, and the anonymous reviewers for their constructive readings of the manuscript.

1. For an early statement on the connection between the two movements, see Ely (1926).

2. This section on the origins and development of the neighborhood idea in planning owes much to the retrospective accounts of two of the major figures in that movement: Clarence Perry (1939) and Lewis Mumford (1954). For a most comprehensive account of the philosophic origins and experiments of community planning, see Conkin (1959). For a concise and definitive history of the principal sources, projects, and accomplishments of community planning in the 1920s, see Lubove (1963).

3. Ward was able to continue his work at the University of Wisconsin in 1909, where he was "to organize school centers on a statewide basis" (Glueck 1927).

4. Mumford (1954) credits Cooley, Perry, Drummond, and Wright and Stein as the principal American architects of the neighborhood idea, but clearly he was one of their company.

5. See, however, Hays (1959) and Lubove (1967).

6. Interview with Lewis Mumford, Feb. 5, 1970, Cambridge, Mass.

7. Both images were latent in the neighborhood unit itself. It was to be a nest for neighborly life and a bulwark against the industrial city. Roy Lubove (1967) has correctly characterized the thrust of modern regional planning as conservation plus community, but he seems not to have noticed that in the American context these two ideals have often proven to be antithetical.

8. There were proposals as early as the 1880s for retaining white labor by "giving laborers cottages for their families" (Taylor 1945, 23).

9. The other members included Harris Weinstock, an internationally known agricultural authority, and Morton Fleishacker, a San Francisco banker (Packard 1970, 42).

10. Interview with Paul Johnstone, Jan. 25, 1971.

11. Interview with Elmer A. Starch, June 23, 1971.

12. For more extensive accounts of the Fairway Farms experiment and its significance, see Kirkendall (1966) and Rowley (1970). [See also "The Land Utilization Movement of the 1920s" in this volume.]

References

Alexander, Christopher. 1965. "A City Is Not a Tree." *Architectural Forum* 122 (April): 58–62; (May): 58–61.

California State Statutes, 1917. Land Settlement Act, 1, 566; 1919, 838.

Columbia Basin Celebration, Inc. 1952. Press Release, 4.

Columbia Basin Herald, March 8, 1955.

Conkin, Paul K. 1959. *Tomorrow a New World*. Ithaca: Cornell University Press.

Cooley, Charles H. 1902. *Human Nature and the Social Order.* New York: Charles Scribner's Sons.

———. 1909. *Social Organization.* New York: Charles Scribner's Sons.

———. 1918. *Social Process.* New York: Charles Scribner's Sons.

Ely, Richard T. 1926. "The City Housing Corporation and Sunnyside." *Journal of Land and Public Utility Economics* 2 (April): 172–85.

Follett, Mary P. 1926. *The New State.* New York: Longmans, Green.

Forbes, George M. 1916. *Hearings on H.R.12653.* Committee on the District of Columbia, House of Representatives, 64th Cong., 1st sess. April 12. Washington: U.S. Government Printing Office.

Glueck, Eleanor T. 1927. *The Community Use of Schools.* Baltimore: Williams and Wilkens.

Guttenberg, Albert Z. 1976. "The Land Utilization Movement of the 1920s." *Agricultural History* 50 (July): 477–90.

Hays, Samuel P. 1959. *Conservation and the Gospel of Efficiency.* New York: Atheneum.

———. 1964. "The Politics of Reform in Municipal Government in the Progressive Era." *Pacific Northwest Quarterly* 55 (Oct.): 157–69.

Hofstadter, Richard. 1955. *The Age of Reform.* New York: Vintage.

Isaacs, Reginald R. 1948. "The Neighborhood Theory: An Analysis of Its Adequacy." *Journal of the American Institute of Planners* 14 (Spring): 15–23.

Jacobs, Jane. 1961. *The Death and Life of Great American Cities.* New York: Random House.

Kirkendall, Richard S. 1966. *Social Scientists and Farm Politics.* Columbia: University of Missouri Press.

Kotler, Milton. 1969. *Neighborhood Government.* Indianapolis: Bobbs-Merrill.

Lord, Russell. 1947. *The Wallaces of Iowa.* Boston: Houghton Mifflin.

Lubove, Roy. 1963. *Community Planning in the 1920s.* Pittsburgh: University of Pittsburgh Press.

———. 1967. *The Urban Community: Housing and Planning in the Progressive Era.* Englewood Cliffs: Prentice-Hall.

MacKaye, Benton. 1919. *Employment and Natural Resources.* U.S. Department of Labor. Washington: U.S. Government Printing Office.

———. 1968. *From Geography to Geotechnics.* Edited by Paul T. Bryant. Urbana: University of Illinois Press.

———. 1962. *The New Exploration.* Urbana: University of Illinois Press.

Mead, Elwood. 1919. "Buying a New Farm in the New Way: The Success of California's New Plan." *Ladies Home Journal* 36 (no. 6): 37.

———. 1920. *Helping Men Own Farms.* New York: Macmillan.

———. 1903. *Irrigation Institutions.* New York: Macmillan.

Merriam, Charles E., Spencer D. Parratt, and Albert Lepawsky. 1933. *The Government of the Metropolitan Region of Chicago.* Chicago: University of Chicago Press.

Mumford, Lewis. 1927. "The Fate of Garden Cities." *Journal of the American Institute of Architects* 15 (Feb.): 37–39.

———. 1965. "The Garden City Idea in Modern Planning." In Ebenezer

Howard, *Garden Cities of Tomorrow*. Edited by F. J. Osborn. Cambridge: MIT Press.

———. "1954. The Neighborhood and the Neighborhood Unit." *Town Planning Review* 24 (Jan.): 256–70.

———. 1925. "Regions to Live In." *Survey Graphic*, May 1, 151–52.

———. 1968. *The Urban Prospect*. New York: Harcourt, Brace and World.

Packard, Walter. 1970. *Land and Power Development in California, Greece and Latin America*. Berkeley: Regional Oral History Office, Bancroft Library, University of California, 38.

Park, Robert E., Ernest W. Burgess, and Roderick D. MacKenzie. 1925. *The City*. Chicago: University of Chicago Press.

Pease, Otis. 1962. *The Progressive Years*. New York: George Braziller.

Perkins, Dwight. 1912. "The Relation of Schoolhouse Architecture to the Social Center Movement." *Proceedings of the National Education Association* (50): 234–39.

Perry, Clarence. 1921. *Ten Years of the Community Center Movement*. New York: Russell Sage Foundation.

———. 1939. *Housing for the Machine Age*. New York: Russell Sage Foundation.

Powell, John W. 1890. "Institutions for the Arid Lands." *Century Magazine* 18 (May): 111–16.

———. 1879. *Report on the Lands of the Arid Region of the United States*. House of Representatives. Washington, D.C.: U.S. Government Printing Office.

———. 1889. Speech before the North Dakota Constitutional Convention, Aug. 5. Reprinted in *Reclamation Era*. Sept. 1936, 201–2.

Reclamation Era. Feb. 1936, 33–34.

Regional Survey of New York and Its Environs. 1929. Vol. 7: *Neighborhood and Community Planning*. New York: The City.

Renne, Roland R. 1935. *Readjusting Montana's Agriculture*. Bulletin 306. Montana State College, Agricultural Experiment Station, Bozeman.

Rowley, William D. 1970. *M. L. Wilson and the Campaign for the Domestic Allotment Plan*. Lincoln: University of Nebraska Press.

Sennett, Richard. 1970. *The Uses of Disorder*. New York: Knopf.

Starch, Elmer A. 1933. *Farm Organization as Affected by Mechanization*. Bulletin 278. Montana State College, Agricultural Experiment Station, Bozeman.

Taylor, Paul. 1945. "Foundations of California Rural Society." *California Historical Quarterly* 24 (Sept.): 193–228.

Teele, R. P. 1923. *Land Reclamation Policies in the United States*. Bulletin 1257. United States Department of Agriculture. Washington, D.C.: U.S. Government Printing Office.

U.S. House. 1917. *National Colonization Bill Hearings, H.R.11329*. 64th Cong., 2d sess. Washington, D.C.: U.S. Government Printing Office.

U.S. Senate. 1915. *Commission on Industrial Relations, Final Report*. Document 415. 64th Cong., 1st sess. Washington, D.C.: U.S. Government Printing Office.

Ward, Edward J. 1915. *The Social Center*. New York: D. Appleton.

———. n.d. *Social and Civic Centers*. Bulletin 23. Boston: American Unitarian Association.

Webb, Walter P. 1931. *The Great Plains*. Boston: Ginn.
Wirth, Louis. 1938. "Urbanism as a Way of Life." *American Journal of Sociology* 44 (July): 1–24.
Yeomans, Alfred B., ed. 1916. *City Residential Land Development*. Chicago: University of Chicago Press.

9

The Land Utilization Movement of the 1920s

The 1920s are memorable in the annals of American land policy as the decade in which the idea of limiting agricultural growth first gained wide currency and seriously challenged the traditional commitment to unlimited growth.[1] Although this phase of the movement for agricultural restraint took its original impetus from the attempt to protect agriculture from the ravages of the post–World War I recession, its policy implications were broad and far-ranging, ultimately involving every facet of American society. Limiting agriculture meant not only extensive land use changes. Implicitly it meant the retirement and reemployment of surplus farms and surplus farmers. Thereby it afforded numerous points of entry for social concerns which went beyond the issue of economic parity for the agricultural sector. The subject of this study is the conceptual structure of the land utilization movement of the 1920s, that is, the system of ideas that prevailed within it, rather than its step-by-step unfolding in time.[2]

Although parity remained the dominant theme, after 1922 the agricultural problem was also discussed widely in terms of the "rationalization of agriculture." In every phase of the discussion, as well as in the research and experimentation which it generated, two concepts were of central importance: marginality and balance. That is, it was always a matter of finding the boundaries between different qualities of land and the balance points between different interests in the land—this for the purpose of arriving at a more rational pattern of national and local land utilization.

Rationalizing agriculture meant, first of all, a thoughtful revision of the industry's external boundaries (those separating it from other major land uses) and its careful containment within these rectified frontiers. Above all, it meant imposing restraints on the expansion of agriculture into forest and semiarid areas. One major objective here was the protection of established farmers from competition, particularly through the

suppression of the land-creating activities of the Bureau of Reclamation
in the western states. The movement for agricultural restraint, however,
was much more than a narrow sectional strategy for maintaining the
vested economic interests of eastern and midwestern farmers. Authentic and long-recognized ethical interests were also involved, namely, the
conservationist interest in sharing scarce soil and forest with future human users and the preservationist interest in sharing them with nonhuman users. Working in the same direction to curb agricultural expansion
were certain changes of a cultural nature affecting American society at
this time—for example, the gradual emergence of a leisure philosophy
and the concomitant relaxation of the work ethic, a trend fostered in part
by industrialization and increased productivity. As one consequence,
certain lands, especially forested lands, were acquiring value as a recreational resource in addition to their value as a reserve for agriculture.

A second cultural change contributing to the restraint of agriculture
was the undermining of the traditional commitment to husbandry as a
superior mode of life. Rhetorically, country folk might still scorn the city
as alien and inferior, yet they were drawn by its glitter (Shideler 1973).
On the farms and in the rural communities men dreamed of having the
advantages of industrialization minus its dangers and discomforts—a
desire matched precisely by the yearning of urbanites for the amenities
of rural life and the eagerness of industrialists to escape, through decentralization, the high production costs associated with urban congestion.
These tendencies were reinforced by (they were not created by) the de-
pressed state of agriculture, inasmuch as the recreation industry and
decentralizing urban industry promised supplementary or alternative
employment opportunities to idle farms and farmers. They prompted
considerable interest in the urban-rural fringe as a special land use zone,
a unique meeting and blending place for the urban and rural economies
and life-styles. Some regarded this zone at the edge of large cities as a
"new frontier" replacing the old frontier of the not-too-distant past.

Rationalizing agriculture also signified rectification of the internal
boundaries of the industry, the drawing, within the agricultural domain
itself, of clearer, firmer lines around each major type of farming area—
this also in the interests of industrial efficiency, price maintenance, and
conservation. Indeed, the decade from 1922 to 1932 was marked by the
most strenuous scientific efforts to define specialized agricultural regions which would serve simultaneously all of these diverse purposes
in agricultural land utilization.

The necessity of curbing headlong agricultural expansion was a note
struck early in the decade. Addressing the National Agricultural Conference convened in 1922 to consider measures for combating the agri-

cultural recession, Richard Ely, the land economist, declared that "there must be a proper proportion between agricultural production and the production of non-agricultural goods and services" (1922, 117). In land use terms the basic question was, Where should agriculture leave off and other land uses begin? No one put this question more insistently nor strove more consistently to answer it than Lewis C. Gray. A former student of Ely's at the University of Wisconsin, Gray had held a number of academic posts before assuming headship of the Division of Economics of the U.S. Department of Agriculture, three years before it was incorporated into the newly created Bureau of Agricultural Economics. Gray's influential views on the external boundary of agriculture found general exposition in an article in the USDA *Yearbook of Agriculture* in 1923. Like all innovators, Gray sought precedents for his proposals. In this article, agricultural readjustment was presented as the second phase of the conservation movement led by Gifford Pinchot and others under Theodore Roosevelt. The premise of the first phase, that certain lands, primarily forests, were affected with the public interest, was now to be extended to crop and pasture land.

The article first attacked the question of the limits of agriculture from the standpoint of a required balance between present and future resource users. Using rough population projections and estimates of future requirements for forest, pasture, and croplands, Gray declared that the nation had reached and passed the high-water mark of land supply three decades earlier. Now it was well into the era of land scarcity, a condition temporarily obscured by the recession and by the long-standing practice of extending cropland at the expense of forest reserves. With timber being cut at a rate almost four times the annual rate of growth, Americans lived in a "fool's paradise" of abundant resources. Consequently, drastic modifications were required "in our rate of consumption of timber, in our rate of growth, or in both" (Gray et al. 1923, 451–55).

Having demonstrated the fact of land scarcity, the article proceeded to a survey of its causes. It noted the tendency of American farmers to increase their productivity by substituting land for labor. The obvious remedy was more intensive farming practices, better crop selection, crop rotation, improved methods of land preparation, and the use of higher-yield strains (Gray et al. 1923, 463–65). As additional cropland would be needed to meet annual growth, reclaimed land from the cutover areas or semiarid regions would suffice. Certainly there was no justification for added acreage by large-scale irrigation or drainage, except in cases "where the economy of reclamation could be demonstrated unequivocally" (497).

This finding set the stage for a direct attack on the western dam builders and their agent, the Bureau of Reclamation. The "evil results" of their shortsighted policies of premature colonization were plain for all to see. The lure of western settlement was no longer the availability of high-quality virgin land, but rather the siren song of profiteers and community boosters leading the ignorant and unsuspecting on to their destruction. Not only were the plains strewn with ruined farmers and ruined land companies, but the prosperity of the established farming industry itself was threatened. To the "sentimental argument" that "we need more farm homes," the unabashed reply was, "We do not need more farm homes than farms." Nor was large-scale subsidy the answer, as some advocates of agricultural expansion proposed. By encouraging profitless adventures, government aid made subsidy increasingly essential. "Thus, like a drug addict, we must go on and on increasing the dose" (Gray et al. 1923, 503–4).

The finale of this remarkable report was a call for a national land utilization policy to replace the sectional policy of the past. Gray and his colleagues recommended a directed system of national land settlement, meaning the supplanting of the reclamation system which favored the West by a system which considered the specific land use capabilities of "all parts of the Nation"; a scientific land classification to be conducted jointly by the federal government and the states; a program for the protection of birds and other wildlife in forests and marshes; attention to the recreational potential of the wild lands; the creation of grazing districts in the public pasture lands to be operated under a permit system; and the recognition of the interrelatedness of all natural resource problems through the establishment of a national administrative agency to ensure unity and consistency of execution (505–6).

Most of these themes were reiterated throughout the decade by Gray and others. Eight years later, in 1931, they were virtually codified in a series of eighteen recommendations by the National Land Utilization Conference convened in Chicago by Secretary of Agriculture Arthur Hyde and attended by three hundred agricultural experts. Their recommendations included the rehabilitation and public administration of grazing lands; watershed protection; an economic inventory and classification of all lands and soils; the decentralization of population and industry; the public retention or acquisition of land for the purpose of achieving wildlife protection, reforestation, and soil conservation; and the reorganization of rural community land use to achieve local public economies (National Conference on Land Utilization 1932, 240–49). To see to the promotion of its policies, the conference concluded with the establishment of a National Land Use Planning Committee, the predecessor of the renowned National Resources Planning Board. But nothing that was said at that conference, or in the subsequent New Deal period, ever exceeded the 1923 report in its reach.[3]

In 1923, theoretically at least, the question of the external boundary of agriculture was not a new one. A century earlier David Ricardo had defined the economic margin as the point where the revenues from the cultivation of land equal the outlays. While recognizing the Ricardian definition as a useful point of departure, Gray rejected this break-even point as a sufficient criterion for delimiting agricultural land utilization and sought to replace it with the concept of a social margin. Even assuming that it was "a reasonably correct interpretation of what occurs in practice (and it is not)," the economic margin did not necessarily "coincide with the line which, in the interest of public policy, should be drawn between lands to be used for agriculture and lands to be used for other purposes" (Gray 1930, 263).

Gray's views on the action implications of the difference between the economic and social margins were marked by humanity and good sense. In some instances, he thought, it would "be well to eliminate from farming certain classes of land which are clearly supermarginal" in the economic sense; for example, good land which is so sparsely settled that provision of adequate services is either impossible or grossly uneconomical from the public standpoint. On the other hand, it would "frequently be found wise to encourage the continued occupancy of land otherwise submarginal, so long as existing improvements are capable of use." Likewise, one should "hesitate to displace [from economically submarginal land] an old or infirm occupant who can exist better where he is than elsewhere, unless perchance his removal may appear essential to the larger aims of the public policy" (Gray 1930, 265).

To the Second International Conference of Agricultural Economists assembled at Cornell University in 1930, Gray enumerated the steps required for the accurate definition of the social margin in local areas: an inventory of physical conditions such as soil type, cover, rainfall, temperature, and topography; the mapping of cultural features, roads, railroads, population centers, and the like; a survey of current land uses; the division of the region into land types "representing complexes of associated physical and cultural conditions"; and historical studies of the area with particular reference to recent changes in land use and possible tendencies to tax delinquency and land abandonment (267).

Throughout the 1920s, farm scientists, land economists, and government officials employed various approximate measures in defining the "social margin." In Appalachia, farm abandonment and living standards were important criteria (Weeks 1929, 603). In New York State, on the basis of comprehensive physical, economic, and demographic surveys conducted at Cornell by Professor George F. Warren and later by Governor Franklin D. Roosevelt's Agricultural Advisory Commission, state land was divided into five classes ranging from land earmarked for public ownership and early reforestation to land rated for permanent retention in agriculture. The latter class was to be developed as highly and served as adequately as possible with good roads, schools, and recreation and health facilities (Ladd 1932, 53–55).

In the lake states of Michigan and Wisconsin, where certain counties were the victims of the lumber industry, the principal criterion was tax delinquency (Weeks 1932, 603). Michigan had entered the Union in 1837, with 35,000,000 acres of virgin forest. Eighty-five years later this store was down by nine-tenths (de Vries 1928, 516). Much of the cutover land might have undergone an uneventful transition to agricultural use, but any remaining hope in that direction was soon foreclosed by the recession. The northern counties remained in a state of arrested development, with the situation growing worse yearly (Wehrwein 1932, 112). As a result, Michigan found itself the unwilling heir of increasing amounts of tax-delinquent acres, some of which had been held by the owners for forty years in the expectation that one day their properties would become part of the "great dairy empire" of the North. The future of the northern counties thus became a matter of serious concern to the wealthier industrialized southern communities of the state, which were saddled with the financial support of northern schools and roads (de Vries 1928, 516–17; Wehrwein 1930, 270–77).

Matters were complicated by much disagreement concerning the true potential of the logged-over land. To resolve this question, the Michigan Land Economic Survey was inaugurated cooperatively in 1922 by the state university and the state departments of agriculture and conservation according to specifications written by the geographer Carl O. Sauer. The executors of this project took pains to avoid the term *land classification*. Its chief theorist, P. S. Lovejoy, explained that "land inventory is one thing, that land classification and planning for use is another thing, and that putting the plans into practice—the political science or engineering of land utilization—is still a different thing." Thus he distinguished among three functions, all of which "are necessary to achieve intelligent land utilization" (1925, 166–67). Michigan concentrated on the inventory, collecting great amounts of data on characteristics as diverse as soil, cover, and timber type; hydrography; and tenure, tax value, and trade area. Writing in 1925, Lovejoy appeared satisfied that this unclassified data "indicated with even greater precision than was to be hoped for" the boundaries between supermarginal, marginal, and submarginal land (170).

In Wisconsin, similar conditions and objectives obtained, and similar methods were employed. The Badger State, however, was disposed to go beyond the inventory stage to the stages of actual classification and legislation. In 1929 a state law, the first of its kind, was passed, permitting county boards to "regulate, restrict and determine the areas within which agriculture, forestry and recreation may be conducted," as well as to determine "the location of roads, schools and industries." At the same time, the right of towns to refuse to build roads for unauthorized or scattered settlement was recognized (Wehrwein 1931, 278). Previously, the laying out of towns to attract settlers and the building of roads and schools to serve sparsely settled areas had been standard practice. Now, armed with zoning powers and guided by land surveys, county boards might, if they wished, interdict the use of submarginal land for agriculture and divert it to alternative uses such as forestry and recreation. They were also empowered to lay out schools, roads, and even whole towns to fit local conditions in the new agricultural, forest, and recreational districts. For example, the size and shape of such towns might be adjusted "to secure an adequate tax base" (Wehrwein 1931, 117). In theory, at least, the implications for local rural community planning were momentous.[4]

The Wisconsin law exemplified the effort to establish agriculture's frontier with a forest region. On the Great Plains, it was a matter of finding a tenable boundary between land suitable for farming and land unsuitable for that purpose by virtue of its excessive aridity. Consequently, the main criterion of marginality was the farmer's ability to wring an adequate living from various qualities of arid soil using scientific farm-management techniques. Here, the critical experiment was the Fairway Farms project in Montana.[5]

In the early 1920s, because of a protracted drought and the market failure, Montana agriculture was plagued with overdeveloped facilities, large farm debts, abandoned farms, and rising tenancy (Renne 1935, 21–22). The nub of the problem was that on the 320 semiarid acres granted under the amended Homestead Law of 1909, a Montana farmer could scarcely hope to produce enough to compensate for declining prices and, at the same time, provide the automobile, radio, and the education for his children, which were now becoming part of his minimum acceptable standard of living. The choice was between cutting costs and cutting his living standard (Starch 1933, 7–12). The aim of the Fairway Farms project was to resolve that dilemma. The basic idea was the "consolidation of small tracts, which are submarginal as family units under present conditions into farms which are still family farms and can become supermarginal with the introduction of new methods that give a larger output per worker" (Wilson 1926, 170). These arrangements were considered a fair way of committing people to the land, hence the name Fairway Farms. The proposition was that, with expert management, a tenant family might be assisted to climb the agricultural ladder to farm ownership (Starch 1933, 17).[6]

In addition to establishing the limits for a viable and responsible agriculture vis-à-vis forest, range, and semidesert, the new external boundary sought by Ely, Wilson, Gray, and others was intended to include a new definition of the urban-rural border. This was the most difficult problem of all, since the line between city and country was more than a geographic boundary. It was also a point of contact between conflicting modes of economic and social life, posing questions as to a fairer division of income and political power between farmers and industrial workers, the sharing of natural and cultural resources, and the establishment of possible new forms of human settlement.

Henry Taylor, first chief of the Bureau of Agricultural Economics, aired his feelings on some of these matters. It was no longer deniable, he charged, that agricultural policy was contrary to the farmer's true interest. Indeed, "Uncle Sam [had] come to view his farmers as the farmer views his cows." Henceforth, the farmer's objective would be not landownership but income, requiring a decisive change not only in urban-rural relationships, but in national economic policy as well. In the future, protective tariff legislation must be enacted only after the most careful scrutiny of its impact on farm welfare. National settlement policy was another matter in need of revision, according to Taylor. Agencies encouraging the holding of excess population on the land must be replaced by agencies fostering their orderly migration to the cities (357–67). These thoughts were written in 1929. A few months later the Crash wrote finis to all talk of sending idle farmers to the city. In fact, for a brief time in the early 1930s, the historic flow of population was reversed, the U.S. Census recording a net out-migration from the cities.

Thus, as the decade ended, farm leaders found themselves confronting what they, and the nation, dreaded: a large underclass of idle farmers whose ranks were augmented by the urban unemployed. Members in good standing of neither agriculture nor urban industry, this class constituted the inhabitants of what was an urban-rural fringe in the social and economic senses. In terms of land utilization there seemed to be only one remedy: the decentralization of urban industry closer to rural communities. For farmers, it promised a solution to the surplus labor problem. For industrialists, it meant lower production costs. For unemployed urban workers, it meant subsistence; for "submarginal" farmers, a chance for supplementary income in the form of part-time factory jobs.

Henry Ford had set an early example by converting an old mill on the River Rouge to a valve shop. Ford was proud of the contribution of his decentralization program to rural welfare. "We have not drawn men from the farm," he boasted, "we have added industry to farming" (Ford 1926, 14–41).

Franklin Roosevelt, whose interest in land utilization dated from his days as a state senator in New York, had all these themes woven into a proposal even before his ascent to the presidency. In 1931, Governor Roosevelt urged the creation of a State Commission on Rural Homes to be charged with finding ways and means to establish "wholly new rural communities . . . on good agricultural land within reasonable distance of . . . new industries aimed primarily to give cash wages on a cooperative basis during the non-agricultural season" (1932, 384). This more diffuse, more problematic, agricultural frontier made the national scene after Roosevelt's election, with the establishment in the Public Works Administration of a Subsistence Homestead Division, with M. L. Wilson as its chief.

A second general question implicit in the notions of rationalization, restraint, and "wise land use" concerned the internal boundaries of the farming industry. Given the accepted domain of agriculture, where should one type of farming leave off and another begin? Within this domain, to what extent and on what basis should regional land use be specialized?

In the 1920s, the prevailing attitudes toward the internal boundaries of the industry and the regional planning concepts derived from them were an amalgam of conservationist thought, efficiency considerations, and antidepression measures. In the shaping of these attitudes, moreover, soil science played a prominent part, as it did in the development of attitudes toward the external boundaries of agriculture. Reviewing the literature in 1929, David Weeks noted the "tendency for soils men to break away . . . from the original objective of classifying soils on the basis of their inherent physical characteristics and to inquire further into their adaptation and use" (1929, 597–98). From observing that soil was a factor in use, it was but a short step to the belief that soil type should determine use. J. G. Lipman, dean of the New Jersey Agricultural College, was expressing the view of many soil scientists when he urged that "systems of farming should be planned for each soil region" (1932, 164).

Certain new findings in soil science were made to order for the conservationists, especially the discovery that soil was not a passive reservoir of plant nutrients, but an entity in dynamic interaction with its environment and therefore vulnerable to adverse changes in that environment. Conservationists were quick to relate this insight to the farmer's economic survival. "Making better use of the soils by using them more in accordance with their adaptations and requirements . . . is a means of improving agricultural efficiency," wrote Hugh Bennett, the reputed father of soil conservation (1921, vi). In addition to specific antierosion measures applied at the individual farm level, soil conservation required a general conformity of agricultural land use to soil type, since it was the maladaptation of the land on the broadest scale which constituted the greatest threat. The most egregious case was the Great Plains, where "land suitable for grazing only [had been] plowed up in an attempt to use it as arable land" (Ely 1922, 115).

The limits of soil conservation as a sufficient organizing principle for agriculture lay in the imperfect correspondence between the farmer's long-term and short-term interests. As F. F. Elliott later wrote, "When the choice lies between an uncertain future and a very real present, the latter usually wins out" (1937, 18). More to the point was the argument stressing the advantages of soil conservation for raising present income. By establishing each major crop upon its most favorable soil, significant production economies might be achieved. But this argument, too, had its shortcomings, since the farmer's income was determined as much by world prices as by local production costs. What had lured many settlers onto the Great Plains was not the prospect of low production costs, but high wartime prices.

Clearly, the farmer had to operate in the narrow limits imposed by two variables—nature and the world market. Correspondingly, within the land utilization movement, there were two major impulses toward the internal rationalization of agriculture. The root of one was the semireligious conservationist belief that agricultural organization ought to reflect the differentiated order of nature, that agricultural land use should conform to land type. The root of the other was the practical necessity of adjusting domestic land use to world economic forces as reflected in price.

Farm leaders were not blind to the benefits in either course. Adjusting agricultural land use to land type, conservation style, could aid the cause of agricultural parity by economizing production. At the same time, recognizing and facilitating the division of arable land into type-of-farming areas conceived as discrete industries based on comparative natural resource advantages could help eliminate inter-area competition, reduce surplus production, and thereby contribute to higher prices for each major farm commodity. In fact, the major agricultural areas actually were, to a considerable extent, discrete industries adapted to their best resource bases in both the economic and the conservation senses. The problems were primarily those of marginal adjustment—

retiring submarginal land and eliminating overlapping production—and the suppression of the programs to create new agricultural land in the West.

Eventually, internal rationalization in the sense of "planning with nature" and in the interest of price maintenance converged in the concept of the specialized agricultural region as a permanent social, political, and economic entity. In 1933, this ideal was stated with singular clarity to certain citizens of Minnesota by M. L. Wilson: "To bring order out of this chaos it will be necessary to set up a type of national economic research to study the comparative advantage of different regions in certain lines of farm production." Each region would have its specialty, and each would be "a little agricultural country in itself" with its own planning board which would "work out the soil and land use classification in their territories" and supply farmers with data for adjusting their operations and reducing their costs. At the summit there should be a national planning board "continually at work on a program for American agriculture," keeping production adjusted to demand, and, insofar as possible, controlling the destructive forces of competition (47–48).

The first legislative steps in this direction had been taken three years earlier with a bill introduced by Congressman Victor Christgau of Minnesota. Its intent was to "aid farmers in making regional adjustments in agricultural production, to assist in preventing undesirable surpluses . . . thereby stabilizing farm incomes." The bill would have authorized the secretary of agriculture to establish regions "based primarily upon the general similarity of crop and livestock production." In each region, the agricultural experiment stations would be organized into research councils for the purpose of conducting studies "to determine the relative advantages, costs and returns of different crops and livestock . . . the best uses of land and the best adjustments of farm operations to these conditions" and to analyze and appraise, for purposes of adjustment, "present and prospective competition between regions in different sections of the country and in other countries" (U.S. Congress 1930, 1–3).

The Christgau bill never got out of committee, but even if it had become law it is doubtful that it could have accomplished what its sponsors hoped for in terms of raising farm income. At the heart of the bill was the amiable notion that flourished on both sides of the urban-rural border in the 1920s—that scientific land use planning, informed by progressive economic and ethical ideals, could be a cure-all for the nation's social, cultural, and economic ills. When the Great Depression came, even the most stringent scientific efficiencies proved to be no match for the general price collapse that engulfed the agricultural sector. As William Rowley has demonstrated, it was this bitter fact that turned farm leaders, such as Wilson, in the direction of another and more powerful form of agricultural restraint, the Domestic Allotment Plan and, ultimately, the Agricultural Adjustment Act of 1933 (Rowley 1970).

Notes

The research for this essay was conducted in part under a Guggenheim Fellowship in 1970–71. It was originally published in *Agricultural History* 50 (July 1976): 477–90, and is adapted with permission. The author wishes to thank Elmer A. Starch for clarifying aspects of M. L. Wilson's role in the land utilization movement.

1. A more precise designation of the period covered by this study is 1922–32. The phrase "the 1920s" is used in the title and occasionally in the text for brevity and also to emphasize the distinctness of the period from the subsequent New Deal period, "the 1930s."
2. For two recent historical accounts of aspects of the land utilization movement, see Richard S. Kirkendall (1966, esp. 11–49) and William D. Rowley (1970, esp. 60, 106–7, 197–98).
3. For an account of Gray's contribution stressing the scientific roots, see Richard S. Kirkendall (1963).
4. For an excellent account of the Wisconsin experience and zoning experiment, see Carstensen (1958, esp. 90–116).
5. Interview with Elmer A. Starch, June 23, 1971.
6. The family theme in land use planning was prominent in urban as well as in rural areas in the 1920s (as it is today). Sunnyside Gardens in New York and Fairway Farms in Montana were contemporary social and economic experiments. Richard Ely (1926), a member of both the Fairway Farm Board and the board of the City Housing Corporation of New York, the builder of Sunnyside and Radburn, drew attention to their relationship. He termed Sunnyside an "urban laboratory," a counterpart to Fairway Farms, the "rural laboratory." Just as the aim of Fairway Farms was to give the rural tenant a leg up on the agricultural ladder, so the purpose of Sunnyside Gardens was, through scientific community planning, to give the urban tenant family a leg up on the ladder of home-ownership. [For additional detail on Fairway Farms and the fate of this experiment, see "City Encounters and Desert Encounters" in this volume.]

References

Bennett, Hugh. 1921. *The Soils and Agriculture of the Southern States*. New York: Macmillan, vi.
Carstensen, Vernon. 1958. *Farms or Forests: Evolution of a State Land Policy for*

Northern Wisconsin, 1850–1932. Madison: University of Wisconsin, College of Agriculture.

de Vries, Wade. 1928. "The Michigan Land Economic Survey." *Journal of Farm Economics* 10 (Oct.): 516.

Elliott, F. F. 1937. "Economic Implications of the Agricultural Conservation Programs." *Journal of Farm Economics* 19 (Feb.): 13–27.

Ely, Richard T. 1926. "The City Housing Corporation and Sunnyside." *Journal of Land and Public Utility Economics*, no. 2 (April): 172–85.

———. 1922. "A National Policy for Land Utilization." In *Report of the National Agricultural Conference*, 117. Washington, D.C.: Government Printing Office.

Ford, Henry, in collaboration with Samuel Crowther. 1926. *Today and Tomorrow*. Garden City: Doubleday, Page.

Gray, Lewis C. 1930. "Objectives and Methods in the Local Definition of the Extensive Margin of Agriculture." *Proceedings of the Second International Conference of Agricultural Economists*, 258–69. Menasha: Collegiate Press.

Gray, Lewis C. et al. 1923. "The Utilization of Our Land for Crops, Pasture and Forests." In U.S. Department of Agriculture, *Yearbook of Agriculture*. Washington, D.C.: Government Printing Office.

Kirkendall, Richard S. 1963. "L. C. Gray and the Supply of Agricultural Land." *Agricultural History* 37 (July): 206–16.

———. 1966. *Social Scientists and Farm Politics*. Columbia: University of Missouri Press.

Ladd, C. E. 1932. "New York's Land Utilization Program." In *Proceedings of the National Conference on Land Utilization*. Washington, D.C.: Government Printing Office.

Lipman, J. G. 1932. "Soil Classification as a Basis for Agricultural Adjustment." In *Proceedings of the National Conference on Land Utilization*. Washington, D.C.: Government Printing Office.

Lovejoy, P. S. 1925. "Theory and Practice in Land Classification." *Journal of Land and Public Utility Economics* 1 (April): 166–67.

National Conference on Land Utilization. 1932. "A National Land Utilization Program." In *Proceedings of the National Conference on Land Utilization*, 240–49. Washington, D.C.: Government Printing Office.

Renne, Roland R. 1935. *Readjusting Montana's Agriculture*. Bulletin 306, 21–22. Montana State College, Agricultural Experiment Station, Bozeman.

Roosevelt, Franklin D. 1932. "Actualities of Agricultural Planning." In *America Faces the Future*, 324–50. Edited by Charles A. Beard. Boston: Houghton Mifflin.

Rowley, William D. 1970. *M. L. Wilson and the Campaign for the Domestic Allotment*. Lincoln: University of Nebraska Press.

Shideler, James H. 1973. "Flappers and Philosophers and Farmers." *Agricultural History* 47 (Oct.): 283–99.

Starch, Elmer A. 1933. *Farm Organization as Affected by Mechanization*. Bulletin 278, 7–12, 34. Montana State College, Agricultural Experiment Station, Bozeman.

Taylor, Henry C. 1929. "The New Farm Economics." *Journal of Farm Economics* 11 (July): 357–67.

Weeks, David. 1929. "Scope and Methods of Research in Land Utilization." *Journal of Farm Economics* 11 (Oct.): 603.

Wehrwein, George S. 1932. "Fiscal Problems of Local Communities Resulting from Changing Conditions of Land Utilization," 112. In *Proceedings of the National Conference on Land Utilization.* Washington, D.C.: Government Printing Office.

———. 1930. "The Problem of Land Utilization in the Cut-over Regions of the Lake States." In *Proceedings of the Second International Conference of Agricultural Economists,* 270–77. Menasha: Collegiate Press.

———. 1931. "A Social and Economic Program for Submarginal Agricultural Areas." *Journal of Farm Economics* 13 (April): 270–79.

Wilson, M. L. 1926. "The Fairway Farms Project." *Journal of Land and Public Utility Economics* 2 (April): 170.

———. 1933. *Farm Relief and the Domestic Allotment Plan.* Minneapolis: University of Minnesota Day and Hour Series 2, 47–48.

U.S. Congress. 1930. *A Bill in the Congress of the United States to Aid Farmers in Making Regional Adjustments in Agricultural Production.* H.R.13275. July 3.

10

The Nation as Family: The Winning Plan of Prestonia Mann Martin

Planning is often defined as rational decision making oriented to the future, a technical procedure the same for all times and places. However, when it is considered not with respect to its means but to its ends, it appears that there are as many kinds of planning as there are types of societal forms to plan for. The farm, the firm, the family, the factory, the neighborhood, the city—these are more than just the names of the various institutions that comprise the nation. Each of them is a design for living, working, and governing that at some point has been held up as a model for the nation itself. Planning history is, in part, the story of how such models have arisen and vied with each other for primacy.

In an age when industry is king, it is not surprising to find the business firm and the factory among the top contenders. So it was at the turn of the century. Social reformers stood in awe of industrialism and welcomed its gifts. All was not well, however. The factory, with its demand for the labor of women and children, threatened health and morals. A deeper problem was that, by its very success, industrial technology had detached the producing side from the consuming side of life. Work had far outdistanced leisure and the other domestic arts.

In 1912, Wesley C. Mitchell, future member of the National Planning Board, noted the basic schism in modern life: "We have let the factory whistle, the time table, the office hours impose their rigid routines upon our money making days, but our homes we have tried to guard from intrusion by the world of machinery and business" (271). The protection of the home had been achieved, but at a cost. The buying and enjoying of goods had become "backward arts," while the art of producing had forged ahead. Mitchell thought the answer lay in a "socialized spending of money"—for common wash tubs, cooperative kitchens, day nurseries, parks and playgrounds, etc.—facilities for which the consuming unit would be the neighborhood rather than the individual family. In this way, work and the domestic side of life might be put on an equal footing with regard to the efficiency that comes from larger-scale organization.

In addition to the firm and the factory, there was the city. The reformers loved the city, but they also feared it. If only the city's advantages could be separated from its material and moral dangers! For the purpose of good government, people struggled to wrest control from the ethnic bosses. Social workers strove to subdue the unruly neighborhood and to make of the city a larger neighborhood safe for rural values.

Community planners also were discovering the neighborhood and experimenting with it as a counterpoise to the city and the factory. Out of their efforts came the Neighborhood Unit, an arrangement of streets, dwellings, and community facilities to provide a haven for family life in the thick of the city. Lewis Mumford and his colleagues of the Regional Planning Association were never in doubt about the nature of a regional plan. It was "a framework for neighborly association."

In the personalities of Al Smith and Franklin Roosevelt the neighborhood idea widened to embrace the nation. Neighborliness was the essence of the Roosevelt style—the fireside chat, the famous grin. "My friends" is the way he began even his formal speeches. Engaging manners these—who could object?—yet to some they smacked of effrontery. Listen to one John Coar, an economist, addressing the American Political Association in 1935: "Three years ago, a candidate for nomination at the National Convention of the Democratic Party; then a Presidential candidate in the campaign immediately following; and since then, the incumbent of the highest office in the gift of the American people, won the affectionate regard of this people and still continues to hold this regard, in part, by beginning every public address with the simple, yet very human phrase, 'My Friends'" (193). Coar recoiled at the president's misplaced neighborliness and its implications. "The Chief Magistrate of the American People has, in his capacity as such, no call to administer, or to seek to adjust, the nonpolitical relations of the millions of human beings who as citizens constitute the 'American People' even though . . . these same millions assume . . . that the difference between citizen and human being [read 'friend,' 'neighbor'] is no more than the difference between Tweedledum and Tweedledee" (193).

After decades of propagation by reformers, the neighborhood idea had triumphed and seemed unassailable. All the more surprising that its supremacy was so short-lived. Not that it was ever overthrown; eclipsed is the better word. It was suddenly eclipsed by another model. The Great Depression abruptly diverted attention from building the framework for neighborly association to fixing the broken economic machine. Making a living, producing, and consuming became the dominant themes. This change marked a turning point in American planning thought. The forte of the American planner has always been the planning of public space. The space between neighbors is close, closer than the space between citizens. But even between neighbors, there always remains, however small, a gap, a commons, free for improvization, for cooperation and healthful conflict—a public space to be bridged by public works. The space between producer and consumer, on the other hand, is internal, private space, separating not two families but different members of the same family, or even two activities of the same individual. Here is no meeting ground for sovereign families. Here is only the specialized parts of a single entity. In short, with the depression, the family replaced the neighborhood as the basic social model, with a corresponding change in the meaning of planning. Henceforth, to an increasing extent, the subject of planning would be a person's economic relationship to self, spouse, and child, a subject beyond the competence of the neighborhood planners as it was beyond the engineer and the architect. Ironically, the same F.D.R. was the symbol and instrument of the change.

In time, the depression began to lift, but the family sense remained, indeed, it was greatly reinforced by economic nationalism and approaching war. Here is Stuart Chase's Swiss Family Robinson image of the nation in 1942:

> The family has passed over a range of mountains in the southwest, let us say, and come to rest in a fertile valley. Essential tools and seeds are in the covered wagons, and livestock has been driven over the mountain trail. Here are Ma and Pa, the sturdy sons, the younger children, assorted relatives, and some Mexican helpers. All the natural resources for survival are at hand—a stream of pure water, timbered slopes, rich bottom lands. Assume the family to be cut off for the time being from all contact with the outside world. Life depends on their own labors and skill. (27)

Erstwhile neighbors had become members of a single family, a national family.

On Pa's and Ma's farm, everyone works. "The children contribute to the family budget almost as soon as they can walk. The duties of every man, woman and child are clear. There is game to be hunted, fish to be caught, corn to be raised, houses to be built, firewood to be fetched, meals to be cooked, wool to be spun. . . . Everybody works on Pa's ranch . . . though not . . . with the hair-shirt fury of early New Englanders. The Mexican helpers make an admirable distinction between work which must be done and work as a variety of moral gymnastics. The latter philosophy escapes them" (27).

In addition to the depression and war, a third factor contributed to the ensconcement of the family as a model for national planning—the feminist movement. When feminism became a serious issue earlier in the century, there were plenty of prophets around to foretell its probable long-term consequences. "One of the supreme values of feminism," wrote Walter Lippmann in 1914, "is that it will have to socialize the home. When women seek a career . . . they will have to market through associations. They will do a great deal more of the housework through associations. . . . If they are not satisfied with the kind of work that is done for the home but outside of it, they will have to learn the difficult business of democracy which consists in expressing and enforcing their desires upon industry" (1961, 131).

Not so clearly anticipated by Lippmann or anyone else was the reciprocal effects of the process he described. As families lost their functions to industry and government, the nation itself ineluctably took on the character of a great family. The "familiarization" of industry and government would soon progress from affecting the kinds of goods and services produced to the division of the product.

These tendencies were adumbrated in the writings of a woman whose ideas achieved a certain fame in the 1930s. Prestonia Mann Martin was born in 1862, the daughter of a New York physician, John Preston Mann, a relative of the great educator Horace Mann. As a girl she attended the School of Philosophy at Concord, Massachusetts. Here she knew Walt Whitman and Ralph Waldo Emerson. When her parents died, she established a summer home in Keene, New York, called Summerbrook. In 1900 Prestonia Mann married an Englishman, John Martin, an ex-Fabian and friend of Sydney and Beatrice Webb and of George Bernard Shaw. At Summerbrook in 1936, the Martins founded "A Little Summer School," to which famous intellectuals of the day were invited. Among her guests were the journalist Ray Stannard Baker and the distinguished economist E. R. A. Seligman. Here, too, three times a week, she expounded her own views on national planning.

Mrs. Martin was a champion of women, but she was not a feminist in the contemporary sense. In 1910 she had written a book, *Is Mankind Advancing?* She held that not only should women remain in the home, but it was also their positive duty to do so, for upon this depended the survival of the family. She argued just as vigorously for progressive measures in the areas of employment security, education, and public health, for these, too, contributed to the strengthening of the family which she extolled as the "garden in which ideal human beings are produced." Indeed, it was the proper "function of the state to protect and foster the family; to prevent its debilitation either by luxury or want, to cast about it the sheltering mantle of collective power and to supplement its ordinary functions by the services of experts" (293).

In addition to her reverence for women as "the priestesses of the inner life" and for the family as the garden of the race, Mrs. Martin cherished the advancement of the common people, for "There can be no real light and air and freedom . . . where the common people are not" (301). Consequently, "all persons who separate themselves from this class do so at their own peril, and sooner or later racial starvation confronts them." The common people are called "the main column" of society and are distinguished from the "runaways," capable persons who have abandoned the common people, the "dropped-outs" (i.e., the poor and the incompetent), and the "stragglers" (296, 300). The column must not remain strung out and fragmented in this manner. It must stay together as "a solid, compact body" (302).

Such themes were common enough in 1910. More important is what Mrs. Martin did with them twenty years later, adapting them to New Deal and Depression themes in a little tract entitled *Prohibiting Poverty*. Printed privately in 1932, it was soon taken up by commercial publishers and by 1939 had reached its thirteenth printing.

Prestonia Mann Martin was one of those reformers for whom our social evils were, in Frederick Howes's phrase, "economic not personal." She quoted Rexford Tugwell to this effect. "'Our current systems are not sacred; the ingenuity of man can devise something better. High adventure awaits the daring. It should be attempted by the youth of the nation aided by those of the elders who retain the energy and confidence of youth'" (1933, 60). Fine words, but what was needed was an actual road map, a blueprint, a plan. Here Henry Ford seemed to point the way. "'Our problem,'" he had said, "'is one of housekeeping. We have got to arrange the machinery of life so that it shall deliver the goods without breakdown or uncertainty. We must settle the question how to maintain an even flow of the necessaries to all men.' Having 'reorganized society on an industrial basis,' we have got to see to it that our industries offer a place to every man to earn a living. This is primary humanity'" (1933, 60–61).

Following Ford, Mrs. Martin deplored the insufficiency of the distribution machinery. What point in turning out vast amounts of goods if the goods cannot be delivered correctly? The trouble is that the channels of distribution are the "channels of Buying and Selling—which are controlled by the money market" (1933, 36). For goods to reach people, the consumers, the impediments must be removed, and this means, above all, doing away with the market as the allocator of basic resources. But what is to replace it? Here is where the woman comes into her own: "It has been women's lot throughout the ages to be the Distributing member of the human family and in the home she has developed a technique of distribution which can serve well as the model for the nation to adopt in distributing Necessaries" (1939, 36). "Man in his outside world is engaged in a fierce fight and struggle to obtain the means of livelihood, but, when he brings his plunder home, the woman adopts a very different method in distributing it. She distributes according to need; she does not fight or contend or struggle, nor does she permit contention among the children. In the home, competition and fighting cease. There is no buying and selling; needful things are distributed for use not for sale. A capable mother keeps her young employed and thus out of mischief. She demands from them co-operative helpfulness" (1939, 37).

Family collectivism thus provided the model for what she called "the winning plan," the National Livelihood Plan. In some of its features it is reminiscent of Edward Bellamy's social science novel *Looking Backward*. It differs markedly from the influential utopian's vision in the rather large compromise with capitalism that her plan allows:

All of the nation's young people of both sexes, between the ages of eighteen and twenty-six, as a continuation of their public school education, shall be industrially organized to produce, under scientific direction, a sufficiency of the necessary goods and services to constitute a decent livelihood and to distribute these goods and services without buying or selling them. . . .

At the end of eight years the Young People, having served their term, would pass out of the organization, and would be succeeded by fresh relays of young recruits coming up in turn from the schools and taking their places in the ranks. Thus a continuous stream of necessary goods and services would be kept flowing steadily from the hands of the Young Workers and, pouring out over the entire population, would furnish a basic livelihood for everybody for life.

This organization composed of Young Workers in the public service, together with their leaders and directors is called . . . "the Commons."

Their patriotic, public industrial service completed, the Young Commoners—still young at the age of 26—would graduate, or demobilize and, leaving the service, as free men and women would thereupon disperse to their homes. For the remainder of their lives they would receive from the relays of Young Commoners who would succeed them a full supply of the Necessaries of life constituting a competence. Thus there would be conferred upon the nation, for the first time in history that any people have attained it—complete economic emancipation.

Having graduated, the Young People would be no longer Commoners, but would be free citizens—potential capitalists. The world they would enter then would be constituted precisely as is our present-day capitalistic system, i.e. competitive, individualistic, profit-seeking—a world in which buying and selling for profit is the prevailing practice. . . . In this sphere . . . the "Capitals," the individual citizen is at liberty to engage in the pursuit of wealth, fame, power, leisure, sport, trade, culture, pleasure—or any other aim that attracts him. . . .

One restriction, however, follows him here in the Capitals. He may not traffic in the Necessaries of Life—for they are handled by the Commons alone. In the Capitals his trade is limited to the production and sales of Luxuries and Surpluses—i.e, staple and manufactured goods over and above what are needed by the Commons in their task of providing basic livelihoods for the people. These may be exported for profit or sold to the Luxury trade at home. Thus the National Livelihood Plan is a project whereby collectivism would be applied to the production of Necessaries while individualism would be reserved for production and sale of Luxuries and Surpluses for profit. . . . This arrangement would give a *subsistence basis* to economic society which nothing could impair or imperil. The Plan provides economic safety while at the same time retaining a huge measure of economic liberty. (1939, 7–9)

Prohibiting Poverty was received with widespread and, in some cases, extravagant praise by many educators, preachers, scientists, bankers, and businessmen. If the book made a certain splash, this was because it reflected something essential in the public thought of the period. Mrs. Roosevelt is reported to have said, "The germs of ideas in 'Prohibiting Poverty' are in some of the administration projects today" (Martin 1939, 140). Her comment was not unfounded. The New Deal was, indeed, a mixture—one might say a marriage of state and market economies—of "Commons" and "Capitals." In this light, "Prohibiting Poverty" appears as a study in the psychosocial structure of a reform era. Underlying the Capitals and the Commons, the familistic basis of the dual society is discernible. The Commons, with its adult leadership, represents the role that mother played in the traditional "well-regulated family." The stereotype of father—aggressive, competitive, ready to risk all in a poker game (the market)—survives in the Capitals.

As a reform program, though, the "Winning Plan" is a period piece. It smacks of CCC camps, Townsend Club meetings, and subsistence homesteads. The conditions—severe depression—which would make the concrete arrangements feasible no longer exist. Especially in an inflationary era, one would be hard put to find, let alone to hold, the line between "necessaries" and luxuries. But even though the answers are dated, the questions are still the vital ones: How to reconcile security and freedom? What do the generations owe each other? Can youth be given an enduring sense of social usefulness other than military? Most piquant of all, Is it possible for Americans to think of themselves as members of a national family? Is it desirable for them to do so? And, if so, what new institutional arrangements are indicated?

Nor, considering current debate, is there anything dated about the idea of the nation as a substitute parent. Recent social history appears to be a search for alternatives to the family and resistance to that search. The notion of a "motherly commons" looking after the needs of all is not unappealing, assuming it could work in the economic sense. However, there also is danger in the idea. That danger is, as some point out, in the destruction of those "mediating institutions" that stand between the individual and the state, and in their replacement by administrative artifices that have the name but not the souls of real families, neighborhoods, and cities.

Note

This essay is adapted from "The Nation as Family: The Winning Plan of Prestonia Mann Martin." *Planning and Public Policy* 9 (Aug. 1983): 1–4.

References

Bellamy, Edward. 1951. *Looking Backward*. New York: Random House.

Chase, Stuart. 1942. *Goals for America*. New York: Twentieth Century Fund.

Coar, John Firman. 1935. "Democracy and World Trade." *Annals of the American Academy of Political and Social Science* 180 (July): 192–202.

Lippmann, Walter. 1961. *Drift and Mastery*. Englewood Cliffs: Prentice-Hall.

Martin, Mrs. John [Prestonia Mann Martin]. 1910. *Is Mankind Advancing?* New York: Baker and Taylor.

Martin, Prestonia Mann. 1939. *Prohibiting Poverty*. Winter Park, Fla.: National Livelihood Plan.

Mitchell, Wesley C. 1912. "The Backward Art of Spending Money." *American Economic Review* 2 (June): 269–81.

11

Regions in Time: Are There Cycles in American Planning History?

Planning which purports to be about social change has very little to say about how it, itself, changes. There is the hero theory and its concomitant, hero worship: Great prophets have arisen from time to time and have pointed the way (Ebenezer Howard, Patrick Geddes, Lewis Mumford, etc.). But was it the man who caused the change, or was he merely the instrument of larger social forces?

Other questions concern the possibility of patterns of change. Is planning history divisible into distinct eras? Although, a certain phasing is widely assumed (City Beautiful, City Functional, etc.). Professional literature which addresses the question of periodicity in planning history directly and critically (that is, as a subject in its own right) is difficult to find, if it exists at all.[1]

Repetition or recurrence is a particular type of patterned change. Are there cycles in American planning history? The very question is discomfiting. We have, so to speak, been brought up in the faith that planning is progressive. We believe that it arose at a certain point in our social history, has developed linearly, and, although suffering setbacks, has grown wiser and more competent. If there have been failures, these are due to inexperience, or "politics," or the anti-planning bias of American society. With such excuses to lean on we can reconcile ourselves to a planning that fails. We know what went wrong and hope to do better the next time. But what about a planning that is essentially directionless, that is going nowhere, that may be going in circles?

But let us suppose that planning is cyclic. What is the nature of the cycle? Is it perfectly regular and predictable, like night and day? Or is it erratic, as is the weather cycle? And how fast does the wheel turn? Every decade? Every generation? Most important, what is driving this wheel? Economic forces? Cultural forces? Whatever the answer, the possibility that planning is driven by something outside itself is, from a professional viewpoint, disquieting. Planning is supposed to determine events, not be determined by them. If planning is no more than history's creature, then it hardly deserves the name *planning*.

Finally, we are driven by this question (Are there cycles in planning?) to an examination of planning itself. What is this thing called planning that either goes or does not go in circles? Is it so simple that we can classify it as either progressive or nonprogressive? Or are there some aspects of planning that are progressive while others are nonprogressive? The present inquiry can take us only a little way into this unexplored subject with results that some may regard as simplistic, but better to deal with it even in an inadequate manner than to ignore it entirely.

According to the cyclic paradigm, planning changes not by becoming more or less effective, more or less competent, but by undergoing a fundamental alteration with regard to both its ends and means. Discontinuity and oscillation are its essential characteristics, the sudden or gradual supercession of one social state of mind by another of opposite character and the consequent transvaluation of previous policies and programs. Today's solution is tomorrow's problem and vice versa. Examples are not difficult to come by. Planning in the 1940s and 1950s meant land use planning. In the 1960s "land use" became, virtually, a dirty word. By the 1970s, it was acceptable once more to be a land use planner. In the teens and 1920s of the present century we were all for the protected, sequestered neighborhood and anti-street. Later, the design was turned inside out. The bustling, turbulent, democratic street was extolled as the ideal focus for local community life as against the exclusionary neighborhood. Now neighborhoods are back in vogue. Or, consider the case of America's most famous planning exploit, the Tennessee Valley Authority. In the 1930s, TVA was regarded, in the word of one scholar, as Hercules, the rescuer of impoverished farmers and the restorer of devastated land. Half a century later it is decried by some as the dragon of the valley, a despoiler of the environment, the exterminator of the defenseless snail darter, a burden on the backs of its luckless residents (Chandler 1984). Turnabouts like these threaten to make nonsense out of our lives and careers, consequently, we tend to ignore them.

Even so, the cyclic phenomenon is not necessarily the nemesis of the idea of progress in planning. There are those aspects of planning, the technical ones, that do increase their effectiveness from era to era. Model-building, survey techniques, management models, land and land use classifications, these and many other techniques in common use show progressive capabilities.[2] Most important, knowledge of the cycles can itself be a means of deliverance from the wheel, a way of breaking out of the cycle. We are never more the play thing of encompassing historical forces than when we are unaware of their existence. Consequently,

	Progressive Era (1900–1920)	Depression–New Deal–War (1929–45)	Modern Period (1950–)
Setting:	Prosperity inflationary spiral consumerism overconcentration of wealth Social conflict over material resources farmer vs. urbanite native vs. immigrant feminism	Economic collapse deflation National unity in face of emergency	Prosperity inflationary spiral consumerism overconcentration of honor and power Social conflict over honor and power black vs. white generational conflict women's movement
Mood:	Shame over material success discovery of poverty (Riis) self-accusation through muckrakers for failure to live up to middle-class values	Hunger for success experience of poverty little tolerance for deviance from middle-class values Deemphasis of individuality (what counts are masses and classes)	Guilt over affluence rediscovery of poverty (Harrington) self-accusation through children for observing middle-class values Celebration of individuality and deviance
Challenge:	Moral costs of success How to share prosperity How to limit large-scale organization (trust-busting)	Material costs of failure How to restore prosperity Large-scale organization a requirement	Moral costs of affluence How to extend affluence How to limit large-scale organization ("beware of military-industrial complex")

	How to restore a lost public morality Life as a problem (Now that I can afford it, what do I want?)	How to restore morale No choice, necessity rules	How to restore a lost public morality (ethics question) The future as a problem (What worlds shall we choose?)
Response:	Private crusades social service social justice foreign missions making the world safe for democracy	Federal programs Political isolationism Economic nationalism	Public crusades Great Society War on Poverty Peace Corps as international settlement-house work Containing communism
	Natural resources water and forest conservation public health and sanitation	Industrial recovery planning Agriculture planning	Natural resources air and water conservation wilderness, coasts, preservation
Planning Movements:	Human resources social work aimed at immigrants settlement houses	Rural and suburban resettlement Public housing Human resource planning Watershed planning (TVA)	Human resources community action programs in cities (for minorities) programs for lagging regions (Appalachia, etc.)
	Metropolitan reconstruction zoning city and metro-regional planning neighborhood planning landscape architecture		Metropolitan reconstruction comprehensive planning urban renewal historic preservation

Table 11.1   Some Time-regions Relevant to American Planning

planners ought not to shy away from exploring the cyclic aspect of their profession's history. The study of planning as a human activity subject to, not superior to, the societal forces we aspire to control is a healthful activity, helping to keep us in touch with reality. It will increase our capabilities vis-à-vis these forces. And, since the cyclic aspect of planning cycles appears to be associated to some extent with generational change, studies such as these can serve to improve intergenerational communication and understanding.

To explore the notion of cycles in planning history, I have begun with what seems to me a reasonable assumption—that planning is a sociocultural phenomenon, and that if general social history is cyclic, planning history will reflect this cyclicity. Drawing upon and building upon the works of noted historians, particularly those of Richard Hofstadter, table 11.1 presents a synoptic schema showing the several periods that constitute an hypothetical framework of recent American planning. These are the Progressive Era; the era encompassed by the Great Depression, the New Deal, and World War II; and the modern era. Hofstadter has limned the nature of the Progressive Era and the New Deal in comparative terms (1955, 272–78). In table 11.1, I attempt further to define those periods and to extend the analytic framework by adding to them characterizations of the modern period. The aim is to evoke the essential character of each great era, to indicate its material and ideational basis, the moral and psychological problems which it presents to American society, the general societal response to those problems, and the specific planning response.

The terms *Progressive Era* (roughly 1900–1920) and *depression-New Deal-World War II period* (1929–45) are well established in American historiography. Each of them comprises a kind of region in time, a "time-region," a constellation of social, economic, and psychological factors that are responsible for quite diverse understandings of the nature of planning and its means.[3] As a foil to these better-defined periods and for the purpose of exploring the question of societal change and its impact on planning, I have postulated a third era beginning with the end of World War II and continuing to the present day. Valid questions about this modern era flood immediately to mind. How can so long a span of time, encompassing so many social changes, be regarded as a single era? Surely, it is composed of several smaller periods? However, if it is unitary, a single time-region, what is its nature? Is it an extension of the New Deal period which preceded it closely? Is it, instead, a resurgence of the progressive period following the New Deal interruption—a kind of grandson to the progressive period? Or is it a period *sui generis* with its own character and its own principle of coherence? I lean to the middle hypothesis (i.e., that what we are living through today is a kind of second coming of progressivism), although there are, as we shall see, enough differences between the two eras to call that hypothesis into reasonable question.

A first approach is to ask, What do the Progressive Era and the modern era have in common? Table 11.1 suggests that they have much in common. Both are periods of inflation, prosperity, and rising expectations. Things are getting better for all. The poor look forward to higher living standards, while the well-to-do have the leisure to take stock of their moral as well as their esthetic situation. As a result, the idea of living well, consumerism, gains ground against the idea of merely making a living. Both the city and rural areas, once the scenes of back-breaking toil, now hold forth the promise of becoming noble settings for human life. Enter environmentalism, a desire for ambient beauty and safety as well as a concern with man's relation to the world of nature. An uneasy conscience is another hallmark of both periods. Americans, with their penchant for moral introspection (a derivative of Protestantism) are an easy target for foreign detractors who like to point out the discrepancies between our stated ideals and our actual practices.

However, when it comes to accusations of hypocrisy, we need no help from outsiders. Hofstadter observes that the muckrakers, those inquisitorial journalists of the Progressive Era, never had to fight their way into American communities. They were generally invited in by community leaders to expose their own corruption (1955, 164). Today's investigative journalists (the media) play a role similar role to that of the muckrakers. In the guilt-ridden 1960s, the middle class was denounced, often by its own children, for holding to and practicing middle-class values, this, ironically, in contrast to the corresponding accusation in the first Progressive Era, where the charge was failure to live up to middle-class values. Corruption and hardness of heart with respect to the poverty of their fellow citizens are the sins reformers in both periods strive to expiate.

There are differences, however. For the old progressives, poverty meant lack of decent food, clothing, and shelter. Contemporary reformers have broadened the definition of poverty to include inequity and have added women, the young, and the handicapped as well as ethnic and racial minorities to the list of those to whom restitution is due. If on no other grounds, the latter are deemed poor in the sense of having been deprived of the respect and honor due them.

With regard to material poverty, corresponding figures for the progressive and modern periods are found in Jacob Riis (*How the Other Half Lives*, 1890) and Michael Harrington (*The Other America*, 1962). (Note the similarity of the titles). Both authored consciousness-raising exposés of the plight of the urban poor of their days. Similar, also, are the remedies touted in the two periods: increasing overall economic resources and redistributing existing resources. In the first period, it is increasing the size of the pie through greater productive efficiency (scientific management) that receives the greater stress, whereas in the second period the emphasis is on equity—dividing the pie more evenly. In both periods, better times foster a sense of personal freedom from traditional constraints. One's nature and identity become qualities to be chosen rather than to be inherited or dictated by society. This provides a strong impulse to utopian planning and futurism.

The federal government plays a larger role in the modern period (the War on Poverty) as compared to the first period in which governmental involvement, to the extent that it existed at all, was mainly at the state level. Reformers in both periods are tempted to make use of large-scale organization, public and private, but at the same time they fear it. Trust-busting was a favorite objective in the Progressive Era. Correspondingly, in the 1950s, President Eisenhower identified a growing "military-industrial complex" as an object for national concern. On the other hand, the ideas of humanizing the work place and of industrial democracy in the work place, although they were by no means absent in the Progressive Era, were never as prominent or effective as they are today. The old Progressives put their faith more in scientific management. They tended to regard the workers as extensions of machines, although the unions of the day certainly fought this idea.

So there are significant differences, but the overall ethical similarity between the two periods is evident. Reformers in both eras are essentially conservative. They seek to retain the benefits of industrialism but to render it less harsh, to foster kindlier relations between citizens estranged from each other because of racial and ethnic diversity, or because of their different functional roles in the industrial order. If one had to use a single word to characterize the ethical posture which reformers in both periods strive for that word would be *neighborliness*. The nation—and even the world—as a great neighborhood is their vision. Correspondingly, the purpose of territorial planning at any scale is, in Lewis Mumford's words, to build a "framework for neighborly association."

Consider now the entirely different psychological and material foundations of the years 1929–45: economic collapse, deflation, falling expectations, and war. Hunger, want, and fear are no longer conditions to be experienced (and, to some extent, enjoyed) vicariously. They are the daily lot of millions of Americans. Guilt and shame recede as motives for social reform—they are not needed when one-quarter of the workforce is unemployed. Dreams of personal achievement are suspended; what counts now is masses and classes. The first order of business is economic recovery, a task beyond the competence of local, voluntary groups such as those that spearheaded reform in the earlier and later period. Enter large-scale governmental organization and action.

But the most remarkable consequence of the Great Depression is of a more subtle and far-reaching nature than any mentioned thus far. The collapse of the world economic order sends every nation, the United States included, tumbling back into itself. In place of international trade there is economic autarchy, in place of expansiveness there is retrenchment, in place of unlimited production there is the curtailment of production to match drastically reduced consumption. It would be astonishing if this sudden loss of power, this inward turning, did not also result in a profound change in the way the nation defined and understood itself. But, of course, it did. Making a living, producing, and consuming became the dominant themes. Economic relations took priority over social relations. Accordingly, the terms of public discourse changed. People came to be thought of, to think of themselves, less as citizens or as neighbors and more as mutually responsible producers and consumers satisfying each other's needs in a way similar to that in which the members of a family are responsible for satisfying one another's needs. Another way to express this change and to comprehend its significance is to say that the family, an economic unit, came to supplant the neighborhood, a social unit, as the model for territorial organization and for the organization of society itself. The idea of the nation as a great family replaced the idea of the nation as a great neighborhood. And, of course, World War II, which followed hard on the heels of the depression only heightened the sense of national familihood.

References to the nation as a family and to the conduct of national affairs as housekeeping were common in this period. One might challenge the significance of this fact on several grounds, first that we are dealing here with metaphors and not with realities. Certainly, but metaphors are not to be taken lightly. As William Leuchtenburg reminds us, "The metaphors a nation employs reveal much about how it perceives reality. The unconscious choice of symbols bares the bedrock of its beliefs. Moreover, the words people use are not neutral artifacts; they shape ideas and behavior" (Braeman, Bremmer, and Walters 1966, 81).

A second objection that might be raised is that the alleged familization of the nation never really took place. But, of course, it never took place in the sense that the American people actually became a great family. On the other hand, who can deny that there were some significant movements in this direction. Much New Deal legislation had to do with making the national public responsible for functions that were still, for the most part, family responsibilities, whether for all Americans or for particular groups: old age insurance, housing, employment, and education, etc. At the very least, some seeds were planted which have blossomed and born fruit since that day.

A third possible objection is that the distinction between family and neighborhood is a matter of degree only and is perhaps being greatly exaggerated here. Those who would hold that family/neighborhood is essentially a distinction without a difference have some good arguments. The two social forms which they represent are closely related. Neighborhood and family seem to go together like bread and butter. Neighborhoods are composed of families. Both terms connote intimacy, mutual trust, and interdependence. And the more intimate and more tightly interdependent neighborhoods become, the more closely they resemble large, that is to say extended, families. Nevertheless, the distinction drawn here between the two models is not a trivial one. A family and a neighborhood differ in political character. A neighborhood is implicitly republican—it is composed of nominally equal units, sovereign families that meet on common ground and parley with each other on matters of joint or mutual interest (*res publicae*). A family, by contrast, is inherently authoritarian, if not totalitarian. The members are not even nominally equal. Parents in the traditional family do not parley with the children—they dictate to them. Families and neighborhoods differ also in their economic nature. Each family in a neighborhood fares according to its capacity to earn. It may choose to curtail its consumption and share its resources with a neighboring family, but this is a matter of sentiment or prudence, not of necessity. The members of a family, on the other hand, live by each other's work. Moreover, they are fed according to their need, not their product. Who needs what and how much he or she gets is, of course, determined by the family head. In short, collectivism is the economic principle natural to the family.

Consider the effect of these two models on the meaning of planning. Plans on the neighborhood model are arrangements serving the common good arrived at by debate, bargaining, trading—in the end by voting. The source of their validity, the only source, is that they were freely arrived at and adhered to. A family, by contrast, is an economic and biological system. Plans on the family model are dictated by the logic of the system. What is there to vote about? To paraphrase Frederick Winslow Taylor in his defense of scientific management against the unions: One might as well vote on the rising and setting of the sun. Consequently, the meaning of the verb "to plan" where the model is the neighborhood must forever differ from its meaning where the family is the model. Likewise, planning in democratic countries must forever differ from planning in collectivist countries.

To sum up, every American generation faces the same question and defines itself by its answer: How are we Americans related to each other? How should we be related to each other, as fellow citizens? As neighbors? As members of the same family? I would like to assert that planning is cyclic, and that its cyclic nature is caused by the passage from citizen to neighbor to family member as societal models, particularly between the latter two. And I believe it is valid to argue that it is the difference between the nation as a great neighborhood and the nation as a great family that marks the essential difference in ethos between the depression-New Deal era and the Progressive Era. To a considerable extent, it is also what distinguishes the New Deal from the modern period. Following World War II, as the conditions that undergirded the national family idea (depression, economic autarchy, war) receded, the way was cleared for the resurgence of pluralism, political decentralism, and voluntarism, all features of the renascent neighborhood model.

Nevertheless, the neighborhood model, although still the dominant one, is far from being supreme. There are two reasons for this. First, although the postwar period has enjoyed a remarkable overall prosperity, there have nevertheless been periods of political and economic adversity when the nation's self-confidence has been shaken, particularly in the decade from 1970 to 1980 (Watergate, the Vietnam calamity, the Arab oil embargo, recession, and the hostage crisis), inducing a depression-like mood, to the extent that one might say that the 1970s constituted a little New Deal parenthesis within a broader Progressive Era.

More important are the women's movement and its effects. Contemporary American social history is largely the story of the struggle for and against the making public and nationalizing of functions that formerly were performed by women and were internal to the family: the care of the young, the aged, the ill, and the handicapped. In effect, it is the story of the attempt to substitute the nation as a family for the actual families of the nation. From small beginnings in the 1930s and continuing through Great Society days, this purpose has made great strides, with a thriving agenda for parafamilial institutions and the construction of a national family—social security, day care, national health insurance, national youth service, etc. In light of this fact, our conclusion must be that the modern era is neither New Deal nor progressive, but has some of the traits of both. It is like the Progressive Era in its ethos: its sense of material well-being; its optimism; its emphasis on individual achievement and personal self-realization, on equity, on neighborly relations; and in its sense of guilt as a motive force for reform. It is more New Deal-like in the persistent demand for institutional reform and its tendency toward family-like relations at the national level. The great family idea may win out in the end not as a result of economic collapse, as many predicted, but rather as a result of the decay of the traditional American family. That transformation is largely a consequence of the changed role of women in American society, the most momentous societal event since the Great Depression. Its effect on the American idea of planning is only just beginning.

Notes

This essay is adapted from a paper presented at the Third National Conference on American Planning History, Cincinnati, Dec. 1, 1989, and published in the *Proceedings.*

1. The literature on economic cycles, however, is vast. For a recent example, see Peter Hall's and Paschal Preston's 1988 study of long waves of economic development triggered by new information technologies. If planning cycles exist, they are surely carried on the backs of such Kondratieff waves.

2. The development of planning techniques offers fertile fields for historical research, but I am not aware of any major methodological histories of planning in progress.

3. I owe the term and concept *time-region* to Kenneth Boulding (see "Classifying Regions: A Conceptual Approach" in this volume).

References

Braeman, John, Robert H. Bremmer, and Everett Walters, eds. 1966. *Change and Continuity in Twentieth-Century America.* New York: Harper and Row.

Chandler, William U. 1984. *The Myth of TVA—Conservation and Development in the Tennessee Valley, 1933–1983.* Cambridge: Ballinger Publishing.

Guttenberg, Albert Z. 1983. "The Nation as Family: The 'Winning Plan' of Prestonia Mann Martin." *Planning and Public Policy* 9 (Aug.): 1–4.

Hall, Peter, and Paschal Preston. 1988. *The Carrier Wave.* London: Unwin Hyman.

Harrington, Michael. 1962. *The Other America.* New York: Macmillan.

Hofstadter, Richard. 1955. *The Age of Reform.* New York: Vintage Books.

Riis, Jacob. 1890. *How the Other Half Lives.* New York: Charles Scribners.

12

Transnational Land Use

Literature of a taxonomic nature on transnational land use is scanty. To our knowledge, the only investigators who have preceded us are Russell and Landsberg (1971, 230–41). Their illuminating essay is very sharply focussed on the environmental and economic aspects of land use. Our approach attempts to take a larger number of land use relations into consideration.

Twenty years ago, the eminent American anthropologist Ralph Linton wrote: "We are prone to think of environment in terms of natural phenomena, such as temperature, terrain, or available food supply. . . . Between the natural environment and the individual [however] there is always interposed a human environment which is vastly more significant. This human environment consists of an organized group—i.e. a society, and of a particular way of life which is characteristic of this group" (1945, 11–12).

One of the most fateful features of contemporary group life is nationality. Membership in a nation determines culture, which is to say that it determines a person's social identity, his relationship to his fellow man as well as to the nonhuman environment. Consider only the land. Is there an inch of habitable land on this planet which does not fall within the domain of some nation? And is there any sense in which the use of that land is not attributable to the fact that it constitutes a part of the national territory? Accordingly, it is not stretching things too far to find a basic cause of all land use in the present order of nation states.

Nations are the fundamental units of the existing world order. They are also the largest legal units of land use. Alternative forms of world order, that is, departures from the nation-state system, would bring in their wake far-reaching changes in the nature and scale of land use organization. Conversely, changes in the nature and scale of land use relationships portend new forms of world order. It is the close correlation between land use and world order that we conceive to be the primary subject of our paper. Hardly less important is the identification of the basic land use issues arising out of the clash between the nation-state system and its rivals.

Land Use Relationships

Land use is not the simple concept that many suppose it to be. Great care has been taken to analyze this concept into its component dimensions and to subclassify them in considerable detail. While the number of possible dimensions is virtually limitless, among the most important we would include the land user, the land use, and the land use effects. Two or more sites may be related through their users, their uses, or their use effects. They may also be related by location and by nature herself [columns 1 and 2, table 12.1].

User Relations

The sites may be owned or occupied by the same person (real or corporate), by different members of the same family, or by strangers of the same race, ethnic group, religion, class, tongue, occupation, or profession. Insofar as there exists some affinity between the site users, an actual or potential bond also exists between the sites they own or occupy.

Use Relations

Where the relationship between the users is one of personal identity, the potential land use relationship is strongest. For example, two sites in one ownership constitute a single legal entity, the owner's property—himself extended. But even if the sites are separately owned, their diverse owners may commit them to various functionally related uses. Thus, the facilities and activities on one site may be complementary or supplementary to those on the other, as where the cotton is grown on the plantation and converted to cloth in the urban factory.

Not all functional relationships are of the type involving the complementarities of production. Of equal importance are the consumption complementarities, those which obtain, for example, in a single residential area between a house site, a school, and a playground. From a community planning standpoint, most important, perhaps, are the relationships between production and consumption activities and facilities reflected in the journey to work. Production and consumption sites tend to separation as the seats of two different phases of the human experience, but the physical distance between them, however great, in no way diminishes their complementarity. In a special sense, home and workplace constitute a single site composed of functionally interdependent parts.

Use Effect Relations

A third possible type of site relationship is through the use effects, those physical influences emanating from the first site which impair

	(1) Land Use Factors	(2) Basis of Land Use Relations	(3) Transnational Land Use Models	(4) Transnational Land Use Issues
Users:	Owner	Property rights	Cosmocorp	Capricious nationalization
	Occupant	Cultural affinity of occupants	Diaspora	Denial of access to land and occupants Impious land use
Uses:	Activities and facilities	Functional complementarities of activities	Geo-centric firm	Autarchic land use Trade barriers
Use effects:	Material and nonmaterial	Transmissibility of activity effects	Spaceship Earth	Externalization of costs Antisocial land use
Location:	Physical and time distance	Propinquity or mutual accessibility of sites	Global Village	Communication and travel barriers
Nature:	The Elements Physiography Quantity and distribution of natural resources	Unity of a natural region	Spaceship Earth	Destruction of land and resources Excessive appropriation of resources

Table 12.1. Transnational Land Use

(or enhance) the functioning of the facilities and activities on a second site.

Location

Every site has a position in a total land use surface which renders it near to or far from every other site. Two sites (and, therefore, their occupants) may be "neighbors" in the physical sense. Neighborhood, however, whether of sites or of people, is not a function of physical distance alone, but also of time distance, that is, travel or communication time in which the critical factors are transportation or communication efficiency. Owing to a special communication link, the two sites and their occupants may be virtual neighbors even though many miles separate them (Webber 1963, 23–56).

Nature

Nature herself is the basis of a fifth type of site relationship. The two sites may be located in the same heavily wooded area, the same watershed, on the same river, or on the same arid plain. In these cases natural events and conditions on one site are likely to be affected by events and conditions oh the other (e.g., fire, flooding, erosion). Moreover, occupants of sites in the same natural region may be subject to the same natural hazards (e.g., flood, drought) or the same natural benefits (e.g., temperate climate, fertile soil).

Transnational Land Use

Land use relationships are transnational if two related sites or parcels are separated by a national boundary. The most obvious example is that of two contiguous sites on either side of a national border. But this is a special case. The border is a line of demarcation not only between adjacent sites or parcels, but also between any two related sites insofar as they lie in different political domains. An example of a transnational relationship among parcels related by ownership is the multinational corporation, a single proprietary unit composed of many sites divided by national boundaries.

Transnational land use relationships frequently spell trouble. Thus, Hugh Stephenson predicts a coming clash between the multinational corporation and the nation-state (1973). Clashes between the nation-state and the transnational cultural unit, on the other hand, are a familiar story. It is a commonplace that borders sever long-standing historical and cultural ties. The result is stranded minorities demanding territorial integration with the main body of their coreligionists or compatriots.

Transnational land use in other relational dimensions is equally con-
flict-producing. The American "energy crisis" and the conflict with the
Arab oil producers stem in part from the relationship of those sites in the
Mideast, where the crude oil is mined, to those midwestern sites where
much of it is consumed. From the standpoint of the complementarity of
their uses (facilities and activities), such sites belong together; they comprise a functional unit. The same is true of those Calabrian and Sicilian
villages where Italian laborers are raised and the German factory sites
where they are employed.

Potential interdependency also characterizes sites in different nations
bound together by, let us say, nuclear fallout, although in this case the
nexus between the physically remote sites are the activity effects rather
than the activities themselves. One place is the source of the poisonous
waste, the other is the recipient. Together they comprise an environmental unit.

The classic case of the transnational land use relationship, the one
harped on most frequently, is that which exists between sites related by
nature. For example, Great Lakes sites in the United States and Canada
constitute part of a natural unit, an "eco-unit." Europe itself is a vast eco-
unit. To a considerable extent, the political history of Europe is the
chronicle of the struggle of the European nation-states for possession of
strategic sites in a system of naturally interdependent sites. In the same
light the current European integration movement appears as an effort to
overcome the political fragmentation of the European eco-unit.

Finally, there is the transnational social or civic unit, not to be confused with the cultural unit (although the two types, for obvious reasons, frequently coincide). The former is based on the propinquity of
sites (either physical or by time distance); the latter on the common characteristics of the site occupants themselves (occupation, language, race,
etc.). In Europe, as elsewhere, it is not unheard of that a national boundary runs down the main street of a single village or even intersects a
street, thereby rendering it a transnational village. Such communities
often display neighborly or civic relations among the inhabitants of different nationality, religion, or tongue. On a much larger scale, a noteworthy example of a transnational civic unit is the Regio-Baseliensis, a thriving transnational metropolitan region centered on Basel and straddling
the French, German, and Swiss borders.

Models of Unity

"Something there is that doesn't love a wall," wrote Robert Frost. National boundaries are walls. That is, boundaries are divisive. They inter-

rupt vital ties between related sites, those which by criteria other than political belong together (Merritt 1968, 165–98). As shown above, the complexity of land use relationships is such that many types of land use unity are severed by national borders. The following types have been identified: the functional unit (sites with complementary facilities and activities); the proprietary unit (sites in common ownership); the social or civic unit (propinquitous or mutually accessible sites); the environmental unit (sites linked by activity effects); the natural unit (sites subject to the same elemental forces); and the cultural unit (sites occupied by persons of the same, race, tongue, etc.).

We can now identify a series of transnational land use models, each of them based on one of the above types of unit idealized and magnified to world proportions, thus the social or civic unit corresponds to the global village; the functional unit to the geo-centric firm; the proprietary unit to Cosmocorp; the cultural unit to the Diaspora; the natural unit to "Spaceship Earth"; and the environmental unit to Spaceship Earth. Each of these models aspires to supplant the national state in some sphere of its authority. Collectively, they are the source of a new land use morality, a transnational morality whose implicit prescriptions foreshadow a new land use code. Before stating this code, let us review the models on which they are based [columns 3 and 4, table 12.1].

The Global Village as Civic Unit

We may begin with an image made famous by Marshall McLuhan. His essential point, now a familiar one, is that the size of the world is not a fixed quantity. Rather, it varies with the ability of our bodies and senses to traverse it. In recent years, owing to jet aircraft, satellite technology, and the electronic media, the time required to traverse the world has undergone a cataclysmic reduction. Space itself is virtually abolished, making us all neighbors in a global village. McLuhan holds that the new technology is a powerful solvent of all earlier structural forms including the nation: "Every extension [of the senses] or acceleration effects new configurations in the over-all situation at once. . . . The wheel and the road are centralizers . . . but acceleration beyond a certain point, when it occurs by means of the automobile and the plane, creates decentralization in the midst of the older centralism. . . . All electric forms. . .have a decentralizing effect (1964, 167).

The Geo-centric Firm, the World as Functional Unit

The global village has its counterpart in the visions of certain businessmen and professors of business administration. Time was when land use reflected the competitive advantages of a unique geographic location. National industries offered the fruits of their soil—grain, coffee, petroleum, rubber—in return for the products of other nations favored by the close proximity of coal and iron ore. Now, industry is becoming increasingly freer to locate wherever it finds the requisite manpower, service skills, and markets assembled. Giant stateless enterprises today roam the earth in search of such convenient assemblages to which they can then add their own managerial ability and organizational culture (Benoit 1970, 21). *Geo-centrism* is the word used to characterize the behavior of these vastly enlarged and world-centered forms of business enterprise.

The geo-centric firm purports to be a leveling social force. Its executives "do not equate superiority with nationality," writes Howard Perlmutter. On the contrary, such firms "seek the best men, regardless of nationality, to solve . . . problems *anywhere in the world*" (emphasis added). The avowed aim is "to build an organization in which the subsidiary is not only a good citizen of the host nation, but is a leading exporter . . . in the national community"—this for the purpose of increasing the host nation's hard money supply, its skills, and its technological capacity (1970, 72–73).

The attitude of the geo-centric firm is further explained by Perlmutter, who invented the term: "The ultimate goal is a worldwide approach in both headquarters and subsidiaries. . . . The question asked in headquarters and the subsidiaries is 'Where in the world shall we raise money, build our plant, conduct R & D, get and launch new ideas to serve our present and future customers?'" (74).

As with men, so with sites—ostensibly, at least, the geo-centric firm is a leveler. The question, Where in the world? which recurs repeatedly is no mere rhetorical device. Rather, it proclaims the potential equivalence of all world sites. Above all, it precludes a privileged functional relation that heretofore has existed between particular sites by virtue of their location within a single nation. Therefore, it signifies the denationalization of land use and the emergence of the world as the ultimate legitimate functional unit.

Cosmocorp as Proprietor

Who owns the geo-centric firm or, more important, who should own it? This question pertains to the proprietary as opposed to the functional unit. By and large, the utopian literature of business is silent on this point. Richard Robinson, however, provides the basis for an answer in his illuminating classification of firms. Robinson distinguishes between an international firm, a multinational firm, a transnational firm, and a supernational firm:

An international firm is one in which international operations are consolidated in a line office on the division level and, as a matter of policy, is willing to consider all potential strategies for entering foreign markets—up to direct investment.

A multi-national firm is one in which, structurally and policy-wise, foreign operations are co-equal with domestic (and) management is willing to allocate company resources without regard to national frontiers to achieve corporate objectives. Decision remains nationally-based for ownership and headquarters management remains uni-national.

A trans-national firm is a multi-national firm managed and owned by persons of different national origins. Decisions thus become free of national bias.

A supranational firm is a trans-national firm legally denationalized by permitting it exclusively to register with, be controlled by and pay taxes to, some international body established by multi-national convention. (Rolfe 1969, 12)

The foregoing is more than a static classification of types of business enterprise. It is also a dynamic model describing the historical march of business attitudes, from "ethnocentrism" to "geo-centrism." The critical phrase is "legally denationalized," indicating that no one nation can or should presume to own or control the geo-centric firm. George W. Ball carries the idea to its logical conclusion. Ball heralds the advent of "Cosmocorp," an emancipated corporate proprietor "evolved to assert the "requirements of the modern age" as against the claims of the nation "which are still rooted in archaic concepts unsympathetic to the needs of the modern world." He suggests that world corporations should become free to pursue "the true logic of the global economy."

What this implies is the establishment by treaty of an international companies law, administered by a supernational body, including representatives drawn from various countries, who could not only exercise normal domiciliary supervision, but would also enforce anti-monopoly laws and administer guarantees with regard to uncompensated expropriation. An international companies law could place limitations . . . on the restrictions nation-states might be permitted to impose on companies established under its sanction. The operative standard defining those limitations might be the quantity of freedom needed to preserve the central principle of assuring the most economical and efficient use of world resources (Ball 1970, 332–33)

"Spaceship Earth" as Natural and Environmental Units

A fourth avatar of the transnational land use idea, its manifestation in the realm of "sites related by nature," is the image shown to us by our astronauts and poetized by Adlai Stevenson: "We travel together on a little space ship, dependent on its vulnerable resources of air and soil; all committed for our safety to its security and peace; preserved from annihilation only by the care, the work and, I will say, the love we show our fragile craft" (1965, 610–15).

The same idea has been rendered a little more prosaically by Kenneth Boulding with the terms *cowboy economy* and *spaceman economy* to distinguish between the "open earth" of the present and past and the "closed earth" of the future, "the cowboy being symbolic of the illimitable plains and also associated with reckless, exploitative, romantic and violent behavior." Whereas in the cowboy economy, production and consumption are both valued as ultimate ends needing no further justification, "in the spaceman economy, what we are primarily concerned with is stock maintenance, and any technological change which results in the maintenance of a given total stock" (Boulding 1966, 9). In other words, the objective is less production and consumption.

In the Spaceship Earth model the bond between any two transnational sites is a double one: First is their inclusion in a total system of sites related by nature. The abuse of any one such site could constitute a breach or lesion, so to speak, in the closed system from which irreplaceable resources could "bleed," never to be recaptured. Second, effects emanating from a misused site might disturb those delicate and intricate ecological balances among all sites, to the detriment of all species, including man. Thus, Spaceship Earth embraces both what we have called the natural or eco-unit and the environmental unit.

The Diaspora as Cultural Unit

Thus far, everything seems to fit. The natural unit of the future is the earth itself. The earth's human population resides in a global village. Their wants are met by the geo-centric firm under the direction of "Cosmocorp," properly mindful of the limits of growth. But not all is harmony. For cutting across the One World concert "like a bagpipe in a symphony" (the phrase is McLuhan's) is a somewhat dissonant model of transnational unity. Arnold Toynbee has named it the "diaspora" after the classic dispersion of the Jews, but, in fact, there are innumerable dispersions, each of them comprising the cultural space of a group sharing a single segmental trait or interest. Such realms cross national borders almost haphazardly. A modern instance is the realm of the Anglophones of North America divided by United States–Canadian border.

Peering into the past, Toynbee foresees the time when "everyone, besides being a member of his local neighborhood, will also be a member of some worldwide diaspora, or, indeed, of more diasporas than one. There will be worldwide associations of Jews, Christians, Buddhists, doctors, lawyers, teachers, engineers, physicists, psychologists, historians, bird-watchers, dog-breeders, rose-growers and what not" (1966, 79–80).

A Taxonomy of Transnational Land Use Issues

Having identified the reigning models or images of world unity, let us now turn to an enumeration of those land use attitudes and practices with which they are in sharp conflict. Although the following list reads like a catalogue of sins, no judgment is intended. The virtues of a system are never more apparent than when it is dead. If the present world order of nations should ever succumb, time might well show that there are many and good reasons for resisting the various transnational models.

Destruction of Nonrenewable Natural Resources

Most obvious is the disposition of a nation to squander, that is, to destroy land and resources or to countenance their destruction by refusing or neglecting to enact appropriate conservation measures, thus risking the reduction for all time of the total stock of usable land.

Excessive Appropriation of Land and Resources

A second type of transgression is the disposition of a nation to consume more than its fair share of the land or of other scarce nonrenewable resources.

Capture and Impoundment of Transnational Resource Flows

A special type of inequitable consumption of nonrenewable resources is the disposition of a nation to excessively divert transnational resource flows to its own uses (e.g., water, migrating animal species), as by dams and other impoundments, a frequent effect of which is the remote modification of the quantity and quality of a neighboring nation's land resources.

Externalization of Costs

More central to the subject of adverse effects is the disposition of a nation to transfer the costs of its land use facilities and activities to sites and their occupants in other nations by refusing or neglecting to suppress such effects at their source.

Antisocial Land Use

The above is an instance of adverse material effects. An example in the realm of nonmaterial effects would be the use of land for purposes widely acknowledged to be illicit or immoral, as in the case of the surreptitious cultivation of poppies for the export of opium, heroin, and other hard drugs.

Autarchic land use is the disposition of a nation to impose trade restrictions by tariffs, quotas, or in some other manner contriving to interfere with or disrupt the world system of land use specialization and exchange in the name of national self-sufficiency.

Capricious Nationalization of Land and Resources

Insofar as the global organization of industry may have benign consequences in mobilizing world resources, maximizing the world product, distributing its benefits most widely, and allowing the greatest participation and ownership by persons of diverse nationality, the disposition of a nation to abrogate foreign or supernational ownership capriciously and without indemnification also constitutes a transnational land use infraction.

Denial of Access to the Land and to Its Resources; Denial of Exit

Not to be overlooked is the disposition of a nation to interpose a barrier between a minority group and its parental or fraternal bodies in other lands by denying the right to emigrate or to travel freely, or by refusing to allow a free flow of traffic and information across its borders (e.g., jamming, roadblocks, gates, walls, refusal of visas, etc.). In effect, by such practices the nation resigns with its population, territory, and resources from humanity (the Global Village).

Impious Land Use

Finally, there is the disposition of a nation to neglect, destroy, or desecrate relics, shrines, holy places, or ruins held sacred by all or some other nations as representing their cultural heritage.

The correspondence of these transnational land use issues to the various land use factors, relationships, and models of world unity is indicated in table 12.1.

Trans-State Land Use: A Concluding Note

Even within its own borders, the United States is no stranger to the problems of planning across national boundaries. The nation itself is the product of a decision by once-sovereign powers to plan jointly. But after two hundred years, the various states of the union are still far from having achieved a clarification, let alone a resolution, of the land use issues that separate them. Like the world itself, the United States is shrinking, with a consequent growing involvement of the states in each other's land use affairs.

Interstate land use relations are trans-state relations. A trans-state relationship may be defined as one in which two or more related sites (adjacent or not) are separated by a state boundary. Trans-state relationships are significant because they subject related sites to variable political and legal controls.

Every type of transnational land use relationship identified above also operates domestically as a trans-state (i.e., interstate) relationship. Thus, the related sites may constitute all or part of 1) the trans-state *property* of a single owner (e.g., the Standard Oil Company); 2) the trans-state *functional space* of a single national industry (e.g., the oil fields, refineries, transportation, storage yards, and retail outlets of the oil industry); 3) the trans-state *cultural space* of an ethnic group (e.g., the northern urban ghettos and the rural areas of the South); 4) the trans-state *civic space* of a great metropolitan community (e.g., New York, Philadelphia, St. Louis); and 5) a trans-state *natural or environmental region* (e.g., the Great Plains, the Upper Mississippi Valley).

In light of this classification of trans-state land use relationships, the following are matters for discussion at future conferences on national and state land use policy:

1. Although the state is still the major subnational political and administrative unit, it is less and less the functional, cultural, civic, and environmental unit. As a result, interstate (i.e., trans-state) land use relationships may soon surpass intrastate relationships in importance.
2. Environmental space (the "eco-unit") is only one dimension of trans-state space needing attention. The modern task of both state and national land use planning is to recognize and respond sensitively to the *diversity* and full range of trans-state land use relationships.

Considering the growing importance of trans-state relationships, what reciprocal concessions should the states make to each other and to the federal government? Specifically, what new legal and administrative mechanisms are contemplated to facilitate the fine meshing of efforts required by modern interstate planning? Such determinations are not to be made massively, but rather categorically, that is, with due regard to the different types of trans-state land use relationship identified. The role of the individual state must vary with each category of trans-state land use relationship.

These are difficult issues not to be settled in a day, but unless they are raised more pointedly and eventually answered, we are not likely to see much progress in [interstate public] land use planning.

Note

This essay was coauthored by Raffaella Y. Nanetti. It is partially based on research made possible by a grant from the Center for International Comparative Studies of the University of Illinois in the summer of 1972. It is adapted with permission from an article of the same name published in *Land Economics* 50 (Feb. 1974): 3–14.

References

Ball, George. 1970. "Cosmocorp: The Importance of Being Stateless." In *World Business*, 330–38. Edited by Courtney S. Brown. New York: Macmillan.

Benoit, Emile. 1970. "Interdependence on a Small Planet." *World Business* (21): 13–28.

Boulding, Kenneth. 1966. "The Economics of the Coming Spaceship Earth." In *Environmental Quality in a Growing Economy, 9*. Edited by Harry Jarrett. Baltimore: Johns Hopkins University Press.

Guttenberg, Albert Z. 1959. "A Multiple Land Use Classification System." *Journal of the American Institute of Planners* 25 (Aug.): 143–50.

———. 1965. *New Directions in Land Use Classification*. Chicago: American Society of Planning Officials.

Linton, Ralph. 1945. *The Cultural Background of Personality*, 11–12. New York: Appleton-Century-Crofts.

McLuhan, Marshall. 1964. *Understanding Media*, 167. New York: Signet.

Merritt, Richard L. 1968. "Political Division and Municipal Services in Postwar Berlin." In *Public Policy* 17, ed. John D. Montgomery and Albert O. Hirschman, 165–98. Cambridge: Harvard University Press.

Perlmutter, Howard V. 1970. "The Tortuous Evolution of the Multinational Corporation." *World Business*, 66–82.

Rolfe, Sidney. 1969. *The International Corporation*, 12. New York: United States Council, International Chamber of Commerce.

Russell, Clifford S., and Hans H. Landsberg. 1971. "International Environmental Problems—a Taxonomy." In *International Environmental Science*, 230–41. *Proceedings of the Joint Colloquium before the Committee on Commerce, U.S. Senate and the Committee on Science and Astronautics, House of Representatives*. 92d Cong., 1st sess., May 25 and 26. Washington, D.C.: Government Printing Office.

Stephenson, Hugh. 1973. *The Coming Clash: The Impact of Multinational Corporations on National States*. New York: Saturday Review Press.

Stevenson, Adlai. 1965. "International Development: Hope of the World." In *Vital Speeches of the Day* (31): 610–15. New York: City News Publishing.

Toynbee, Arnold. 1966. "Man and His Settlements: An Historical Approach." *Ekistics* (Feb.): 79–80.

Webber, Melvin M. 1963. "Order in Diversity: Community without Propinquity." In *Cities and Space*, 23–56. Edited by Lowden Wingo. Baltimore: Johns Hopkins University Press.

Inventions in Urban Structure

Social invention may be a kind of dreaming, but it is not fantasy. It is practical dreaming which is responsive to the needs and problems of a real time and place. As needs change, the appropriate inventions change with them. The history of cities is the story of a succession of inventions reflecting changing needs. For many ancient and medieval cities it was military defense that counted. For the Rome of Sixtus the Fifth, it was the holy processional. For nineteenth-century Pittsburgh, it was steel production. For modern America, the city is neither a fortress nor a church, nor a factory, but a larger home to be arranged for the convenience of all. The instinct of the age is to understand the city as a means of organizing space so as to provide all citizens with access to facilities of all kinds in order to achieve the widest possible, that is, the most democratic distribution of urban goods and services.

Credit for the first statement of accessibility, of overcoming distance or "the friction of space," as a great organizing principle in urban spatial structure belongs to Robert Murray Haig. But having stated that principle with remarkable clarity and conciseness, Haig left us with some open questions. Accessibility for what purpose or purposes? And how do those purposes relate to the elements of urban structure? The selections in this section attempt to provide some answers. They posit two ideal types of accessibility within the ambit of a single city: bringing people to facilities and bringing facilities to people. The result in one case is the meeting of all needs at a neighborhood scale, thereby minimizing the need for travel; in the other case urban organization is citywide or regional, requiring people to travel considerable distances to meet their needs, including the need for work. It is precisely out of the contention and necessary compromise between these two possibilities of access that urban spatial structure arises and its major elements are defined. The same elements constitute the planner's tools for creating and modifying spatial structure. Although not all planners would accord to accessibility the pride of place it enjoys here, an instrumental view of urban structure is characteristic of planning and distinguishes it from the various social sciences (economics, sociology, geography, etc.), whose definitions of urban structure are derived from a description or analysis of what is rather than from what could or what should be.

The essay entitled "Urban Structure and Urban Growth" and the graphic essay on Philadelphia, interpret the city as an invention for creating access. The "Tactical Plan" and the essay on the Dutch *woonerf* illustrate the need for modifying access in line with other community objectives, such as protecting the economic base and protecting the quality of urban life. The final two essays take the problem of accessibility to a deeper level. The spatial and functional order of the modern city imposes inordinate strains upon the human personality. As a person travels about a city for whatever purpose—to work, to shop, to attend school, to visit a doctor—they are undertaking parallel internal trips from one region of the self to another. In some cases this can be enjoyed as a relief, a refreshing change of scene and role. Under other circumstances, the stress of the trip, as well as the distance and contrast between settings that it entails, can be experienced as so great as to be jangling and disintegrating—a tearing of the unitary self into numerous discordant roles. The final two essays explore some of the economic, social, and technological forces that have contributed to the self-separation of urban Americans in the past century, and a few of the social inventions designed to make them whole again.

13

Urban Structure and Urban Growth

The effects of the automobile on urban life and on cities which achieved their present structure in horse-and-buggy days are well known. The private automobile makes possible a wider spatial range of personal activity. With its speed and flexibility, the automobile is also changing the time-distance relationships among established activity centers, with the result that a new pattern of urban centers is emerging. As growth takes place, old links are broken, new ones are sought, and problems of future structure arise which involve the fortunes not only of individuals but of whole communities.

The present article offers no solutions. Instead, the purpose here is to identify some of the critical elements and relationships of urban structure so that the probable consequences of different solutions can be better investigated. I hope it will be received as it was written—not as a mere exercise in the theory of urban structure, but as an analytic aid in city and metropolitan planning.

The discussion is presented in three parts. The first explains how structure and form result from an effort to relate people and facilities over metropolitan distances. The second part discusses briefly the mutual influences of structure and form on the one hand, and community size and growth on the other. The third part is an attempt to derive the major features of the future metropolis from the present by analyzing the effects of a change in transportation efficiency. No doubt, the results are questionable, inasmuch as the analysis manipulates but a few elements whose relationships are more surmised than known. Even so, I hope this material will be of some interest as an attempt to grasp the dynamic interdependency of urban phenomena and systematically to explore the consequences of planned change.

Also of some interest, I believe, will be the method used here. Too frequently, one gets the impression that planning concepts include two kinds of statements of necessarily independent origin, that is, theoretical statements about the nature of the city, and practical statements or objectives. I propose to show here what an intimate relationship can exist between these two kinds of statements. For example, I begin with an objective—that of overcoming distance between people and facilities—and use it to produce a definition of urban structure.

Urban Structure

The Elements of Structure

Assume the spatial separation of all people and of all the kinds of facilities that they need in order to live in both the biological and cultural senses of that word.[1] The sum of all distances between each person and each kind of facility is total distance. The objective is to overcome total distance.[2] In working toward this objective, there are only two means available. People can be transported to facilities, or facilities can be distributed to people. Each method applied in the extreme produces a distinctive kind of city.

In figure 13.1, the function of transportation is to overcome total distance between people and facilities.[3] In figure 13.2, transportation has no function, total distance being overcome by means of distribution.

Actually, neither transportation nor distribution can do the whole job, because not all people are mobile and not all facilities can be distributed. People may be place-bound because of their age (the young and the old) or because of their social role (as women with young children). Some facilities can't be distributed because they are underpinned by natural resources or because, to exist at all, they must exist at a physical or economic size which prevents indefinite multiplication.

These constraints require the use of both transportation and distribution to overcome total distance between people and facilities. Part of the distance must be overcome by means of local facilities. The remaining, or residual, distance must be overcome by means of the transportation system. Accordingly, we combine figures 13.1 and 13.2 to give a truer picture of urban structure (figure 13.3).

In this brief analysis we have identified the major functional parts of urban structure and given them a meaning in relation to a single objective. The major parts are the distributed facility, the undistributed facility, and the transportation element. In overcoming distance, the first and the third have complementary roles: more distributed facilities mean less residual distance and less need for transportation capacity; fewer distributed facilities mean more residual distance and greater need for transportation capacity. Practical limits to both concentration and distribution are set by place-bound people and place-bound facilities. Figure 13.3 shows the anatomy of the human settlement conceived as a system of relating facilities to people. It also represents the fundamental elements in any plans for the settlement. Certain facilities can be distributed throughout the area in close physical proximity to their users.[4] Other

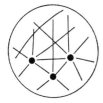 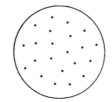 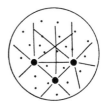

Figures 13.1, 13.2, 13.3

facilities can be distributed only in the sense of being made accessible through the transportation system.[5]

Urban Structure and Urban Form

Our first objective was to overcome total distance between people and facilities. A second objective, related to the first, is to reduce residual distance, that is, the distance remaining between people and facilities after some facilities have been localized.

Residual distance can be reduced by adjustments in the spatial form of the community. Form is used here to mean the way the structural components just described are arranged on the ground—the pattern they make. The effects of this arrangement on residual distance are depicted in figures 13.3, 13.4, and 13.5.

The obvious effect of the arrangement in figure 13.3 is much movement back and forth between people and undistributed facilities. Consolidate these facilities at one point, and the distance to be covered will decrease (figure 13.4). It will decrease even further if the consolidated facilities are put at the center of population (figure 13.5). The pursuit of the objective, namely to reduce residual distance, requires that one activity center in the urban field be privileged with respect to size and location. This fact gives functional meaning to the core of the city or metropolis and to the radial shape of the transportation system serving it.[6]

The Hierarchial Aspect of Structure

Limits to both concentration and dispersion are set by immobile persons and by facilities which cannot be distributed. But not all persons are equally immobile, and not all facilities are fixed or concentrated in the same degree. Mobility differs according to age, sex, and income, whereas distribution is a matter of economic plant size or of the spatial scatter of natural resources. These facts explain the hierarchical tendency of

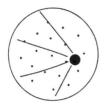 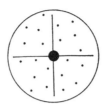 

Figures 13.4, 13.5, 13.6

urban structure: people must travel different distances to facilities, and the facilities themselves have different service radii. Also, they account in part for the existence of central places of several sizes and the corresponding differentiation of the highways which serve them into major and minor arterials and local streets (figure 13.6). As there is more than one level of community, community planning must be carried on at more than one level.

The Whole and the Part

Bringing people and facilities together creates three urban structural elements. Of these, one, the distributed facility, becomes the basis for a local organization of human activities. The undistributed facility and the transportation element become the basis for regional organization. The existence of these two levels of community is responsible for the development of a regional, as opposed to a local, interest in local land. For the local community, the local area is "home." For the regional community, the local area is a unique geographical resource to be used for its own purposes. Where these different viewpoints produce conflicting demands on the same land, a technical solution is required in the form of a set of defined land use relationships which permit the simultaneous expression of both local and regional functions in the same area with as little friction between them as possible. Of course, the possibilities are different in different parts of the field. Structural accommodation is more difficult toward the center where the great regional paths converge and where regional facilities come to predominate.

Density

We consider next the factors which give to any location in the urban field its value. These factors bear upon another dimension of urban structure—density. By the value of a location, we mean here its desirability as a place of residence or business.

In figure 13.7, let X represent the locus of one kind of facility and Y another. If a person (or establishment) needed access only to X (or Y) he would locate there. What about the person whose needs or preferences require him to be close to both X and Y? This is a question as to whether the several possible locational requirements of an individual are practically compatible and if so, how so.

As a matter of fact, the needs of our hypothetical individual are not beyond compromise. He can reconcile them spatially to some extent by locating at a point where access to both opportunities is adequate but where access to neither is optimal. If X is one point of opportunity and Y is another, then there is likely to be a point B from which both are accessible in proportion to the needs or interests of the person who seeks them. In this simple example the relationship of B to X and Y constitutes a good part of its value as a location to the individual or establishment in question.[7]

If all persons had the same needs or preferences, then all would try to locate at one point, for example at point B. But all persons don't have the same needs and preferences, and this fact accounts for the value of points A, B, C, . . . N, and for the population of the whole field.

But the whole field is not evenly populated. For, although every point is valuable to some people, not all are valuable to the same number of people. There are two reasons for this. In the first place, social forces operate so as to create in most persons like needs and interests. Second, certain points in the field, because of their locations, offer better access than others. Such points are able to accommodate diverse locational interests.

Where, in terms of access, one place is supreme, as in a metropolitan region (figure 13.5), every other place acquires a value which is some fraction of the value of the chief place, the amount depending on how well it is able to substitute for the chief place. The better it can substitute, the more desirable it becomes as a place of residence or business. Hence, it tends to be more intensively occupied with households, other establishments, or structures. As places differ in their ability to substitute for the chief place, or center, they differ in their crowdedness, that is, their density.

As a rule, as one leaves the center of a region, ease of access declines, and, with access, substitute or referred value also declines (figure 13.8, line BP). A region ends where it is no longer possible to substitute for the center in any respect or any amount. The rise or fall of referred value with distance from the center is the basic economic density gradient which underlies all forms of the physical density gradient.[8]

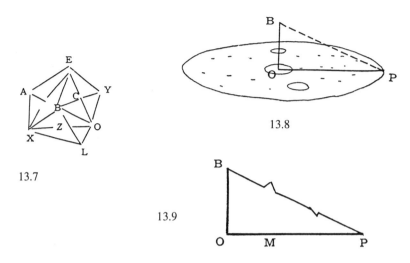

Figures 13.7, 13.8, 13.9

The general slope of the economic density gradient depends mainly on transport efficiency in substituting more peripheral for more central location. Irregularities in the slope are of two kinds. Positive deviations are caused by transport advantages (e.g., an expressway ramp which gives quicker access to the center from a point M, figure 13.9, than from other points at about the same distance from the center); negative deviations, conversely, are caused by transport disadvantages (e.g., a bad stretch of road).

The relation between economic density and physical density is not necessarily direct. Whether or not high economic density at a given point is translated into high physical density depends on local site conditions, on whether or not prospective users need a lot of space, and on their ability to pay for space. High economic density may go with low physical density, and low economic density with high physical density, but these combinations are exceptional.

Urban Structure and Urban Growth
The Spatial Extent of a Community in Relation to Its Structure
Place-bound persons and place-bound facilities cause the community to have a stable spatial structure. In turn, this structure affects the community's spatial extent. Figures 13.10 and 13.11 are similar to figures 13.1 and 13.2, except that symbols have been used to represent loci of differ-

   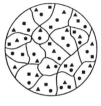

Region 1   Region 2

Figures 13.10, 13.11

ent classes of major activities. A characteristic of Region 1 is the separation of place of work, play, and residence at a regional scale. In Region
2, separation of activities is local.[9]

Corresponding to these structural differences, there are implied differences in the spatial range of personal activity. Whereas in the second
region a person would hardly have to travel at all, daily routine might
require him to traverse Region 1 several times over. One can imagine
that the size of the second region, no matter how great it might be,
would impose no strain on the time or energy of any of its inhabitants.
On the other hand, the size of Region 1 is subject to a practical limit—a
limit determined by the ability of people to reach unique activity centers
and represented in figure 13.10 by the circumference of the circle.
Growth beyond this limit requires structural changes in the form either
of faster of more far-reaching transportation, or of new regional centers.
These considerations permit us to give to the concept growth a definite
meaning.

Growth and Its Consequences

Growth involves an increase in size and an adjustment to size. In biological forms these two processes occur at the same time, or so close together that they can hardly be distinguished. Cities, however, increase in size
first and adjust to size only gradually. As a result, transitional relationships often confuse the features of the old and new equilibriums. But
always emerging in the growth of a city is the perduring structure of the
human settlement at a larger scale—that is, distributed facilities, nondis-
tributed facilities, and highways, usually with more space between
them.

The emerging scale involves the welfare of individuals as well as of
whole communities. The political community is affected when, as a re-

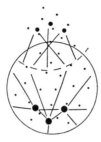 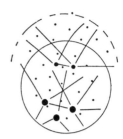

Figures 13.12, 13.13

sult of adjustments to scale, its boundaries cease to coincide with the boundaries of the functional community. Figure 13.12 illustrates the possibility: a vacuum caused by excessive distance comes to be served by centers outside the city. The influence of the new centers ranges deep into the service areas of the old, causing the reorientation of considerable numbers of people. Such a situation poses problems of conflict which are beyond a merely technical solution [see "The Tactical Plan" in this volume].

Or the new centers may rise within the political community. In this case, also, old established centers may lose their supremacy, but this loss must be weighed against the advantage to the political community of retaining its custom and winning new customers beyond the boundaries (figure 13.13).

Older centers may keep their importance by means of better transportation—transportation being, as we have shown, the functional equivalent of distributed facilities.

Whether they occur in the form of new centers, or as improved transportation facilities, structural adjustments to greater scale affect individuals by changing the positions of their homes or places of business relative to the locations of other homes and other business places and to the great activity centers of the community. Any point in the city derives its personal, economic, or social value in part from its position in the total structure. When the structure changes, all points are thereby dislocated. This fact implies loss for some individuals and gain for others, depending on their interests and on the relationships of the points they occupy to the emerging structure.

When growth occurs, population movements ensue, caused by many

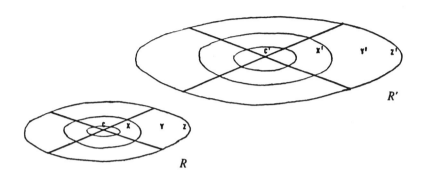

Figure 13.14

people seeking points in the new structure corresponding to points in the old. As a result, some areas develop and others decay, both process-es giving rise to social and economic problems to be met by means of development and redevelopment.

Translocation

The Meaning of Translocation

Growth and the adjusting movements of populations mean a new re-gion—new in the sense that the absolute locations of people and activi-ties will be different even if the relative locations are the same or simi-lar. If the community is to proceed from the present to the future without wasting effort or resources, then the corresponding parts of the present and future region must be identified ahead of time. But how can places in different regions be compared? A prior question must be, How can we compare different places in the same region?

Suppose we say that places can be compared in terms of their access to other places, especially to central places. Then places in the same re-gion are comparable if they have equal access to the regional center. Places in different regions are comparable (correspond) if they have equal access to their respective regional centers. In figure 13.14, C can be reached from X as easily as C' can be reached from X'. Therefore, X and X' are corresponding locations. In like manner, Y and Y' and Z and Z' are corresponding locations.

If R is the present region and R' the region of the future, is it reason-able to expect that the function now performed at X will one day be car-ried on at X'? Perhaps. Units of different kinds of activity, as well as dif-

Figures 13.15, 13.16, 13.17

ferent units of the same kind, compete for a site. The site goes to that activity which can best use it, in the sense of realizing from its use the highest material return. As activities differ in their ability to use different sites, that is, in their ability to survive at different time-distances from the center, they become spatially sorted [Haig 1927]. In this way originate those broad areas over which one kind of activity prevails, or one quality, or one density, or a typical mix of different activities, or, perhaps, no activity at all. Insofar as time-distance is the sorter, we can expect locators in R to take up corresponding positions in R' unless they have changed their time-distance requirements in the meantime.

Of course, in the interval between R and R' it may happen that the economic composition of the region changes, in which case R' will be not just a larger version of R, but will be a somewhat different animal. If such a metamorphosis does occur, then it will not be enough to identify corresponding parts in terms of time-distance from the center. In fact, in this event, the idea of translocation is open to question, since it presumes the identity of the translocator.

But suppose that the economic composition of the region doesn't change and that within it all locators keep their relative time-distance requirements. Then we can expect that, relative to the center, the time-shapes of the two regions will be alike.[10] Does this mean that the space-shapes must also be alike, as we have made them in figure 13.14? Here, too, the answer must be conditional. It depends mainly on the transportation system in the two regions. The transportation system, to repeat, is a means of substituting one place for another. As transportation systems differ in their design and these designs differ in their substitution effect, the spatial pattern of activities differ.

Where there is one big center of overwhelming importance and transportation efficiency is equal in all directions, the rate of substitution in

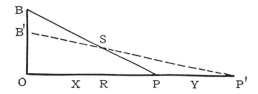

Figure 13.18

all directions is also equal, and the prevailing form of the city will, theoretically, be circular (figure 13.15). Simple radial form appears where there is one big center and a few of the routes serving it offer superior transportation (access). Displacement from the center is more intensive along these routes, and there is less demand for the area between them (figure 13.16).

Displacement of activities from the center along major radial routes will be continuous if access to these routes is continuous, otherwise it will concentrate at points of superior access (e.g., at interchanges with major circumferential routes). In this case, the prevailing spatial pattern of the activities will be not merely radial, but also nodal. This is the kind of form which a radial freeway system is likely to induce (figure 13.17).

Insofar, then, as the transportation system in R' is similar in design to the system in R, the spatial pattern of activities in the two regions will be similar, unless the pattern comes to be distorted by other factors such as accidents of terrain, public or private intervention, or by the influence of other regions and their centers; for as regions expand in area, the possibility of their bumping into each other grows.

Size and Density Changes

If R' does remain similar to R in its space-shape, it will be different in two other important respects—first in its size, and second in its density distribution.

As with location, changes in the densities at which all activities are carried on follow as a matter of course from changed time-distances. The general slope of the density gradient depends upon transport efficiency in substituting more peripheral for more central location (figure 13.18, line BP). A new level of efficiency means a flatter slope ($B'P'$), a territorially larger region, a more spread-out center, and a lower regional density, assuming, of course, that the total population increases less than proportionally to the increase in area and that there are no unusual restrictions on space supply.

New time-distances change potential in every part of the region, throwing it into conflict with actual densities which are past values realized. The choice is to put things where they belong once more (i.e., in the right amount) or else, in the public interest, deliberately to bear the cost of not doing so in the form of unrealized value, inflated value, or subsidy.

The curves in figure 13.18 illustrate some of the basic relationships assumed to hold here between the regional center, the size of the region, transport efficiency, and density distribution. The line segment RP' represents that range of the region where new conditions of accessibility will cause future density (SP') to exceed present density (SP) by a definite amount. For the range represented by the segment OR, the reverse is true; there, future density will be lower than present density. By this criterion then, the range OR is overdeveloped, RP' is underdeveloped, and at point R where the two curves cross, present and future development are identical.

For every point (X) on the line OP' it would be possible to specify a difference between present and probable future density representing the relative demand for redevelopment. Thus, of all points in the overdeveloped range of the region depicted in figure 13.18, the demand for change is greatest at O, the regional center. The demand for change in the underdeveloped range is greatest at P, the edge of the present region. At R very little change, if any, would be required.

Figure 13.18 suggests that, theoretically, the question of redevelopment priorities is not a valid one. The reason for this is that redevelopment means redistribution. A reduction of development at point X requires a corresponding change at other points. All would have to be undertaken at the same time.

On the other hand, figure 13.18 does give us some clue as to where scarce public redevelopment monies should be concentrated. For example at O, and again at P, the forces for change would appear to be greatest, and we would expect the marginal effect of every public dollar spent there to be correspondingly large.

In this section we have tried to find an intelligible connection between the present and future metropolis by analyzing the effect on the former of an assumed change in transportation efficiency. The shortcomings of this analysis are obvious—above all, its rudimentary character. Even the few relationships presumed to hold here are, as yet, hypothetical and require further investigation. We have, no doubt, made too much depend on a single factor, access, while other factors are omitted from consideration altogether.

A different kind of criticism is possible on the grounds that no account is taken of the financial, social, cultural, and political consequences of structure and of their reactive effect on the total system.[11] Surely, figures 13.15, 13.16, and 13.17 imply great differences in cost, in quality of social and cultural life, and, if the metropolitan area is composed of independent communities, differences in the balance of economic and political power among these communities.

These considerations are beyond the scope of the present article. Here we hoped only to stress the connectedness of urban phenomena and to spur its further investigation—a purpose of more than academic importance. For only when it is accomplished will it be possible for a community to foresee the results of its own actions and to make an intelligent choice among proposed structural alternatives.

Notes

This essay is adapted with permission from the *Journal of the American Institute of Planners* 26 (May 1960): 104–10. This analysis grew out of my work on some of the conceptual aspects of comprehensive planning. Acknowledgement is due to Arthur T. Row of the Philadelphia City Planning Commission, who allocated work program time for the analysis. Intellectual stimulation came primarily from the work of Robert Murray Haig (1927).

1. The term *facility* is used here to mean any fixed physical instrument of artificial or natural origin (e.g., a beach) which people use to meet a need or fulfill a purpose. So defined, the term includes anything from the corner mailbox to a factory but excludes vehicles or anything normally portable.

2. This is a necessary objective since in order for people to live at all, or to participate in their culture, the distance between them and facilities must be bridged.

3. In figures 13.1 and 13.2, dots represent facilities or clusters of facilities, and lines represent transportation routes. People are assumed to be scattered over the whole field and are not represented symbolically.

4. These facilities could include, for, example, a small park or playground, an elementary school, a neighborhood convenience store, or a movie house. A dwelling unit would be the "most distributed" facility.

5. These facilities could include, for example, a beach, a department store, or a regional park; many major workplaces also fall in this category.

6. Residual distance is physical distance. Both physical distance and time-

distance are reduced by adjustments in spatial form. Time-distance may be further reduced by improvements in transportation efficiency (e.g., by new or improved highways, by operational changes which speed traffic flow, etc.).

7. The other component in the value of a site is the intrinsic properties of place: soil, slope, elevation, etc.

8. Economic density is the value of a place as a vantage point for access to all opportunities in the region as a group.

9. The meandering lines in figure 13.11 represent boundaries, not highways.

10. In this context, "time-shape" means the time-distance relationships among all activities, not a sequence of events.

11. However, see "The Tactical Plan" in this volume.

Reference

Haig, Robert M. 1927. *Major Economic Factors in Metropolitan Growth and Arrangement.* Vol. 1 of *Regional Survey of New York and its Environs.* New York: Regional Plan Association.

14

From the General Concepts of the Philadelphia Comprehensive Plan (1960): A Graphic Essay

Formerly, cities were built for the protection and enjoyment of a fortunate few. Others were left to find what advantages they could in city life and, doubtless, even for these the advantages were considerable. In the present democratic era, however, the only allowable objective is that all men be helped to avail themselves of all of the opportunities which the city offers and, if possible, to avoid the more harmful effects of city life. For city planning, which must serve the instinct of the age, this means planning the city in such a way that all people have good access to facilities of all kinds. Here is one of the great technical objectives of contemporary planning.

From the point of view of the Comprehensive Plan, the city is the means for bringing together people and the facilities which serve them. In the pages that follow are set forth the concepts of the plan, the broad principles that should be followed to accomplish this purpose.

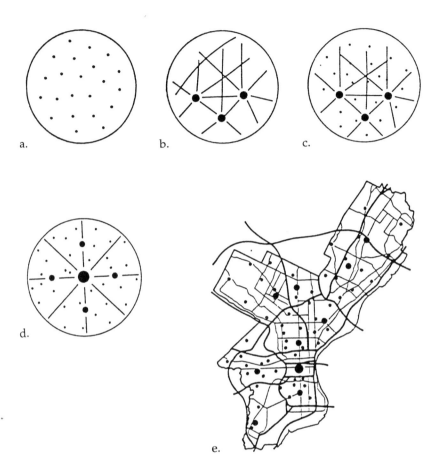

Figure 14.1.   The Elements of Urban Structure

a. Certain facilities are used so often, or are so important to the public welfare, that they must be distributed throughout the city within easy reach of all. Facilities in this category are small parks and playgrounds, neighborhood schools and shopping centers, neighborhood clinics, and community centers.

b. Other facilities—large parks, high schools, and sports stadiums—can be distributed only in the sense of being made accessible to the people through efficient transportation.

c. City structure results from a combination of both methods of distributing facilities. Figure 14c is the anatomy of the plan.

d. The objective of reducing distances between all people and all opportunities requires that one activity center be privileged with respect to size and location.

e. The anatomy of Philadelphia.

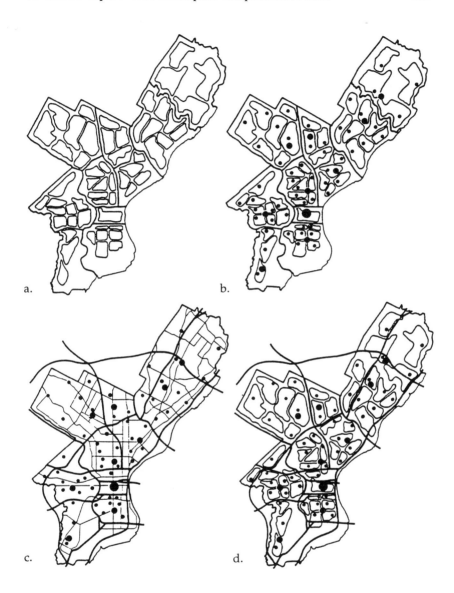

Figure 14.2.   Urban Form

    a. For each set of facilities, a service area.
    b. For each area, a center.
    c. Highways differentiated in capacity and design, according to the centers
they serve.
    d. A hierarchy of communities based upon successively wider interests and
fostering a progressively wider sense of place.

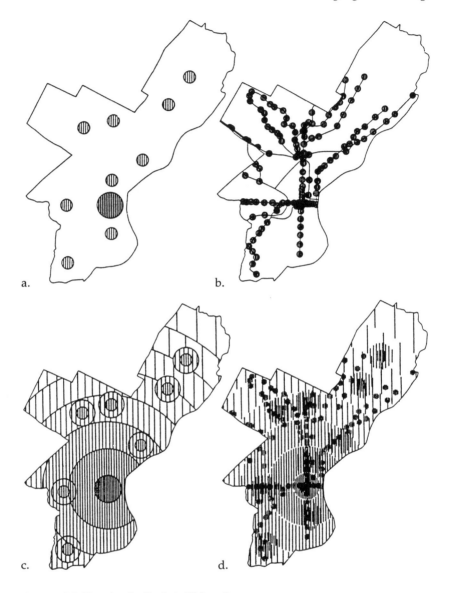

Figure 14.3. Density: Its Basis in Urban Structure

a. The basis of density is accessibility. Accessibility is greater at the regional center and subcenters, and

b. along major transportation routes, and in the vicinity of expressway inter-changes and mass transit stations, and

c. declines with distance from all such access-privileged points.

d. The density proposals of the plan are based on a recognition of the under-lying realities of urban structure and form.

Note

This graphic essay is an abbreviated and adapted version of the General Concepts section of the 1960 Philadelphia Comprehensive Plan. The General Concepts section, a special insert in the plan document, was developed and written by the author of the present volume. It was the product of the interaction of his conceptual work on urban structure (see the preceding essay, "Urban Structure and Urban Growth") with the subject matter and components of the Comprehensive Plan. Its purpose was two-fold: To state the most fundamental objectives of the plan and the logic of those objectives—their basis in the principles of urban structure; and to help unify the diverse perspectives generated by the plan's individual components.

Edmund N. Bacon, at the time executive director of the Philadelphia City Planning Commission, encouraged the development of the General Concepts section and accorded it its distinctive treatment in the format of the published plan.

The Comprehensive Plan itself was prepared under the direction of Arthur T. Row, assistant executive director of the City Planning Commission, and Larry Reich, chief of its Comprehensive Planning Division.

Figure 14.1 a, b, c, and d was drawn by the author. All other figures reproduced in this essay were drawn by Thomas P. Melone.

Reference

Philadelphia City Planning Commission. 1960. *Comprehensive Plan: The Physical Development Plan for the City of Philadelphia.*

15

The Tactical Plan

A question as old as human society itself is how to deal with the apparent contradiction between the private good of the individual and the good of society as a whole. Political thinkers have answered the question in many different ways, some by denying that the conflict has any real basis. For certain philosophers, only the society and its agent, the state, are real, and, therefore, any sense of a purely private good is illusory, an aberration to be suppressed or ignored. On the other side, there are those who argue that individuals and their interests alone are real and that "society" is merely a convenient abstraction.

The mainstream of Western political thought, however, has always recognized both a private person and a public or corporate person, and although the respect given to their different claims or interests may change with time and place, the distinction itself is never wholly lost.

These two "persons" are endowed with legal rights in which their relationship to each other is defined and regulated. To anyone concerned with questions of urban form, their legal relationship is a matter of considerable interest because it determines how public objectives are to be implemented and this, in turn, affects a number of other concrete societal relationships, including spatial relationships. Where the public power is large, the method of implementation is one of direct enforcement. But where the major decisions determining the course of events are for the most part in private hands, the situation is quite different. Here, any idea of enforcement is often out of the question. In this case, government becomes a problem centering on the question, How can private energies be led to contribute to a public objective? One aspect of our own political history has been a search for effective inducements.

Essentially, there are only two ways of securing the cooperation of private individuals when more direct controls are lacking: persuasion and tactics. Persuasion works on the motive of the individual so as to confirm it in the public point of view. By education and argument, he is made to see that, in the long run, self-interest is better served when private action encompasses the public good. The argument is reinforced by holding up vivid images of the objective meant to move the observer by their very attractiveness.

But, while persuasion is useful for winning inner assent to the objective, it doesn't necessarily bring about a corresponding change in behavior. Accordingly, persuasion comes to be supplemented by more effective, if less direct, measures—by tactics.

The essential method of tactics is not to divert the individual from his pursuit of self-interest, but rather to change the field in which he acts so that his private actions are more likely to follow paths which contribute to the realization of the public objective. Thus, to give a familiar example, a government wishing to encourage charitable activities may exempt income donated to those activities from taxation. Or, to give another example closer to our own interests, a city wishing to encourage the use of a certain transit line may lower the fares, improve the service, or avoid building a competing expressway. Perhaps all three. In none of these cases are individuals coerced, nor are they exhorted, but the environment which conditions their behavior is changed and so it is hoped that their behavior may be altered in a way that favors the public purpose.[1]

With tactics, then, the purpose is not to win the assent of the individual. Assent was given when he or his representatives ratified the objective and made of it a goal for himself and others to follow.[2] Tactics are used to overcome the self-contradiction involved when the individual acts publicly and when he acts privately.

American society is one in which the larger part of social and economic initiative is still legally vested in private hands. Our purpose is to trace some of the effects of this basic feature of our national political constitution into a field where they have never yet been described in a systematic fashion—city planning, especially its effects on the notion of urban form.[3] Persuasion and tactics as two different methods of influencing the behavior of private individuals become the bases of two different types of community development plan, a goal plan and a tactical plan, with the result that urban form is made to appear under a double aspect—as an end state to be striven for and as a means of achieving that end state.

As an illustration, I have chosen the case of a hypothetical central city under conditions of metropolitan growth. Although the use of tactical planning is by no means limited to a situation of this type, I thought it desirable not to divorce the concept of tactical planning from an account of the situation in which it usually arises and finds its most dramatic expression. In the crisis of growth, a particular objective often comes to predominate in the tactical planning of the central city. Our first concern here will be with the origin and nature of this objective.

Functional Centrality as an Objective

Ordinarily, a city is viewed in either of two ways—as a society of people seeking opportunities, in which case the industrial establishment appears as a place to work (or to shop, or to play)[4] and its location is judged to be good or bad with reference to the convenience of the worker; or as a society of industries, also seeking opportunities according to their own functional requirements. In this case, people are still in the picture but their value is changed. They appear as localized factors of production (labor supply) along with other factors, or as the ultimate consumers of the industrial product (market). Their human aspirations matter only insofar as these affect their availability or their propensity to consume.

The essential difference between the two societies is this: In one case people are the subjects and industrial establishments the objects, while in the other case the reverse is true—industrial establishments are the subjects and people are objects. Each type of subject is faced with more or less immobility on the part of its object which stems from the latter's proper needs, and each tries to use the other (i.e., locate the other to its own advantage). In the total city, then, we see the struggle of two formative principles or interests, which although opposed are also indissolubly joined, inasmuch as they make use of the same human and material elements—two spirits in the same body.

How do the human and industrial subjects, implying as they do different spatial orders, manage to come into contact in a way in which the requirements of both are generally satisfied? The question goes to the heart of the problem of urban form, but it is not the direct concern of this essay.[5] Here we can only note the obvious fact that neither subject is able to ignore the other's interest altogether. For if a community were organized solely from the standpoint of human convenience, its industrial capacity would suffer. On the other hand, a community organized strictly in the interest of industrial convenience or efficiency would finally injure or alienate its human base. Urban structure, therefore, is necessarily a compromise, a relationship of persons and facilities in which the human and industrial subjects are both served, but neither of them optimally. In short, the total system has its own optimum. This fact rules out the possibility of either human or industrial convenience as a sufficient objective for urban planning.

The political city, as represented by a corporate boundary line, is merely a part of the total arena in which the two subjects meet and work out a relationship to each other. But when, as a result of metropolitan growth, it becomes evident that this meeting can take place equally well

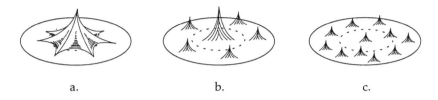

a. b. c.

Figure 15.1

under a variety of spatial forms (figure 15.1),[6] not all of them favorable to the interests of the political community, then the latter becomes a third subject opposed to the unlimited subjectivity of both people and industry (i.e., it regards them both as objects to be used for its own purpose). By political community I mean here the inhabitants of the corporate city, such as the one represented in figure 15.1 by the dotted line, who have in common a more permanent interest in the value of its territory. The political community is impelled to influence metropolitan developmental forces in a direction which would increase that value. In other words, it seeks to retain or increase the economic or functional centrality of its territory in the region, although the objective need not take a crude quantitative form (as in figure 15.1a).[7] More qualitative kinds of centrality may be sought.[8]

In its endeavor to bring about a distribution of metropolitan activities favorable to itself, the political community is hindered by the fact that its control over the behavior of the inhabitants of its own territory is limited, while beyond the boundary it has no control at all. Under these conditions, it has to resort to indirect or tactical measures, a requirement as urgent in the case of physical planning as it is in other forms of public action. In the following sections I have tried, first, to explain the general nature of tactical city planning by comparing it with types of nontactical planning, and then to show how its use in a situation of metropolitan growth can lead to an overall locational pattern in which the elements of urban form are made to subserve the objective of a political community.

Tactical Planning

The Goal Plan and the Tactical Plan

As subject, a polity begins to influence regional events in its own favor by projecting and publicizing an image of its objective. This image is represented by what I have called the goal plan. The goal plan, which may be spelled out in considerable land use detail, is an optative statement of the size and form of the political city for the future year X. Typically, it shows the political city gaining or retaining a position of dominance in the region. The image is credible, it bears some relation to existing opportunities in the region, but apart from its ability to persuade, to move people by its attractiveness, it includes no explicit measures for ensuring that these opportunities will be realized.[9] Therefore, in addition to the goal plan, another kind of plan is also required, one whose special purpose is to prevent the objective from being left behind by events over which the political community has only limited control, events largely determined by the innumerable decisions of private individuals, by market forces. This is the tactical plan.

The Tactical Plan and Conventional Capital Programming

The tactical plan must, at least to begin with, bear a demonstrable relationship to the goal plan because of the fact that the latter is a known and publicized document, and any deviation from it has to be justified. The tactical plan may begin as a statement of the order in which the different elements of the goal plan should be undertaken. In this respect, tactical planning would appear to be identical with ordinary capital programming, but this is not the case inasmuch as capital programming, as it is usually practiced, and tactical planning are dealing with different problems and are guided by different considerations.

The problem of conventional programming is this: Given the goal plan for the year X to be realized over a period of, say, twenty-five years, what part should be carried out in the year X minus twenty-four, what part in the year X minus twenty-three, etc.? Here the guiding criteria, insofar as they are rational, are usually based on existing needs and trends. For example, highway A is prior to highway B because the present traffic pattern indicates a greater demand for A; or A is prior to B because present land use trends indicate it will come into fuller use sooner.

This is quite different from the problem and procedure of tactical planning, which may be stated as follows: Given the goal plan for the year X, what steps should be taken first, not to anticipate present trends but to control them—this to keep the plan from being made rapidly obsolete by a dynamic, changing environment?

Conventional programming, then, is concerned with carrying out the various elements of the plan, subject only to considerations of present or anticipated need, whereas tactical planning addresses itself to shaping actively the background conditions required by the plan (i.e., those general market orientations and locational preferences of the metropolitan community which are consistent with the features of the goal plan and necessary for its realization). For example, if, according to a central city's goal plan, the city's central business district is to continue to be preeminent in the metropolitan region, then the continuing patronage of the regional population is a condition required for the realization of this feature of the goal plan.

The tactical plan would then specify what is to be done first in order to increase the chances that this patronage does in fact continue uninterrupted, on the grounds that patronage once lost is not easily regained. Perhaps it will schedule improvements to the radial highways serving this center before improvements to highways serving other less important centers, even though improvements to all major highways are called for by the goal plan. In this case, highway B is given priority over highway A because it would facilitate trips in the direction of a preferred center and thus help to fulfill a major feature of the goal plan. And it would be given priority despite the fact that, compared with highway A, it may satisfy a smaller number of present or (according to present trends) anticipated total trip requirements. From this example, it will be evident that there can be a conflict between conventional programming and tactical planning (i.e., between needs and goals as a basis for allocating community resources, between the community's present and its planned future).

In addition to prescribing the order in which the different elements of the goal plan should be undertaken, the tactical plan may also call for certain elements not appearing in the goal plan at all. Such elements represent modifications of the objective in the direction of greater realism. They tacitly recognize that, in some areas, conditions have already changed adversely to the goal plan beyond any possibility of reversal. But they are no less tactical, as their purpose is to prevent conditions from changing even more adversely. Corresponding to the tactical plan, there is a spatial form—a configuration of elements comprising those parts of the total goal plan which are given priority or emphasized for tactical reasons plus certain modifications of the goal plan.

Tactical Form: An Example

The point has been stressed that to promulgate a plan is easy enough, but to put it into effect is not so direct nor simple a matter as utopian planning literature has commonly supposed. The main difficulty is in trying to keep market forces from behaving unfavorably to the plan, a requirement which often leads to results different from what was intended or hoped.

The forces of metropolitan growth and change include the following: 1) technological advances, mainly in the field of transportation, which make possible the organization of regional life on a vastly wider geographical scale than has hitherto existed; 2) the numberless private decisions to relocate made in response to the expanding regional framework; and 3) the conscious maneuvers of the politically independent suburb to bring about a shift of wealth and power in its own favor. For this is a common objective, even though it may be stated in far more ingenuous terms as a "workable tax economy" to be achieved by means of "limited and balanced growth." The land use meaning of limited growth is large lot zoning and low density, the social meaning is exclusion of the poor and underprivileged, the fiscal meaning is low service costs. Balanced growth, on the other hand, means the selection of "choice," (i.e., "non-child-producing" ratables), as well as the selection of the skilled and relatively well-to-do. The effect is to make of the boundary a line separating the costs from the benefits of regional growth.

The question naturally arises as to what corrective measures the central city can take in the face of this problem. The more direct measures are beyond the power of the city to impose, for example, the elimination of regional tax disparities, the enforcement of fair housing practices, and any unusual restriction of the right of the individual to buy, sell, or locate where he chooses. Consequently, less direct measures have to be considered. To the planner, the question may appear as a problem in physical form. How can key regional facilities be arranged and programmed so as to bring about a pattern of private locational preferences and orientations more favorable to the central city, more favorable to the goal plan? This is but a specification of the more general question, How can self-satisfying private decisions be led to contribute to a public objective? The question, when it appears, marks a definite change in perspective: overall community form has come to acquire a tactical meaning in addition to its ideal meaning as a right relationship between people and facilities.

The Tactical Variant

The diagrams in figure 15.2 illustrate, in the broadest possible terms, the effect of tactical thought on a central city plan and, through the plan, on the form of the city.

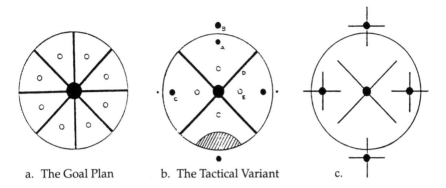

a. The Goal Plan   b. The Tactical Variant   c.

Figure 15.2

Figure 15.2a, a hypothetical goal plan in schematic form, is an optative statement about the year X and after, a symbol of central city dominance in the region. Areas are to be served by radials, which relate them to the regional center, and by interstitial subordinate centers.[10] The purpose of the goal plan is more to state a desired objective persuasively than to plot a course of action for the intervening years.

The tactical variant of the goal plan (Figure 15.2b), on the other hand, is an action plan for the years prior to X and specifies the urgent measures to be undertaken in that period if the city is to retain its dominance. Its objective is to brake the centrifugal tendencies of money and population, in short, to keep the background conditions assumed by the goal plan from changing completely. Therefore, the elements of form become tactical elements. Peripheral substitute centers (such as A) are contemplated,[11] not so much to meet demand as to determine the place at which it will be satisfied, to compete with the substitute centers (such as B) beyond the boundary, or sometimes (as in the case of C) to forestall the imminent development of a suburban center. As an alternative countermeasure, further development of city areas tributary to a suburban center (hatched) may be given a low priority, as compared with other areas of the city, in order to deprive the suburban center of a market. Those radials of the goal plan (such as D) are emphasized which bypass the suburban centers and which would establish the dominance of the regional center over a wider area. Radials feeding suburban centers may be downgraded in design, postponed, or altogether eliminated from the plan.

Tactical form is likely to result in yet other changes to the goal plan. For example, in figure 15.2b (compared with figure 15.2a), the regional center itself has undergone a reduction in planned size in favor of the substitute centers within the city or, to state the effect in terms of time, its improvement has been deferred. Also, the location proposed for subordinate centers (such as E) may change. However, these are the results of secondary adjustments; figure 15.2b shows tactical form to be primarily a combination of certain elements of the goal form, such as the bypassing radials, which are given priority for tactical reasons, and special tactical elements, such as the peripheral substitute city centers, which the goal form doesn't include. It represents a compromise between the two regional alternatives stated in figure 15.2a, the goal form, and 15.2c, presumably the form which unopposed market forces and the action of neighboring communities would produce. Perhaps it represents a stage of regional development intermediate between the present and future forms, likewise represented by Figures 15.2a and 15.2c.

Perspectives

In the preceding section I have sought to make explicit an element present in the planning of large metropolitan areas, a tactical element which owes its motive in part to the political and fiscal disjointedness of an economic region.

Formerly, the major profit-generating functions were concentrated downtown. Now, changes in living patterns and technological advances have resulted in vast dislocations outward of people and economic activity. At the same time, the politically independent suburb has been able to select the more prosperous elements in this migratory wave, leaving the central city with a disproportionately large share of financial and social problems. Consequently, the city is impelled to take corrective measures, even at the price of such departures from its stated physical development goals as may ensue from tactical planning—and this for the purpose of not entirely abandoning the objectives which those goals represent.

We will now carry our examination of this single instance of tactical planning somewhat further to explore the meaning of certain metropolitan planning problems and also to illustrate the problematic nature of tactical planning in general.

The Tactical Variant and the Private Interest

If, as has been done in the case of individual activities (Alexandersson 1956, 14–15), the uses of urban form are divided into two main types, city-serving and city-building, then the tactical variant of figure 15.2b is an example of the latter type, for it represents the primacy of the city-building motives, and only within the narrow limits they set are the city-serving functions of form to be carried out.[12] It is a characteristic of any tactical plan that it set limits other than budgetary and legal limits to the service standards of the community. So doing, it implies that there is a more important objective than the immediate satisfaction of the individual person or industry who inhabits the city. In the case we have considered, the superordinate interest is the value of the common territory, which the tactical variant seeks to preserve. This viewpoint is consistent with the character of the political community as subject. But for the individual resident—person or industry—whose immediate interest is bound up with a particular site which he occupies, it may involve a cost, represented in Figure 15.1b by the planned shift of service from the center to the peripheral areas of the city. It may also involve a cost for the private resident outside the city, for if the tactical variant should succeed, it would curtail service beyond the boundary.

Is the cost justified? The answer depends on two factors; first, the intrinsic merit of the goal or objective in behalf of which a cost may be required. By the merit of the objective, I mean here its power, if achieved, to restore to the individual or to his descendants or successors more than was taken from him, or its power to save him from a greater future loss, and this without depriving another individual. This is the ultimate moral test of any tactical plan.

The second factor is the aptness of the measures of the plan, their ability to achieve the desired objective. A single tactic, or a set of tactics, may be applied at the wrong place or at the wrong time, so that it fails. These failures do not invalidate the objective itself, but they are wasteful, and in this case the cost is not justified. This is the technical test of a tactical plan.

Here, however, we will concern ourselves only with the first criterion, the merit of the objective, as a test of the tactical variant of our example, and our viewpoint will be that of the total metropolitan community. In other words, we shall look at the plan as though it were a proposed metropolitan plan despite the fact that the plan was made by the central city for its own benefit. Cities, like individuals, act in their own interests, but this in no way alters the fact that at the same time they may be acting as the representatives of larger social forces. Metropolitan growth is not a wholehearted process. In certain respects, the tactical variant appears as an effort of the total metropolitan community, a concrete social, economic, and political organism made up of the interlocking lives of multitudes, to preserve itself in the moment of growth, from the pain and cost of disruption which is one aspect of growth.

These comments imply the existence of a fourth subject, the total metropolitan community, whose objective is the metropolitan optimum and from whose point of view the self-interested political communities of the region and their plans may appear as mere instruments, perhaps even as unwitting representatives. This is the light in which we now wish to regard the plan. In order to see it in this way (i.e., in order to avoid the prejudgment likely to be involved in knowing that the tactical variant is, in the first instance, the plan of a single political subcommunity of the region) it will be useful to view it momentarily in relation to a metropolitan problem of major importance—the urban renewal problem. From this point of view the plan will appear as one kind of plan which the metropolitan community may wish to regard as being in the long-term interest of the metropolitan resident, regardless of his location.

The Tactical Variant as an Urban Renewal Plan

As a special kind of planning interest, urban renewal is characterized by a concern with the older portions of a metropolitan region under conditions of growth, represented in Figure 15.2b by the area of the circle.

Metropolitan growth means a farther-flung population to be served, and as a result of the increased distances the older, central areas of the region are no longer entirely convenient places from which to serve them. Losing their normal time-distance relationships to a dispersing population, they become, as it were, dislocated.

Dislocated, the central areas undergo the ordeal of economic and social succession. Their original activities begin to leave them and are replaced by activities of another kind or quality. The process is a costly one with its accompaniment of personal, social, and environmental disorder—blight. As one of the major objectives of urban renewal is to eliminate blight or to prevent its occurrence, it follows that any plan to halt or retard the process of dislocation, or to limit its extent, is a kind of urban renewal plan.

It might be argued, then, that the tactical variant is an urban renewal plan since, in its case, too, the purpose is to retard the dislocation of the older established areas of the metropolitan region. By inhibiting the rise of competing (i.e., substitute) activity centers at the periphery, the radius of regional development is shortened. As a result, the more central areas retain their usefulness as places from which to serve the regional population, and the establishments which use them for this purpose remain in their present locations, with all that this implies for a continuance of healthy economic life at the center. To be sure, the tactical measures themselves involve a planned shift of some activity outward, but presumably the shift is less extensive than what would take place if these measures were not applied (compare figure 15.2b and 15.2c).

Considering the great strength of the forces of dispersal and the weakness of the tactical measures considered here, the stabilization of present central activity is a doubtful undertaking, but not necessarily hopeless. Much depends on the extent to which existing sites are replaceable elsewhere in a region. A good harbor, for example, the base of many activities, cannot be easily replaced, nor can the qualities of site sacredness or historicity. In one case, value depends on physiography and in the other on absolute location. In the possession of rare or unique site qualities, cities differ greatly, but where they exist, tactical planning would have powerful allies.

To be sure, we have considered only one aspect of regional growth—the cost of disrupting the present pattern of development. But what of the benefits of reintegration at a larger scale?[13] From this point of view, the dislocation of the central city, which it is the purpose of the tactical variant to resist, may, in the long run, be a salutary development. This is especially the case when we consider that the metropolitan area as a whole is itself in competition with other metropolitan areas and that a broader, more comfortable, and more efficient spatial setting may be required for its future economic welfare, including the welfare of the central city itself. Steps to hinder the process of dislocation, then, could well be considered retrograde.

Does the greater social waste lie in encouraging the disruption of the existing pattern or in resisting this disruption? Or is the question itself a false one? Is it only through the mutual opposition of these two forces that the metropolitan optimum can be found, or can find itself? These are but different ways of asking if the tactical variant is justified, if it would finally compensate that metropolitan resident who may have to pay the price.

The Tactical Planner and the Public

American government is government for the people, and so the people's values, insofar as they are not satisfied in the market place, become public objectives embodied in great programs of civic improvement. Other values, those that pertain to individual rights, come to government in a negative form as restraints upon its actions. Thus, government is entrusted with broad responsibilities, but it is seldom given corresponding powers of effectuation. It is this disparity of governmental ends and means which is one of the distinguishing features of our society, some of whose effects we have sought to trace here. It has been shown that the very insufficiency of means calls forth a special response in the field of city planning, a tactical use of urban form. We have limited ourselves to a single example, but in this example the essential phenomenon is contained. One is able to distinguish between the tactical method itself and a particular use to which it may be put.

Like persuasion, the basis of the goal plan, tactical methods represent, in the main, the efforts of a community of free men to take a conscious direction or to resist a direction (i.e., not to drift, not to rely on the "unseen hand of the market" to produce a desired social result). But they go beyond persuasion in trying to overcome the frequent contradiction between public and private action.

As a response to an ancient problem of democracy, as a means of combining personal freedom with community planning, tactical methods show great promise. But the difficulties which stand in the way of this promise are also great. Not the least of these difficulties are the demands which tactical planning makes on the planner himself, who must use it as a technician, and on the public, which must authorize its use. If they can be met, then urban communities may look forward to a new era of self-mastery.

For the planner, tactical planning requires a shift of focus from ends to means. With relatively few means at his disposal he is expected to produce large transforming and, of course, predictable effects on community life. This presumes considerable knowledge of urban dynamics in general and of his own community in particular.

From his dalliance with long-range objectives, he is called upon to subject these objectives to the contradictions of time, by programming and putting into effect intermediate arrangements which contribute to the realization of these objectives at the same time that they differ from its popular symbol, the goal plan.

How are these differences to be presented to the public and explained? Here we encounter what is perhaps the major nontechnical problem of tactical planning. Although the goal is fully public and easy to grasp, the tactical means, being largely esoteric, pass out of public view into the hands of the expert, the planner. The criteria of the public as a critic of programming decisions are based on its observations of existing conditions and trends, on obvious needs, and on the dramatic features of the goal plan. Therefore, a purely tactical programming of the objectives, not necessarily meant to meet present needs, is likely to appear quite arbitrary and unreasonable. Here, it should be understood, it is not a question of winning the public's approval of the objective. This, presumably, has already been accomplished with the ratification of the goal plan. What is needed is public approval of the tactical means.

Can this approval be secured? The American public is likely to be impatient with the distance between the present fact and the future goal. It is hardly likely to endure the devious route to be followed in order to reach that goal. In submitting the tactical plan to the public, then, the planner is presenting the implications of a goal plan, and in so doing he is subjecting it to a test far more critical than if he merely presents the "bill" in terms of financial costs. In short, he is testing the seriousness and durability of the public purpose itself, for this is what the goal plan represents. As a result of this confrontation, the public may decide to rethink its objectives a little more carefully, perhaps a little more realistically. But if it retains its objective, then it is better prepared to realize them because it is forearmed with knowledge of their implications in time. These considerations alone are enough to justify tactical thought and planning.

Notes

This essay is adapted from *Explorations into Urban Structure* (Philadelphia: University of Pennsylvania Press, 1964).

1. Strictly speaking, of course, persuasion is itself a kind of tactic, but here I would like to restrict that word to mean a change in the field of action rather than in the consciousness or motive of the private actor.

2. This is only to say that an individual, in approving a goal (i.e., in giving open or tacit consent to it), implicitly approves of its implementation by indirect as well as by direct means. It does not imply that the legality or desirability of any specific tactic is beyond challenge, that an end justifies any and every means.

3. However, see Meyerson (1956, esp. 60–61), in effect a call for a "tactical plan."

4. The term *industrial establishment* is used here most broadly to mean any establishment where a good or service is produced. In this sense even a playground or shop is an industrial establishment.

5. For an approach to the general features of the spatial or structural solution to the problem of duality, see "Urban Structure and Urban Growth" in this volume. [For examples of real-life applications of the solution see the essays "How to Crowd and Still be Kind" and "Taylorism, Unionism, and Metropolitan Spatial Structure."]

6. In figure 15.1, the conical mounds represent densities or concentrations of regional economic activity.

7. In Figure 15.1a, compared with 15.1b and 15.1c, the degree of regional economic and functional centrality possessed by the political city (enclosed by the dotted line) is greater and, presumably as a result, the value of its territory is higher.

8. Compare Foley (1964). Foley sees in contemporary metropolitan planning two different approaches, the "adaptive" approach, which views the metropol-

itan community as process and seeks to influence developmental forces at work, and the "unitary" approach, which aims for a single metropolitan form as a goal, the latter flowing [from the design professions, principally architecture and landscape architecture]. Foley's distinction is a valid and useful one. However, it is apparent that there is a far more powerful force in the field than architecture contributing to the prominence of the "unitary" approach, namely the territorial interest. Metropolitan form is a factor to which a political community can hardly afford to be indifferent because this is the factor which, perhaps more than any other, determines the locational value of its territory. Therefore, the political community, the author of the plan, is impelled to seek a preferred metropolitan form, one which maximizes the value of its territory. In practice, therefore, the two approaches are related to each other, as are ends and means.

Even where metropolitan competition is not a factor, the unitary approach is required, for we have seen that one purpose of a plan is to persuade, and this means projecting a single, unambiguous image which will move private individuals in a desired direction.

9. Most master plans are goal plans in this sense. Mitchell (1961, 169–75) speaks of "wouldn't it be nice if—" plans which do not prescribe methods of attainment.

10. A subordinate center is one of the two basic types of subcenter in the urban field. It corresponds to a lower level of community than the total region and, therefore, in the function it performs for the regional resident, complements rather than competes with the regional center.

11. The second basic type of subcenter is the substitute center. The substitute center is "insubordinate" to the regional center whose functions it duplicates, or attempts to duplicate, for all or part of the region.

12. In the present context, *city-preserving* would be a more appropriate term than *city-building*.

13. While one objective of urban renewal is to prevent the occurrence and spread of blight, another is to give the total metropolitan community a broader and more comfortable spatial setting, one more in harmony with present day living patterns and technical capabilities. Both objectives are very much present in contemporary urban renewal thought but are not necessarily compatible.

References

Alexandersson, Gunnar. 1956. *The Industrial Structure of American Cities*. Lincoln: University of Nebraska Press.

Foley, Donald L. 1964. "An Approach to Metropolitan Spatial Structure." In Melvin M. Webber et al., *Explorations into Urban Structure*. Philadelphia: University of Pennsylvania Press.

Meyerson, Martin. 1956. "Building the Middle-range Bridge for Comprehensive Planning." *Journal of the American Institute of Planners* 22 (Spring): 60–61.

Mitchell, Robert B. 1961. "The New Frontier in Metropolitan Planning." *Journal of the American Institute of Planners* 27 (Aug.): 169–75.

16

How to Crowd but Still Be Kind:
A Dutch Invention in Urban Structure

But all he did was spread the room
Of our enacting out the doom
Of being in each other's way
And so put off the weary day
When we would have to put our mind
On how to crowd but still be kind

Thus wrote Robert Frost of Columbus and the discovery of the New World in a poem entitled "America Is Hard to See." The subject here is a neighborhood design whose aim is to help us to live kindly with ourselves and others under conditions of extreme crowdedness and pressure such as only a large modern city can generate. Not surprisingly, it is found mainly in Holland but is encountered in other countries as well, including the United States. The Dutch call it a *woonerf* (pl. *woonerven*), literally a yard or the immediate premises of a house, although their preferred English rendition is "residential precinct." In a legal sense the *woonerf* was defined on September 17, 1976, when the Dutch government published standards governing its construction and use. Since that date, only neighborhoods that meet these rules and are officially designated as such can legally be called *woonerven*.

From a functional standpoint, the *woonerf* is conventionally defined as a physical design for controlling the automobile in residential neighborhoods. This is accurate, but the *woonerf* is much more than a design for slowing down automobiles. It is also a social invention in urban structure: *invention* because it is a novel arrangement of quite familiar structural elements (dwellings, streets, street furniture, play lots, parking spaces, etc.); *social* because its object is not to save work or money, but to save old valued practices and human relationships from forces that threaten them with obliteration. In this sense, the *woonerf* is a conservative invention. It can also be regarded as an experiment in conservation, that is, cultural conservation.

By calling the *woonerf* a Dutch invention, I do not mean to imply that the idea necessarily originated in Holland. The sources of such complex ideas are usually numerous. Dutch planners, on the other hand, are among the foremost pioneers and practitioners of the design and perhaps its principal conceptualizers. In Holland, moreover, the concept has achieved a very high degree of physical and legal definition as well as strong governmental backing as evidenced by the fact that between 1976 and 1980 more than eight hundred *woonerven* have been brought into existence (ANWB 1980, 3). According to Heeger (1979), the minimum design requirements for *woonerven*, published in September 1976, "were the world's first . . . in this field." To appreciate the significance of this invention for Americans, some background is necessary.

The *Woonerf* in an American Perspective

Europeans have their kings and queens and noble families, but Americans have always gloried in the primacy of the ordinary citizen. The United States is the country of the average man and woman, but their heyday was the first half of the last century.

Although the term *average* can be a pejorative, meaning mediocre, dull, or undistinguished, there is another sense in which average denotes something praiseworthy, a prized quality. It is precisely because a man or woman is average, that is, not extreme in any respect, that they can represent a certain kind of human ideal. Being average, no parts of their personalities are overdeveloped, hypertrophied, disproportionate. They are balanced, healthy, whole. Their common sense, far from being an inferior form of intelligence, is what the Republic relies on for its survival. Herbert Croly, in his seminal work *The Promise of American Life* (1909), traced the origin of this ideal to the western frontier:

> Unlike the French Fraternity, [American democracy] was the product neither of abstract theories nor of a disembodied humanitarianism. It was the natural issue of [the Frontiersmen's] interests, their occupations and their manner of life. They felt kindly towards . . . and communicated freely with one another. . . . The pioneer democracy viewed with distrust and aversion the man with a special vocation and high standards of achievement. Such a man did insist upon being in certain respects better than the average; and under the prevalent economic and social conditions he did impair the consistency of feeling upon which the pioneers rightly placed such a high value. (61, 64)

What did it mean to be an average man or woman? It meant that life had a certain unity to it. You weren't separated from yourself as we are today. You lived and worked on the same few acres or in the same neighborhood. Physical distances separating family from family were not very great. You were neither very rich nor very poor, nor were you much better or worse off than your neighbors. The social distances between neighbors was also moderate. The chances are, they were the same kind in religion, race, and language. In short, averageness betokened membership and participation in a community.

Industrialism and urbanization changed all that. With the "journey to work," men and women became self-separated. Physical distances increased, a process in which advancing transportation technology—the railroad, the tram, the auto—was only one factor. Economic and social distance also increased as some people acquired great wealth and others were left behind. With the progressive rationalization of industry and the division of labor, functional separation from one's fellows became a factor of increasing importance. Not the least irritating consequence of this occupational separation was the division of what had hitherto been a generalized citizenry into the experts and the people. Immigrants from every quarter of the globe were thrown together in American cities to live and work cheek by jowl, aggravating the sense of separation from one's own kind. Finally, rapid social and cultural change separated the generations more than did nature itself.

The turn of the century was a time of great turmoil. To many, it seemed that the country was on the verge of class warfare. This was the time when a special type of urban reform appeared on the scene—city planning. This new movement intended to be a substitute for class and culture warfare—a substitute for politics. Its highest goal was to reconstitute that shattered average man and woman, the scene of this Humpty-Dumpty job being the city itself.[1] How was this to be accomplished? While some reformers wanted to turn back the clock to the preindustrial era, most clung tenaciously to the benefits of industrialism and technology. For them, reform meant adding to industrialism and its requirements a whole set of other values, specifically, those values which had been excluded or suppressed by the industrial system: nearness of nature, opportunity for neighborly association and recreation, a prudent concern for the welfare of future generations, and self-government. Ironically, planning, itself an affair of experts, would deliver the people from the untoward consequences of expertise.

In our own day, other meanings of planning have been gaining ground. Planning is said to be politics, more cynically, the disguised politics of the middle class, that is middle-class politics in the guise of technical expertise. Even so, the original definition of planning still holds. Its method is to substitute technical solutions for raw political conflict, its goal to restore wholeness to the human experience, hence, the call for inventiveness in adapting the functional requirements of an advanced industrial society to accord with the imperatives of small-scale community life. In this respect, the traditional aims of planning are not far removed in spirit from those of the appropriate technology movement.

Two structural elements of cities—the street and the dwelling unit—are crucial in the invention of new types of urban form for reconciling neighborhood life with a wider environment. The dwelling unit serves and represents the human nesting function—home-making, the care and nurture of children, rest and recreation. The street gives access to and at the same time symbolizes the great world beyond home, the complex socioeconomic system in which it is embedded. Consequently, the proper function of both realms of human existence are seen to depend in no small part on how street and dwellings are related to each other. That is why current experiments in Holland for the purpose of modifying this relationship have attracted wide interest in America.

Antecedents

In fact, the *woonerf* has some American antecedents. As a design for bringing about a new relation between the public street and the private dwelling, it is reminiscent of Clarence Perry's Neighborhood Unit. Perry was a New York social reformer who, beginning in the early years of the present century, worked to devise a secure haven for family life in the midst of the "urban wilderness." His idea was to establish neighborhoods of about five thousand souls each, "residential cells" as he called them, lodged between busy arterial streets, which would form their boundaries and conduct the traffic around rather than through the area. Commercial establishments would be relegated to the four corners of the unit where the arterials crossed, while community facilities such as the school and playground were to be ensconced at the center. Thus, all the key institutions of neighborhood life could be safely reached from within the unit without the need for crossing major streets. This fortress-neighborhood he called the Neighborhood Unit was considered the ideal setting for living and raising children (Perry 1929).

Perry's concept was first promulgated widely in 1929. In the 1940s, the neighborhood concept came under attack on social grounds. Critics charged that its effect was not only to keep out traffic but also to keep out "uncongenials" of a different race, religion, or ethnic strain (Isaacs 1948). *Exclusionary* is the word that would be used in condemning it today. Perry envisaged the adoption of his scheme in a variety of locales and densities, but it was in the suburbs that the Neighborhood Unit concept really came into its own. In fact, the adjective *suburban* has come to connote the very type of protected family-life enclave that Perry advocated.

The 1950s was the heyday of suburbanization in the United States, but this did not prevent social critics, such as David Riesman, from observing the symptoms of a growing suburban "malaise." Riesman noted the "aimless quality of suburban life," the lack of meaningful work, and the "tendency . . . to lose the human differentiations which have made great cities in the past the centers of rapid intellectual and cultural advance. The suburb is like a fraternity house at a small college . . . in which like-mindedness reverberates upon itself" (Riesman 1957, 134).

Riesman's critique was mild compared with that of Jane Jacobs who, in the 1960s, launched an acerbic attack on the "monotony, sterility and vulgarity" of the one-class, one-function residential area in its suburban form, which she traced to Ebenezer Howard, Patrick Geddes, and Le Corbusier, with their "anticity" ideology. Among the "city-destroying" ideas let loose by these men, she singled out for special opprobrium the very pillars of the planner's creed: that "the basic unit of city design is not the street but the block"; that "commerce should be segregated from residences and greens"; that "the presence of many other people is, at best, a necessary evil"; and that "good city planning must aim for at least an illusion of isolation and suburbany [*sic*] privacy" (Jacobs 1961, 20).

Jacobs's writings and those of her allies signaled a turning of the tide. After decades of disgrace, the street was beginning to make a comeback as a respectable focus for urban residential planning. The mixing of residences, shops, and traffic was ceasing to be a cardinal sin. Christopher Alexander (1965) carried the heterodoxy a little further in his article "A City Is Not a Tree," meaning that it is not a set of self-contained, hierarchically-ordered neighborhoods and communities. He made the common-sense point that human social groups at any level of territorial organization are too complex, their activities too fluid, to be confined neatly within a single set of boundaries. For Perry, neighborhoods had been safety zones, and streets their boundaries—better not to cross them. Alexander's articles were odes in praise of street crossing.

Street and boundary crossing were all the rage in the late 1960s and early 1970s. The order of the day for middle-class youth was not to wall out the demons of middle-class life in the fashion of their suburban parents, but to meet them head on and work out a new deal with them. In this spirit, Richard Sennett, an American social historian, viewed the turbulent street as a main arena of social and cultural experimentation and the avenue to the future.

Their very mental health required middle-class youth to cast off the "adolescent" dreams of "purity" fostered in the suburban cocoons. Sennett preached a kind of anarchy. Let all the codes, statutes, ordinances, and other legal restraints be lifted that now muffled the conflict in the streets. Life would be tough in the resulting "survival communities"—a bruising street-clash of personalities, cultures, activities—but only out of this encounter could come a broader, more just, healthier social order (Sennett 1970).

A year before Sennett's book appeared, Milton Kotler published *Neighborhood Government*, reviving a theme which had been present in the thinking of the neighborhood theorists of the Progressive Era but virtually dormant since their time—the neighborhood as a political entity (Guttenberg 1978). Kotler paints the picture of the downtown of the typical northeastern city as a kind of Rome which, beginning as Rome had begun, one of many city-states in ancient Italy, had forced down one rival after another and then annexed them. Downtown Philadelphia absorbed Germantown, Pittsburgh devoured Allegheny, and Boston swallowed Roxbury. Each great city is, in fact, an urban empire of subjugated neighborhoods. With this metaphor, functional problems are transmuted by Kotler into political problems. To check and divert the streams of traffic coursing through the prostrate neighborhoods is a step in throwing off downtown's imperial yoke (Kotler 1969). Thus, to mixed land use and a street focus, Kotler added political insubordinacy as a criterion of the good neighborhood.

The teaching of these recent movements was to retain or restore community, but to establish it on a broader, more pluralistic base. No longer were races, classes, life-styles, land uses, etc. to be hermetically segregated. The right of each to exist on its own ground was recognized, and, henceforth, at the very least, they were to exist within each other's sight. Moreover, there was a new and strong emphasis on reclaiming the street and making it the center of the neighborhood stage.

This thumbnail sketch of the development of American neighborhood theory indicates what is at stake for Americans in the Dutch experiment. The *woonerf*, of course, also has a specifically Dutch history, elements of which are discussed in Heeger's excellent article (1979). An examination of the issues on both continents reveals the urban residential neighborhood as a point of conflict between equally deep and authentic cultural traits. On the one side is the love of mobility and openness, the Faustian impulse to adventure in ever wider worlds of industry, commerce, science, politics, and human relations. On the other side is the instinct to create the environmental conditions that protect the family hearth from violence, overstimulation, and the challenge of alien values. Can a stable balance between these contradictory urges be struck through a single neighborhood design embracing both the street and the home? On the answer hangs the hope for the peaceable reintegration of our urban-industrial order. This is what, in the end, the *woonerf* is all about.

Functions of the *Woonerf*: Physical and Legal Characteristics

In the *woonerf*, nothing is present by caprice. All its physical and legal features exist to facilitate the achievement of certain functions. First, it is meant to provide an island of safety and repose, especially in those urban areas assailed by pollution and crisscrossed by dangerous traffic routes. It serves a logistical function by allowing residential support facilities to exist within reach of the inhabitants. It aims to inject a new civility into urban behavior and to add a touch of visual beauty to drab inner-city neighborhoods. It attempts to guard and regulate the passage back and forth between two levels of community organization—the city and the neighborhood. Finally, it aspires to substitute a technical solution for raw political conflict between these communities over questions of land use.

Recess and Access[2]

In technical terms, most of the above social objectives reduce to how to provide access to facilities of all kinds while at the same time providing recess from the deleterious effects of those facilities, especially the motor traffic that flows to them in ever-increasing volume. Reasonable planners can and do differ about the relative value of these two properties of urban structure. The *woonerf* planners come down heavily, although not totally, on the recess side of the argument. They propose to resist the economic and even the geometric forces that press hard upon the residential neighborhoods of the city. This purpose is embodied in the first two articles of the official minimum design standards for *woonerven*, which state respectively that "a *woonerf* must be primarily a residential area," and that through traffic should be excluded (ANWB 1980, 11).

Note that the words are *should be*, not *must be* excluded. For even while affording recess from the urban traffic stream, the *woonerf* is definitely not supposed to choke off or in any way impair access to and from services needed in daily living. Access is maintained in two ways, first by allowing certain facilities to locate within the *woonerf* itself. Although it is primarily residential, other establishments such as shops, schools, and churches are not zoned out of the *woonerf*, provided these remain minor traffic generators and are truly subservient to the residential function (ANWB 1980, 11).

Access to and from facilities beyond the *woonerf* boundaries is also assured by maintaining adequate linkage with the general road network. Although translocal traffic is discouraged, the *woonerf* is not hermetically sealed against motor vehicles in either a physical or legal sense. They are expressly admitted so long as they are not so numerous as to change the character of the road as part of a *woonerf*. The suggested limits are one hundred to two hundred vehicles per peak hour, depending on variable factors such as road width and the distribution of daily traffic flow (ANWB 1980, 11).

The accessibility principle is further fortified in Article 8 of the design standards, which requires "adequate parking facilities for the residents. . . . Before a *woonerf* is created, all the parking problems must be resolved and full account . . . taken of the expectation that the demand for parking will increase" with the years to come (ANWB 1980, 14).

The *woonerf* must always remain accessible to certain larger-sized motor vehicles, such as police vehicles, fire engines, trash trucks, and the like, a provision which necessarily affects *woonerf* design.

Restoring Civic Order: Motorist and Pedestrian

Woonerf planners are traffic engineers and residential designers, but they must also be seen as something more, as latter-day solons who mean to restore an older code of civil conduct that has long been in abeyance. They aim to alter the rules of behavior relating man in his industrial-technological phase, as typified by the motorist, to communal man as typified by the pedestrian. Their viewpoint is reminiscent of Ralph Waldo Emerson's adage, "Things are in the saddle and ride mankind." In the residential quarters at least, the pedestrian is to regain his rightful place as master, and the automobile is to be made to comport itself with the restraint of a well-trained horse. Every physical and legal feature of the *woonerf* is bent toward this purpose. Thus, Article 4 of the standards blurs the sharp line maintained elsewhere by Dutch law between sidewalk and cartway by requiring frequent and lengthy curb breaks. Where a curb is maintained, both ends are to be marked clearly by plant tubs, boxes, trees, shrubs, and the like, features which are also intended to enhance the esthetic quality of the *woonerf*. In every case, however, such curb markers exist to protect the pedestrian, not to limit his rights as in non-*woonerf* territory. In the public part of the *woonerf* there are no limits to the pedestrian's right of entry. The same applies to the play space of a child. Although for safety reasons play areas, especially, are to be clearly demarcated, play is by no means legally restricted to these areas. Article 88a of the Dutch Motor Code for the *woonerf* stipulates that "playing is also permitted on the roadway" (ANWB 1980, 12, 18).

By depriving the heedless driver of his legal protection, it is hoped that every driver will learn self-restraint.

Along with these rules, the motorist acquires new responsibilities. He must slow down to a pace no faster than "a rider allows his horse to walk" (estimated at about fifteen to twenty k.p.h.) as enjoined by Article 88b of the Motor Code (ANWB 1980, 20). The rule is reinforced by actual physical impediments on the roadway, such as humps, bumps, curves, bottlenecks, etc. Article 9 of the design standards requires that these obstacles be located no more than fifty meters apart (ANWB 1980, 14). Besides slowing down to a walk, the auto in its passage through a *woonerf* must at all times keep a respectful distance from any dwelling, the recommended minimum distance being .6 meters (Article 10).

As quid pro quo for these curbs on his freedom, the motorist retains certain privileges. He may enter and even pass through the *woonerf* by right, not by mere sufferance. Although he must always defer to pedestrians, they may not unduly impede his progress (Article 88d RVV). His vehicle is afforded its own rightful resting place. It can be "stabled" in its own "stall," that is, in specified parking spots clearly marked *P* (ANWB 1980, 20). For the vehicles of invalids there are more liberal rules (Article 138 RVV revised). The motorist is never to be suddenly confronted with unreasonable obstacles, so the design standards place much stress on signs and on the proper placement and good lighting of the structural elements (ANWB 1980, 14).

The Woonerf *as Energy Transformer*

A large city is a place where two worlds meet: the wider, higher-speed world of industry and commerce and the smaller, slower, more human-scale world of neighborhood and family life. The *woonerf* design functions as a kind of transformer between the different speed and energy levels of these two worlds. Several of the design standards and legal rules affecting the *woonerf* have specifically to do with this transformation function. If it is to take place smoothly, then the visibility and recognizability of the *woonerf*'s exits and entrances, as well as traffic priorities at these points, become all-important. Article 6 requires signs displaying the symbol of the *woonerf* at every exit and entrance. The commentary to Article 14 adds that "since the concept of *woonerven* is even new in the Netherlands, it cannot be expected that all road users are, or will soon become, acquainted with it." Hence, Article 14 states that "the word *woonerf* must be displayed [on an additional panel] below traffic sign" (ANWB 1980, 18).

Further regarding safe and smooth transition between the *woonerf* and outside, Article 6 mandates the clearest possible design of the exits

Figure 16.1. Amsterdam. Learning how to share space is a must for autos and pedestrians in crowded, canal-bound Holland.

Figure 16.2. The pressure of traffic on an Amsterdam side street.

Figure 16.3. *Woonerven* can be created by converting older streets, or they can be built from scratch. The canceling of the distinction between sidewalk and roadway gives notice that this older Delft street is reclaimed for neighborhood life. Note the textured pavement and the centrally placed lamp standards, saplings, and benches.

Figure 16.4. In a *woonerf* built from scratch, additional design features are possible. The bollards and the bend in the road serve to keep traffic at a respectful distance from the dwellings and slow it down. The low-cut hedges ensure good visibility throughout.

and entrances. For example, where vehicular points of entry or exit cross footpaths, the curb cut should be carried clear across the roadway. With this, the demarcation between *woonerf* and non-*woonerf* will be clearest. Alternatively or additionally, legal restraints may be applied to effect a safe and smooth transition between traffic streams of different volume and velocity. Thus, "when a vehicular exit . . . is onto a [non-*woonerf*] street carrying a considerable volume of traffic, the legal exit can be located inside the side-street [i.e., inside the *woonerf*] so that normal traffic regulations apply on the last section of roadway immediately prior to the junction with the local distributor" (ANWB 1978, Article 6).

Just as the *woonerf* is a device for adjusting two communities which operate at different speed and energy levels, so it is a means for adjusting the conflicting land use claims of the two communities. Shall this street serve the family purposes of the neighborhood residents, or shall it be subservient to the superordinate interests of the city of which it is a part? The answer the *woonerf* planners give is that it can be designed to serve both, although not equally, and they purport to show us how. In this sense, *woonerf* planning is a substitute for political conflict.

Evaluation

Does it work? Is it liked? Is it of, as well as for, the people? The *woonerf* is still new, even in Holland, and a large body of evaluative literature is only now beginning to emerge, most of it in the Dutch language. At the moment one can only draw on personal observation; some limited comments by the *woonerf* planners themselves as to the benefits and drawbacks of the concept; scattered surveys in various parts of Holland reported by Heeger; a study by students at the University of Leiden; and a report by D. de Jonge which has only recently become available.

In most West European countries, including Holland, motorists drive unconscionably fast. Some American drivers also speed through quiet residential neighborhoods, but in Europe it seems to be the general rule to do so. This suggests that in the United States the taming of the motor vehicles which *woonerf* planners hope to achieve mainly by means of physical restraints may have proceeded further by driver education and traffic law enforcement alone.

From the standpoint of automobile restraint, the workability of the *woonerf* remedy seems to be very much a matter of location. A neighborhood off the beaten track may appear tranquil enough, but with one that lies close to downtown and offers a tempting link in a possible route to and from the center at peak hours the result can be quite different. One may be pushed and pulled through it at quite a clip by the cars in front and behind, despite the *woonerf*'s physical features. The designers themselves implicitly acknowledge this effect when they observe that not all streets, especially the heavily traveled ones, lend themselves to *woonerf* treatment.

Dutch planners are also quick to point out that in other respects as well the *woonerf* is no panacea for the ills of the Dutch residential areas. As continuing problems they mention specifically the parking problem, heavy vehicles, and mopeds, all of which evade or in some other way negate the controlling power of the design or limit its effectiveness or applicability. The growing demand for parking makes it difficult to achieve or maintain the aimed-for balance between the traffic and the residential functions (Jonquière 1978, 18). The broad, heavy service vehicles force larger than desirable street widths and other design changes that vitiate the slowing-down power of the lay-out. It is not as though such vehicles can be shut out, since they include the emergency service vehicles of the police, the fire fighters, and the hospitals, as well as the vehicles of the sanitation department. As for the mopeds, barriers which serve to hold back four-wheeled vehicles are no obstacle to them (Jonquière 1978, 178).

Heeger reports the dissatisfaction of some Dutch planners on esthetic grounds. They complain that the *woonerf* design destroys the streetscape and object to its standardization. "The townscape is being flattened," they say, meaning that it is being deprived of its distinguishing features by the standardized treatment (Heeger 1979, 14).

ANWB, the Royal Dutch Touring Club, cites the large cost of creating a *woonerf*. Jonquière, however, reports a cost of only about 40 to 50 percent more than the cost of correcting street subsidences, a frequent requirement in much of Holland because of the watery subsoil and one that provides a good occasion to build a *woonerf* at the same time (ANWB 1980, 26; Jonquière 1979, 25). ANWB also mentions the difficulty and length of time required in winning resident assent for the idea. *Woonerf* building in undeveloped areas has an advantage, since there are no residents whose assent needs to be won.

With regard to acceptance by the people, the situation is not exactly clear. The main opponents of the idea seem to be the merchants with stores in the *woonerf* street who, according to Jonquière, are disposed to equate traffic flow with cash flow. Other opponents are those who lack communal feeling for the street, especially those "groups that have just won the means and opportunity for owning a car" and who are only interested in having a place to park it. A third set of opponents are the emergency services, which are less than enthusiastic because of their great concern for unimpeded access (Jonquière 1978, 20–21).

Even so, most authorities concur that the *woonerf*, if it is built on the right streets (those not dominated by traffic), does what it is supposed to do and is publicly accepted. According to a study conducted by a group of Leiden University students, the design is favorably regarded not only by those who live in *woonerven*, but by residents of traditional neighborhoods as well (Hendricks, Knip, and Meijer 1979). The students studied a hundred people in five *woonerven* in Ede, Huizen, Naaldwikj, Oud-Beijerland, and Spijkenisse, as well as an equal number of traditional neighborhood-dwellers in the same cities. Significantly, most of the *woonerf*-dwellers, although they favor the results, did not think that they had much influence on the decision to convert their neighborhoods into *woonerven* (Royal Netherlands Embassy 1979).

A recent rigorous study by Professor of Architecture D. de Jonge of the Delft University of Technology appears to confirm the findings of the Leiden students. On the basis of his research, which included polls of *woonerf*-dwellers in Nordwijk and of a control group of non-*woonerf*-dwellers in Hoofdorp, he concludes that "most residents of woonerven in new low-rise areas think these neighborhoods are successful" in that they offer "more play opportunities for children and more peace for adults than do conventional streets" (De Jonge 1981, 596). Such criticisms as are made pertain not to the idea itself, but rather to the failure to implement it sufficiently. The continuance of through traffic and the persisting tendency of this traffic to speed are among the chief complaints (De Jonge 1981, 596).

One notable conclusion of De Jonge is his suggestion that traffic rules such as "drive no faster than walking speed" are useless and that they be replaced by a precise and more realistic standard stated in terms of kilometers per hour, since according to his observations no one obeys them anyway, not even cyclists who have to drive faster than most people walk if only to maintain their equilibrium (1981, 596).

Conclusion

The *woonerf* concept seems to offer some hope of reconciling the different societal functions of a residential neighborhood, particularly accessibility and the social protection of the home. In the United States, compared with Europe, the idea of neighborhood traffic restraints through physical design is young, but it shows signs of a growing vigor. Schemes to tame traffic in residential areas are afoot in a number of American cities including Berkeley, California, Boston and Cambridge, Massachusetts, Chicago, Eugene, Oregon, Los Angeles, Minneapolis, San Francisco, Seattle, and Washington, D.C. According to Simkowitz, Heder, and Barber (1978), the most extensive of these projects are found in Berkeley, Madison, and Seattle. One of the interesting contrasts with Holland is that in the American examples the action seems to stem more strongly from local initiatives.

The same authors point out that the measures are not without their cost in the form of inconveniences to those whose travel time is increased. A more serious disturbance is the congestion resulting from displaced traffic in areas peripheral to the controlled neighborhood. While these dislocations are still relatively minor, they opine that with the increasing application of such restraints, particularly in denser areas, one day a threshold will be reached requiring either compensatory adjustments in the shape of a considerable upgrading in the traffic capacity of peripheral roads or a large-scale shift to public transit or car pooling.

Nevertheless, Simkowitz, Heder, and Barber conclude that "the neighborhood traffic restraint schemes are highly suited to the prevailing planning and political styles of American cities" since they "can be identified with the interest of a particular constituency that can effectively lobby for them through local politicians. They are relatively inexpensive and can be implemented quickly" (Simkowitz, Heder, and Barber 1978).

Meanwhile in Holland, the *woonerf* idea does not remain static. The new order of civility envisioned by the Dutch planners is beginning to claim ground beyond the residential quarters. In Delft, the *woonerf* principle has been applied to at least one commercial street. Delft planners now think of the city center itself in *woonerf* terms: "Pedestrians, cyclists and cars sharing the same space is more or less a commandment" in tiny, overcrowded, canal-bound Holland (ten Grotenhuis and Jonquière 1979, 7). Our situation is a far cry from that of the Lowlands, but with the ongoing energy shortage, the movement to conserve farmland and combat urban sprawl, and the need to cut development costs, the same thought may one day occur to Americans.

Notes

For much of the factual information herein I am indebted to the following individuals: Ir. de Jong, Public Works Service, Delft, Holland; Peter Jonquière, head, Department of City Planning, Delft; and Robert Haslach, Information Officer, Royal Netherlands Embassy, Washington, D.C. The Royal Netherlands Embassy provided the photographs. The interpretation of the *woonerf* is based on a paper presented at a conference of Europeanists sponsored by the Council of European Studies in Washington, D.C., October 1980, and subsequently published in the *Humboldt Journal of Social Relations* 9 (Spring–Summer 1982): 100–119, which has permitted it being excerpted here.

1. The fall of Humpty Dumpty is Marshall McLuhan's apt image for the shattering experienced in modern times by Western man, a disaster he, too, attributes to inventions in transportation technology—the steam engine, the automobile, the jet plane. McLuhan claims that Humpty Dumpty is being made whole again through modern advances in telecommunication—telephone, radio, television, satellites, etc. (1964, 162–69).

2. For the paired antinomous terms *access* and *recess*, as applied to urban structure, I am indebted to Anshel Melamed.

References

Alexander, Christopher. 1965. "A City Is not a Tree." *Architectural Forum* 22 (April): 58–62, (May): 58–61.

ANWB [Royal Dutch Touring Club]. 1978. *Woonerf: Revised Translation of the Minimum Standards and the New Traffic Regulations for Signs.* The Hague: ANWB.

———. 1980. *Woonerf: A New Approach to Environmental Management in Residential Areas and the Related Traffic.* The Hague: ANWB.

Bakker, J., D. H. ten Grotenhuis, K. Havinga, and M. de Jong. Undated. *Helping Pedestrians in Urban Areas.* Delft: Department of Public Works.

Croly, Herbert. 1909. *The Promise of American Life.* New York: Macmillan.

de Jonge, D. 1981. "Waardering van Woonerven—de Opinies van Bewoners in Nieuwe Laagbouwijken." *Verkeerskunde* 32, no. 12, 592–96.

Frost, Robert. 1969. "America Is Hard to See." In *The Poetry of Robert Frost,* 417. Edited by Edward Connery Latham. London: Jonathan Cape.

Heeger, H. P. 1979. "The Dutch Solution to the Problem of a Residential Environment." *Planning and Development in the Netherlands* 11, no. 1, 3–16.

Hendricks, Corry, Judy Knip, and Peggy Meijer. 1979. "Een Onderzoek Naar de Houding T.A.V. Woonerven, Leiden." *Vakgroep Sociale Psychologie* (Ryksuniversiteit Leiden).

Isaacs, Reginald R. 1948. "The Neighborhood Theory: An Analysis of Its Adequacy." *Journal of the American Institute of Planners* 14 (Spring): 15–23.

Jacobs, Jane. 1961. *The Death and Life of Great American Cities.* New York: Random House, 1961.

Jonquière, Peter. 1978. *Woonerf: An Environment for Man and Transport Together.* Delft: Department of Works Service.

Jonquière, Peter, and Dirk H. ten Grotenhuis. 1979. *The Woonerf in City and Traffic Planning.* Delft: Traffic Department, Public Services.

Kotler, Milton. 1969. *Neighborhood Government.* New York: Bobbs-Merrill.

McLuhan, Marshall. 1964. *Understanding Media.* New York: Signet.

Orski, Kenneth C. 1979. "Transportation Planning as if People Mattered." *Practicing Planner* 9 (March): 22–25.

Perry, Clarence A. 1929. "The Neighborhood Unit." In *Neighborhood and Commu-*

nity Planning: Regional Survey of New York and Its Environs. Vol. 7, 22–132. New York: Regional Plan of New York and Its Environs.

Riesman, David. 1957. "The Suburban Dislocation." *The Annals of the American Academy of Political and Social Science* 314 (Nov.): 123–46.

Royal Netherlands Embassy. 1979. *Netherlands Study Reveals Appreciation for Woonerf.* Press release. December.

Sennett, Richard. 1970. *The Uses of Disorder.* New York: Knopf.

Simkowitz, Howard, Lajos Heder, and Edward Barber. 1978. "The Restraint of the Automobile in American Residential Neighborhoods." *UMTA/TSC Project Evaluation Series Final Report.* Cambridge: United States Department of Transportation Systems Center.

17

Taylorism, Unionism, and Metropolitan Spatial Structure

There are two fundamental moments of life—work and rest (which includes the enjoyment of the fruits of work, that is, recreation). At work, man treats himself as an object, an instrument for the satisfaction of his future needs, but at rest he reaffirms his subjectivity. Ideally at least, he becomes Adam before the Fall, free of care or want.

This dual relationship to self is reflected in the organization of space and time. In time, it takes various forms: workday and sabbath, weekday and weekend, etc. The two alternate: now man as object prevails, now man as subject. In space, one of its forms is the separation of place of work and place of residence.

It is not often that these two phases of human being have faced each other so starkly and in such open debate as at the turn of the century in the United States. Although, in essence, the debate was a philosophic one, its venue was not in musty books or ivied halls, and it was not conducted in the arcane language of philosophers. The protagonists were "practical types": engineers, union organizers, businessmen, and lawyers. In fact, their encounter began as an important episode in American labor history.

The effects of the encounter did not remain within the confines of what is called labor and industrial relations, but spread outward from that point of origin to join with other forces that were giving to American society, including its cities, its general shape. The same encounter, or rather its outcome, helped set the main agenda of the American city planning movement for most of its career.

The twentieth century, which Henry Wallace was later to proclaim the century of the common man, began auspiciously for the American laborer. The previous fifty years had seen tremendous changes, which were to convert a nation of farmers into a predominantly urban nation and the world's foremost industrial power. But, in Walter Lippmann's image, big industry made little men. The urban worker, like the western settler, was dwarfed in a vast new environment. Seeming to promise him all, out of it, too frequently, came storms and droughts to defeat his best hopes. Finally, he set himself to subdue it, just as the western settler was attempting to subdue the unruly arid regions of the West. At least some of those who sympathized with him saw his struggles in that light. "The virtues of labor today are frontier virtues," wrote Lippmann. The unions were "the first feeble effort to conquer the industrial jungle for democratic life" (1961, 59–60).

One of the skirmishes at this new frontier which the workers won was entirely symbolic. "The labor of a human is not a commodity or article of commerce," proclaimed the Clayton Act of 1914, challenging a basic premise of classical economics. *The American Federationist*, official organ of the American Federation of Labor, hailed this pronouncement as one of the greatest legislative declarations of all times: "It sweeps away legal precedents and legal philosophy that have served to impede Labor's efforts to rid itself of all vestiges of the conditions and relations that existed when human workers were . . . held as slaves. . . . It demolishes that . . . economic theory that had been built up upon the concept that human power to produce is a commodity to be bought, owned and controlled by employers" (Gompers 1915, 665).

These words were written in 1915, when the "efficiency craze" was at its height in the United States. It would have been remarkable if, by legislative fiat alone, human labor had escaped definition as a resource subject to efficiency considerations like any other resource. And it didn't. The man who gave perfect expression to the idea of human efficiency was a Philadelphia engineer.

Frederick Winslow Taylor was born in 1856, the son of Quaker parents. In childhood he was educated in part in France, Germany, and Italy. Later, he attended Phillips Exeter Academy, but bad eyesight forced him to change course; rather than entering Harvard College as planned, he went to work as an apprentice in a small pump works. At the age of twenty-two, he took a job with Midvale Steel Company as a laborer, a move which Samuel Haber suggests (1964, 6) may have been dictated more by the ideal of hard work as a builder of manly character than by actual need (Drury 1915, 88–89). He quickly rose in the ranks from laborer to foreman. After receiving the degree of mechanical engineer from Stevens Institute of Technology in 1883, he finally arrived at the position of chief engineer. The principles of scientific management began to take shape in his mind during his gang boss days at Midvale, when he became interested in finding out how long it should take a man to perform a given piece of work.

Years later, Taylor compared his method to the conservationist prin-

ciples preached by Gifford Pinchot. It was his appointed task to save
human energy as Pinchot was saving natural energy: "We can see our
forests vanishing, our water-powers going to waste, our soil being carried by floods into the sea; and the end of our coal and iron is in sight
[this in 1911!]. But our larger wastes of human effort, which go on every
day through such of our acts as are blundering, ill-directed or inefficient,
and which Mr. Roosevelt refers to as a lack of 'national efficiency' are
less visible, less tangible, and are but vaguely appreciated" (1911, 5).

Taylor's method consisted of the substitution of expert for lay judgment in the conduct of common work or, as he himself put it, of science
for rules of thumb. The laborious and exacting process of discovering
these truths was laid down in a number of precepts: 1) "Find, say, 10 or
15 different men . . . who are especially skillful in doing the particular
work to be analyzed"; 2) "Study the exact series of elementary operations which each of these men uses in doing the work . . . as well as the
implements each man uses"; 3) "Study with a stop watch the time required to make each of these elementary movements and then select the
quickest way of doing each element of the work"; 4) "Eliminate all false
movements . . . and useless movements"; and 5) "After doing away
with all unnecessary movements, collect into one series the quickest and
best movements, as well as the best implements" (1911, 117–18).

Daniel Bell alludes meanly to the "compulsive character that Taylor
stamped onto a civilization": "Playing croquet, he worried his fellows
by plotting the angles of his strokes. When he walked he counted his
steps to learn the most efficient stride. Nervous, high strung, although
he neither smoked nor drank, not even coffee or tea, he was a victim all
his life of insomnia and nightmares; and fearing to lie on his back, he
could sleep in peace only when bolted upright in bed or in a chair. He
could not stand the sight of an idle lathe or an idle man. He never loafed,
and he was going to make sure that no one else did" (1965, 226). One
might as well say that Pinchot wasted nothing and was going to make
sure that no one else did. That Taylor was neurotic is, in the end, no more
significant than that Karl Marx suffered from boils, which made him
irascible and misanthropic. His foibles detract nothing from the man's
stature as a social thinker who attempted to square the requirements of
industrialism with the claims of humanity.

Taylor believed that the time and motion study was a just method of
task-setting because it offered what nothing before it had succeeded in
providing, a scientific definition of a fair wage. Moreover, scientific
management was, in his view, a democratic method because by means
of it the elements of personal force were finally eliminated from the industrial relationship. Where, formerly, employee served employer, now

both might serve the scientifically defined standard. Thus, the way was cleared for a remarkable "mental revolution." In place of their customary hostility, man and boss could now find a new comradeship around the common task. As for their temporarily lost freedom, as a consequence of increased efficiency, the workers would receive it back in the form of a higher wage to be disposed of as they pleased.

Many business leaders welcomed Taylorism in principle because it seemed to justify their resistance to unionism. It also appealed to Progressive social thinkers, for whom increased social efficiency appeared to promise the best means of staving off class warfare. Theodore Roosevelt saw in it the "application of the conservation principle to production" (Gilbreth 1914, 2). Louis Brandeis, the future Supreme Court justice, believed it offered the working man his greatest opportunity to boost his earnings, as well as a "satisfaction with his work which in other lines of human activity accompanies achievement" (Gilbreth 1914, vii). In fact, it was Brandeis who gave scientific management its name (Drury 1915, 16).[1]

Nevertheless, Taylorism was far from having its own way. It drew fire, especially from unionists. A typical criticism of the day, and one of the most pungent, appeared in the *Journal of Political Economy*, the work of Frank T. Carlton of Albion College. The worker's ideal, Carlton held, was not necessarily maximum productivity as Taylor had assumed, "but a condition in which work and recreation are blended for each and every individual. . . . And if economics is 'the seasonal activity of a people tending to the satisfaction of its needs,'" then what right had the economist to dismiss the wage-earner's ideal needs as unworthy (1912, 837)? Carlton flung at Taylor that his own ideal was a "human machine rather than a man," one who spends all his time and energy preparing for tomorrow's work (1912, 838).[2]

Carlton did not rest his case on the alleged heartlessness of scientific management alone. He widened his attack to include Taylor's definition of efficiency. The search for human efficiency required the "engineer to go outside the shop" to study the worker's home life, his food, housing, and recreation (1912, 845). Moreover, scientific management would have to be supplemented by some form of collective worker action to ensure that the benefits derived from greater efficiency would be more equitably distributed (842–45). Carlton's critique was a clear call for industrial democracy: "The average American citizen looks askance upon an arbitrary government which is no way under the control of the mass of the governed. . . . The Louis XIV view of government is obsolete, but absolutism in industry is still characteristic in the business world" (1912, 841).[3]

Carlton's critique of Taylorism was given a more official expression by Robert Hoxie, a professor of political science at the University of Chicago. In the hearings of the U.S. Commission on Industrial Relations held in 1914, the leaders of the scientific management movement and the leaders of the A.F. of L. clashed head on. The Taylorites claimed that scientific management was democratic as well as scientific. Indeed, it was democratic because it was scientific. For the rule of opinion and whim had they not substituted the rule of scientific law? In a shop where no man served another but all served the requirements of the job, no room remained for unions and bargaining. One might as well bargain about the rising and setting of the sun, said Taylor. The labor men retorted that the "scientific management cult" was neither scientific nor democratic. It was unscientific because it left out of its efficiency calculations the worker's humanity, regarding him more as a machine than as a man. Far from establishing the basis of a just economic order, it was plainly a reversion to the principle of the survival of the fittest.

The inevitable investigating machinery was set up "to test the validity of the opposing claims and to determine what, if anything, can be done to harmonize the relations of scientific management and labor" (Hoxie 1915, 1). Hoxie was put in charge of the investigation, with Robert G. Valentine, a Boston industrial councillor representing management, and John P. Frey, editor of the *International Molder's Journal*, representing labor, to assist him.

Although Hoxie was a specialist in unions, his definition of unionism was exceedingly broad. "Unionism," he thought, "is not confined to wage earners; it is one of the most fundamental and pervasive of social phenomena, and is prevalent in every social class. . . . Trade unionism is distinguished from other forms of unionism simply by the fact that it is the unionism of the wage workers, but it does not differ essentially . . . from the unionism of other social classes and groups" (1915, 358). Trade unions, no doubt, were interest groups, but interest groups were the elementary stuff of social reality. Therefore, if Hoxie, the student of unionism, was opposed to scientific management, it was not out of narrow partisanship but from his view of society as a system of interest groups. Here, Taylor the engineer and Hoxie the social scientist were clearly at loggerheads.

In his report, Hoxie quickly disposed of Taylor's claims that scientific management left no room for bargaining. He cited seventeen factors, "variable with the judgement and will of those immediately concerned," which were not subject to scientific determination, ranging from the intelligence of the time and motion study man to atmospheric conditions (1915, 46–47). His main objections to scientific management, however, concerned its demoralizing effect on the laboring man. The difference between types of worker would grow less and less as all jobs were reduced to their elements. Soon, every man who walked the street would become interchangeable with every other man. The ultimate result could only be the end of collective bargaining, lower wages, and unemployment (1917, 321–23).

But Hoxie faltered when it came to pushing his indictment of scientific management to its conclusion. True, unbridled efficiency would crush the humanity out of the working man. On the other hand, how could we "afford to give up the vast possibilities of increased productiveness" latent in scientific management? "Your Commission," the investigator wrote, "is dealing . . . with two forces, neither of which may or will be sacrificed to the other. . . . It is inherent in the nature of things that they both live and fructify" (1915, 138). The need is for a "method by which the intellectual and moral content which the worker is losing through the destruction of his craft training and the loss of his craft knowledge can be restored to him" (1917, 324). How might this be done? Hoxie thought the answer lay in "an adequate system of industrial education, socially launched and socially controlled . . . an integral part of our public school system. With such a system . . . we might hope . . . that what the workers lose intellectually and morally in the shop under the modern, specialized workmanship, they would gain in the school, and that through this moral and intellectual gain they might become universally organizable and organized, and might develop policies and methods which, while not interfering with productive efficiency, would secure for them as a class improved conditions and a reasonable share in the social dividend which the development and spread of scientific management promise" (1917, 325).

The encounter between the union leaders and the scientific managers is significant because it illuminated the field of social forces around it. Even as Hoxie was writing his report, the metropolitan area was undergoing profound changes in response to the same forces that were convulsing the life of the laboring man. Planners and social workers might prate of metropolitan decentralization, decongestion, and reconstruction, but what they were advocating were schemes that were the spatial analogue of what Hoxie was proposing. Henceforth, there would be a division of the world between the place of the machine where efficiency ruled and those places where the humanity of man could assert its primary claim. Even before Hoxie's death in 1916 many of the contemporary themes of city planning made their appearance for an indefinite future: the work place, the place of man as object, where the requirements of the job prevail; its counterpole, the suburban neighborhood as the inviolable precinct of man as subject; the rapid transit line as the material and metaphysical link between the two worlds; zoning as the means of protecting the residential neighborhood from industrial intrusion; and dreams of garden cities where the tension between man and machine would be overcome.

Notes

This essay is adapted from a paper published in the Proceedings of the First National Conference of American Planning History, Columbus, Ohio, March 13–15, 1986.

1. Brandeis's interest in the movement which he named appears to have been connected with his involvement in the Eastern Rate Case as one of the lawyers for the shippers who were contesting the effort of certain northeastern railroads to raise freight tariffs. Thompson observes that "the application of the railroads to the Interstate Commerce Commission for permission to raise freight rates was met by the shippers, under the advice of Mr. Louis D. Brandeis, with the counter argument that, instead of raising the rates . . . they should make their operation efficient to get more out of their present expenditure" (1914, 26).

2. This frequent allegation was always much disputed by Taylor and Taylorites. See, for example, Drury (1915, 239–42).

3. Ironically, the Taylor Society eventually became a forum for industrial democracy ideas (Haber 1964).

References

Bell, Daniel. 1965. *The End of Ideology.* New York: Free Press.

Carlton, Frank T. 1912. "Scientific Management and the Wage Earner." *Journal of Political Economy* 20 (Oct.): 834–45.

Drury, Horace Bookwalter. 1915. *Scientific Management.* New York: Columbia University Press.

Gilbreth, Frank B. 1912. *Primer of Scientific Management.* New York: D. Van Nostrand.

Gompers, Samuel. 1915. "Labor's Mission: The Achievement of Freedom." *American Federalist* 22 (Sept.): 665–66.

Haber, Samuel. 1964. *Efficiency and Uplift: Scientific Management in the Progressive Era, 1890–1920.* Chicago: University of Chicago Press.

Hoxie, Robert F. 1915. *Scientific Management and Labor.* New York: D. Appleton.

———. 1917. *Trade Unionism in the United States.* New York: D. Appleton.

Lippmann, Walter. 1961. *Drift and Mastery.* Englewood Cliffs: Prentice-Hall.

Taylor, Frederick Winslow. 1911. *The Principles of Scientific Management.* Norwood: Plimpton Press.

Thompson, Clarence B. 1914. *Scientific Management.* Cambridge: Harvard University Press.

18

A Note on the Relation of the Concepts of Science, Democracy, and Community in the Progressive Era

In keeping with the theme of this conference, resources and resource distribution are my topics, although the type of resource dealt with here is not material goods or political power. It is knowledge, expert knowledge in particular. If expert knowledge is a resource, then there is a question as to how it can be distributed most widely and in such a manner as to be subject to democratic control. Here is a problem as old as society itself. On the one hand are the priest, the shaman, and the learned Ph.D. On the other hand are the laymen, the people. How bridge the gap? How relate the expert's specialized intelligence to the people's wisdom? These are questions that go to the heart of science as well as of politics. They are also questions of particular moment to Americans, given our double heritage of democracy and technocracy.

This is the story of several twentieth-century social scientists and social reformers who explored the relations of experts to themselves and to the people and came up with insights which even today illuminate the nature of science, democracy, and community.

Historians might question the title, inasmuch as some of the works cited appeared long after the Progressive Era is considered to have ended. Historical periods, however, are notoriously fuzzy. Certain books referred to were published in the 1920s or even the 1930s, but there can be no doubt that the concepts they deal with stem from earlier decades and are the authentic fruits of Progressivism.

Charles Merriam and Luther Gulick: Social Science and Public Administration

The story begins with Frederick Winslow Taylor, originator of scientific management. Taylor, the engineer, had extended the machine principle to human labor. He was, to use the language of the day, a social inventor, but his inventiveness was confined to a single phase of the economic process, production. His union critics chided him for this and pointed out that the present social need was less for scientific production than for scientific distribution: "If Mr. Taylor or Mr Brandeis . . . can only tell us how this can be done," said one, "they will do more for humanity, as it exists in organized society, than any one economist or engineer, who has ever walked this planet" (Thompson 1914, 739).

The idea of scientific consumption also came in for its share of attention. According to Wesley C. Mitchell, then a young professor of economics at the University of California, the producing unit, the business enterprise comprised of members of many families, had proven to be vastly more efficient than the consuming unit, the individual family, which "has remained substantially where it was in colonial days" (1912, 270). The problem was how to secure the benefits of scientific consumption while preserving human dignity, community, and democratic control. Mitchell thought the answer lay in a "socialized spending of money with a neighborhood instead of a family as the unit" (1912, 280).

Consuming was a "backward art" as compared with the art of producing. If the art of consuming was ever to be advanced, more would be required than the broadening of spending from the family to the neighborhood. The enlarged family would also have to be brought into effective relationship with those groups whose special knowledge was indispensable to scientific spending—the professionals and experts of the community. The more so as the experts themselves were engrossed in extending the science of management to the realm of public affairs.

One of the experts of the day was Luther Halsey Gulick. In 1928, looking back at the twenty-year history of public administration in which he played so important a part, Gulick observed: "It is no accident that the efficiency movement in industry and the research movement in government should have arisen in the same decade within the boundaries of a single nation" (10). He explained that both movements sprang from the same national faith in science and efficiency, and it was only through the application of scientific methods to human affairs that we could hope to "adapt our institutions and our habits to conform to changing conditions so that we may at least limit war, crime, exploitation, poverty, preventable disease, corruption, superstition, and ignorance." To control the runaway forces of industrialization and urbanization, "Must we not . . . encourage social, economic, and political invention? Must we not discover the principles and laws which govern men through the same techniques that we have used to discover the laws that govern atoms? Surely, we must through science develop human engineering as we have, through science, mastered our environment with mechanical, chemical, civil, electrical and industrial engineering" (1928, 101–2).

As an embodiment of this high purpose, Gulick and others had founded the National Institute of Public Administration. The institute was the offspring of an earlier agency, the Bureau of Municipal Research, organized in 1895 and two years later incorporated with financial assistance from John Rockefeller and Andrew Carnegie. The bureau was itself the successor of still earlier reform associations of a more spontaneous and transitory kind, which had sought to achieve good government in New York by ridding the city of dishonest officials and replacing them with capable administrators.

When the Bureau of Municipal Research was formed, Tammany Hall "was in full control" of the city government, and almost from its inception the fledgling organization found itself embroiled with that formidable political machine. Gulick recalls that it won its first fight when it secured the removal for incompetency of Manhattan Borough President Ahearn, who had sought to block its right to access to public resources. In subsequent years, the bureau was in the forefront of numerous reform campaigning and counted among its successes not only the removal of dishonest political appointees (which earned from its enemies the title "Bureau of Municipal Besmirch"), but also more positive achievements: the establishment of a Bureau of Child Hygiene, of a central purchasing department employing efficient business procedures, and the reorganization of the city's accounting system. As word of its success in New York reached other cities, a demand arose for its counsel and services, and the bureau responded within the limit of its staff resources, although Gulick denies that it was ever the bureau's intention to engage in missionary work (1928, 14–28). Nevertheless, by 1929, there were in the nation seventy-four accredited municipal research agencies, sixty of which had full-time staffs.

One of the bureau's favorite devices was the governmental survey. Neither the term nor the practice of surveying was invented by the bureau. In the nineteenth century, fact gathering and analysis was one of the few ways available for marshalling public opinion and generating demands for reform (Hurst 1967, 106). As early as 1866, the Council of Hygiene of the Citizens Association of New York in their crusade for housing reform had conducted a door-to-door survey of housing and sanitary conditions in the tenement slum districts. The most famous survey of all was the Pittsburgh Survey undertaken by the Russell Sage Foundation for the purposes of showing the impact of industrialism on the life of that city (Lubove 1962). In the twenty years following its establishment in 1909, the bureau surveyed more than fifty cities in addition to New York and studied the administrative set-up in twenty-seven counties. The surveyor "went at a city government much as an engineer goes at a tract of land before laying out streets, sewers and water pipes" (Gulick 1928, 31). The thoroughness of a bureau survey is indicated in the queries for which it sought answers: "What was the object or purpose of the agency from a practical as well as a legal standpoint? Had the agency kept pace with the growing demands of the work which it was performing?" What was the value of the work and how suited was the organization to its accomplishments? Did it use modern methods? Was it overstaffed? Were the employees well trained for their work? Were they adequately paid?" (Gulick 1928, 38–39).

Laboratory was another recurrent term in the vocabulary of the social scientists and public administrators of the day. Connoting experimentation with isolated variables under controlled conditions, the laboratory concept in public administration was first introduced in the Training School for Public Administration founded in New York in 1911 with the aid of Mrs. E. H. Harriman. The school aimed at fostering the use of business methods in government. Its teaching staff was the bureau staff, and bureau studies provided the practical problems, while the city and its departments became the laboratories for solving the problems (Gulick 1928, 52, 54).

The year after Gulick's progress report appeared, the Local Community Research Committee, a group of social scientists at the University of Chicago, published an account of their own experiments and accomplishments after five years of intensive study of the Chicago region. Under the editorship of T. V. Smith and Leonard White, the book was entitled *Chicago: An Experiment in Social Science Research*, and in its first chapter Robert E. Park explained that "whenever fact finding precedes legislation and reforms are conducted by experts rather than by amateurs," progress does indeed acquire "something of the character of a controlled experiment" (1).

The Local Community Research Committee was an interdisciplinary group of social scientists headed by Charles E. Merriam, professor of political science. It was founded with a grant from the Laura Spelman Memorial Foundation. "The character of the grant made to the University of Chicago presupposed an intimate relation with the city." Part of it was put to immediate use "for the study of local problems." The remainder was to be spent on a matching basis, the idea being to attract groups and individuals seeking expert advice and assistance in the solution of specific social problems (Smith and White 1929, 33).

The social scientists of the Local Community Research Committee devoted a considerable portion of their resources to the collection of basic urban social data. Their method of collection and analyzing data was influenced by their conception of themselves as scientists, and this, in turn, influenced their conception of the city. "In scientific research,"

wrote Ernest Burgess, "an object is studied not as a whole but by breaking it up into its parts which are then described and analyzed in their
interrelationships. . . . Therefore, social science research should focus its
magnifying glass . . . upon these local communities, if for no other reason than to understand the life-processes of the larger community"
(Smith and White 1929, 59). Chicago was broken down for study purposes into eighty local communities, and these were further subdivided
into four hundred neighborhoods. At the same time, more mechanical
methods of data assembly were used. A map of 935 census tracts was
prepared, which facilitated the assembly of data by square miles and by
political subdivision. Later, a committee drew up a social science research base map showing basic land uses upon which were plotted
many varieties of demographic data, including poverty, crime, and disease, revealing all manner of hitherto unsuspected relationships between the physical structure of the city and its social structure. "The
map exhibit room," wrote Ernest Burgess, "soon became a Mecca for
class and conference groups as well as for research students, social
workers and visitors interested in examining and studying the basic
social data which they presented" (Smith and White 1929, 54–57).

Charles Merriam and his associates were dedicated promoters of social science as an attitude toward society. There is no evidence that this
energetic group was ever much concerned with the effect its rendering
of the city as a scientific object might have on the local sources of urban
life and vitality. There was among them, however, a philosopher, T. V.
Smith, who raised the question in an indirect way. "One way of seeing
what . . . the community may expect from social science research is to
make clear what such research does for those who pursue it as a voca-
tion." Smith believed that there is no greater benefit in knowledge than
that it brings peace to the knower. "It shows one his place in the vast
universe: it deflates his pride, but also gives him a sense of being a part
of an encompassing system which he may contemplate in its majestic
motion." Self-knowledge is more difficult but, when achieved, its rewards are greater. "To objectify oneself upon social data" was the modern form of self-knowledge (Smith and White 1929, 227–29). What social
science research offered the community, the new thing that had not yet
existed in all history, was the opportunity to contemplate itself disinter-
estedly. And yet, let no one fear that the researcher's disinterestedness
betokened lack of interest. "Enough of the public spirit" has informed
his training to ensure a continuous devotion to the public interest. Nor
was his love of the community to remain platonic; "The community
needs nothing else so much as men who, even though they themselves
be not scientists, can understand science and adapt its results to commu-

nity needs." A link would be forged "between those devoted to pure research and those with engineering minds who order the business of the day and bring to pass whatever of the dream is workable in the world of affairs" (Smith and White 1929, 233).

"A whole community pictured in the mind of each scientist" as a "prized object," a "gorgeous pattern," this was the scientific and esthetic aim of social science research. As for the scientist, "sufficiently detached...to organize his own life around a vision of social unity," he will be "sufficiently implicated in common concerns as to work against whatever disrupts the community and thus disturbs his own personality synthesis" (Smith and White 1929, 231–32, 245). Probably no nobler defense of the ethical and esthetic aims of social science has ever been uttered. Smith's imagery, the researcher saint contemplating creation, the engineer-priest, was strictly out of the Middle Ages. Twentieth-century Chicagoans, certainly, could never be as interested in maintaining the social scientist's inner repose and personality synthesis as Smith from his lofty heights had supposed. As for the scientists, in their innermost councils, they soon showed that they had little respect for the people's institutions, however much they might prize them as scientific objects. Three years after *Chicago* was published, Leonard White, the political scientist, was addressing his colleagues at a university research conference on local government. Local governments as presently constituted, he is reported to have told them, were obsolete. There was an "excessive number of local governments," administrative areas were "badly adjusted to their functions, . . . there is a spread between what the people want and what they can afford, . . . a spread between what the people want and what the experts think they need." To Professor White, the answer was self-evident: Local jurisdictions should be erased and replaced with scientifically defined areas. "We must forget the . . . local government as an organ of democracy and consider it rather as an area of administration. . . . We should analyze the ways and means of manipulating local rural attitudes" (1932, 34–35). Technocrats and democrats were on a collision course.[1]

Mary Parker Follett and the Group Process

Luther Gulick's retrospective account of the origins of the public administration movement, a book in which he confidently advocated government by experts, was subtitled, "An Adventure in Democracy." To many progressive reformers there was nothing paradoxical in this fact. In their view, the public administration movement was a democratic movement because it was clearing the way for the substantive work of democracy. There was good authority for this viewpoint. Herbert Croly, editor of the *New Republic* and a leading progressive thinker, held that American democracy had an historic mission, which was to free the broad masses of the people from the social and economic restraints that bound them. Croly called this goal "the promise of American life." It was to be realized through national planning, a program in which efficient municipal organizations were indispensable elements (1965). There were, nevertheless, many urban reformers for whom the paternalistic imperatives of the "new nationalism" were quite unacceptable. They were no less dedicated to the fulfillment of the American promise than were the public administrators, and they were as opposed to corruption and waste, but, when it came to sacrificing government by the people to government for the people, they halted. One of these was a Boston settlement worker and friend of Justice Brandeis. In the *New State*, which gained worldwide recognition, she had given notice that "the ordinary man is not to do his work and then play a little in order to refresh himself, with the understanding that the world of industry and the government of his country are to be run by experts" (Follett 1926, 339).

Mary Parker Follett had majored in economics, philosophy, and government at Radcliffe College (Cabot 1934, 81–82). She graduated in 1898 and soon became immersed in settlement work in Roxbury Neighborhood House and later in the Municipal League. It was in Roxbury that Miss Follett developed the personal and political philosophy that brought her international fame and made her the respected friend of philosophers, statesmen, and business leaders. Roxbury, in those days, was a typical immigrant section of Boston, the home of poor Jewish and Irish families whose children worked in the nearby shops and factories but were sadly in want of adequate educational and recreational opportunities. Later associates credit Follett with "the idea of opening up the Schoolhouses of Boston after school hours" for neighborhood use. This innovation soon gave rise to a "widespread social movement. For many people came to see the Boston School Center and went away inspired to work for the same objectives in their own cities" (Metcalf and Ruwick 1941, 11–13).

In the school center a place was provided where children and grownups alike might meet together voluntarily and through their interaction in the pursuit of common interest learn the art of self-government. In her days of fame as a political thinker there is nothing that Mary Follett said or wrote that differs essentially from this simple process. As she later defined it in the *New State*, the group is a collectivity whose members by an honest exchange of ideas attain a higher level of thought and will than each could have reached alone. She was careful to distinguish the vital group from those false and dangerous collectivities the crowd and the mob, whose principles of association are not creative interplay, but mechanical imitation. She illustrates the process of group formation as follows:

> Let us imagine that you and I, A, B, and C are in conference. Now what from our observation of groups will take place? Will you say something, and then I add a little something, and then A, B, and C, until we have built up, brickwise, an idea, constructed some plan of action? Never. A has one idea, B another, C's idea is something different from either, and so on; but we cannot add all these ideas to find the group idea. They will not add up any more than tables and chairs add. But we gradually find that our problem can be solved, not indeed by mechanical aggregation, but by the subtle process of the intermingling of all the different ideas of the group. A says something. There upon a thought arises in B's mind. Is it B's idea or A's? Neither. It is a mingling of the two.
>
> We find in the end that it is not a question of my idea supplemented by yours, but that there has been evolved a composite idea. But by the time that we have reached this point we have become tremendously civilized people, for we have learned one of the most important lessons of life: We have learned to do that most wonderful thing, to say "I" representing a whole instead of "I" representing one of our separate selves. The course of action decided is what we all together want, and I see it is better than what I had wanted alone. It is what *I* now want. (1926, 24–25)

Follett believed she saw the triumphal emergence of the group spirit on all sides: in the idea of adult education "as a continuous process," preventive criminology and the idea of community responsibility for crime, city planning, the trade association, and collective bargaining. The foundation of this whole movement was the revolution in law theory represented in the United States by the sociological jurisprudence of Roscoe Pound, which spelled out in legal terms the theory of the superiority of community life to particular rights (Follett 1926, 105–23).

Democracy was the aim of the group process. Thus far, American and English history had accomplished the "extensive work" of democracy, brought the suffrage to all, and provided the machinery of representative government. Now the time for "intensive" democracy was at hand—the deeper democracy, the interpenetration of the minds and hearts of all the people (Follett 1926, 256).

Follett's approach differed from that of other political reformers. Whereas they took at face value the powerlessness and separation of people and sought to overcome them with objective political devices such as the initiative, the referendum, and the recall, she regarded separation as a subjective malady. Consequently, the cure must be subjective. People were estranged, first of all, because they misunderstood their own nature. The primary cause of misunderstanding was the false doctrine of laissez-faire, which taught the isolation of person from person. It pitted each person against the state. The truth is that this opposition, insofar as it exists, is sustained only by our belief in it. For in a healthy society, the individual and the state are one (Follett 1926, 238).

Her ideas, of course, were derivative as she herself acknowledged. Their sources could be found in the writings of Marx and Hegel, James and Dewey, Henri Bergson and Charles Cooley. But to point this out is by no means to deny the original force of the woman. Indeed, Follett's intensity and passion are matters of more than stylistic interest. Historians have referred to the appeal to conscience that underlay the approach of the progressives, but it is questionable whether this gets to the root of the difference (Haber 1964; Graham 1967). More germane perhaps is the conversion phenomenon of which William James (1936) wrote in *Varieties of Religious Experience,* the sudden switch from the objective to the subjective mode of experience. What some reformers knew from the outside, for others was a vivid internal excitement. They were not satisfied just to *do* reform; they wanted to *be* it. This "turning on" (in modern slang) was both the unity sought as well as the means of achieving unity. Certainly, no amount of scientific management or public administration could provide that.

Out of this subjective reform style came a new ethics and a new politics, which although not modern is surprisingly current. Politics is no longer a story of the isolated and atomic individual owing duties to a state. First, the state as the promise of the ultimate wholeness is not a present reality, but an ideal to be striven for. Second, its sole means of coming into being is the individual acting joyfully and passionately to create it; hence, the accent on activism as the only genuine form of politics: "As God appears only through us, so is the state made visible through political man. We must gird up our loins, we must light our lamps and set forth, we must *do* it"—Jerry Rubin's slogan (Follett 1926, 335).

A political doctrine which held that the local community must grip its own problems, fulfill its own needs, make effective its own aspirations was at clear variance with the idea of social control by a special cast of experts. Follett was quite emphatic on this point. It would never do "to say, 'we are good men, we are honest officials, we are employing experts on education, sanitation, etc.: you must trust us'" (1926, 234). Something quite different was indicated for the relationship between the experts and the people. This "something different," moreover was predicated on a quite special understanding of the nature of social science research. Follett recorded her ideas on this matter in *Creative Experience*, her last and, in the opinion of some, best work. She held that in successful social science research two different kinds of accurate information were required. The information provided by the scientific expert was indispensable, but no less important was the experience of the ordinary citizen as a test of the scientist's data and the administrator's prescriptions. How did these prove out in the laboratory of actual life? Since on this question only the ordinary person was qualified to speak, social science research could never be just an affair of experts. It was necessarily a cooperative endeavor involving the experts and the people. To be scientific, research must be democratic—the diametric opposite of Taylor's prescription (Follett 1924).

As an example of undemocratic, and therefore unscientific, research, Follett cited the case of the southern cooperative movement:

> This movement emphasizes the expert. The cooperative tobacco associations frankly tell the farmer that he is not an expert. . . . In other words, a high value is put on technical experience, but there is no effort to add the farmer's experience. The field service department gets information *to* that farmer; there is no recognized method of getting information *from* the farmer. Even if you should think the farmers' experience of little value . . . it could be made more valuable if the farmers were told that one of the principles of the cooperative movement was to make use of their experience, that they were expected . . . to watch their experience . . . to take an experimental attitude . . . to try experiments and contribute the results . . . for the benefit of all. Thus would the southern farmer be answering the problem which we must solve: how to live life scientifically. (1924, 214–15)

The farmer's case was not the best that Follett could have chosen to state the problem of scientific living. Farms are business enterprises. They exist to make money. A family, farm or nonfarm, endeavors to make money, too, but it encompasses in addition a host of nonpecuniary functions that are not so easily measured in terms of efficiency— health, connubial satisfaction, filial affection, domestic contentment, the enjoyment of culture, and tradition. Of these, only health, perhaps, is capable of scientific measurement.

Difficult or not, scientific family living was the goal that Follett advocated. Science, she insisted, was not to be dismissed, but to be retained as a tool of democratic neighborhood life. When it came to saying just how this ideal was to be realized, she referred to the Cincinnati Social Unit Plan, an experiment that had come to an unnatural end some years before *Creative Experience* was published: "In that plan the expert had a recognized place and a recognized relation to the rest of the community, a place which instead of separating him from the community in order to operate upon it, gave him an integral part therein by means of which he could both influence and be influenced by the community. Through such experiments, humble as they may seem to the political scientist, must we work our democracy" (1924, 214).

The story of the Cincinnati Social Unit Plan is the story of an attempt to bridge the chasm that was opening between the average man and woman and the expert, an attempt to combine objective and subjective reform, to democratize expertise.

Wilbur and Elsie Phillips and the Social Unit

Wilbur Carey Phillips was born in the village of Nunda, New York, the son of a scholarly but impecunious Baptist minister. He attended Colgate Academy and, later, after his father's death, entered Harvard College, where he supported himself and his mother as a member of a student business firm which handled the Harvard correspondence for eighteen newspapers (Phillips 1940, 10). In this connection he met his classmate Franklin Roosevelt, but his acquaintance with the editor of the *Harvard Crimson* was never more than casual. Looking back, Phillips recalled that it was not fondness for his classmates, nor even book-learning, that he took with him from Harvard, but loneliness, estrangement, and a conviction that the knowledge of "how to bring daily life into line with deep verities" would come, if at all, from his own "dogged persistence in thinking things through for myself," standard doctrine in the days of William James and John Dewey (1940, 14).

Phillips's chance to learn by doing came unexpectedly when, following his graduation from Harvard and a brief bohemian escapade in Europe, his cousin, Dr. Margaret Doolittle, got him a job with New York's famous Association to Improve the Condition of the Poor as secretary of its Milk Committee. The New York Milk Committee was a roster of great names, including Richard Harding Davis and Nicholas Murray Butler, but it was a paper committee, only too glad to leave its affairs in the hands of the young secretary. Phillips leaped at the task with the alacrity of one who has recognized his life's work.

In those days, a war was raging among medical reformers of the city over the correct way to secure a safe and clean milk supply for tenement babies, and Phillips played an important organizational role in resolving that question through the establishment of a National Commission on Milk Standards. With Dr. Charles E. North, he helped set up an experimental milk station that dispensed not only pure milk, but also precise instructions to mothers for modifying the milk in accordance with the special needs of each child. It was in this work requiring the cooperation of doctors and tenement mothers that he glimpsed the possibility of a new social form. On the one hand were the doctors and nurses, on the other the mothers and babies. As he later phrased it, "Why not . . . bring experts and people together . . . through representatives selected by each, to make a joint study of their common needs; to develop practical plans for meeting those needs, . . . each educating the other in the process?" (104). The first opportunity to try out the idea was in the poor Polish parish of St. Cyril's in Milwaukee, where Phillips and his wife Elsie had gone directly to a children's health center.[2] Before they could put the plan into effect, however, the city's socialist administration, which had hired them, was voted out and the couple lost their jobs.

Almost penniless and subsisting on the gifts of wealthy friends, Wilbur and Elsie retired to the College Settlement Farm in the Catskills to write a book on the social unit idea, as they had named the plan for citizen-expert research. When the manuscript was complete, they submitted it to eminent social workers for criticism, one of whom was Felix Adler, the founder of the Ethical Culture Society. Adler sent them to Herbert Croly, who, in turn, introduced them to Dorothy Straight. Mrs. Straight started the ball rolling with a contribution of $45,000. Finally, enough financial backing was secured for a three-year experiment, and in 1916, a National Social Unit Organization was established, with Gifford Pinchot, the conservationist leader, as president (Phillips 1940, 148).

National news coverage of the organization and its purposes brought forth responses from many cities eager to become the site of the experiment. Cincinnati was finally chosen because of the high development of its social service community, its reputation as a city of neighborhoods, the favorable state of public opinion, and, not least important, the readiness of the city fathers to pledge $15,000 a year for the backing of the experiment. The neighborhood singled out to become America's first social unit was Mohawk-Brighton, an innercity neighborhood of about fifteen thousand, comprised mainly of workers of German-American extraction (Devine 1919–20, 20).

Prior to going to Milwaukee, the Phillipses had become socialists. Although they always denied that their "invention" owed anything to European theorists, the unit idea, as they envisaged it, bears a strong resemblance to guild socialism. Ideally, each neighborhood in the nation should be organized along bicameral lines, with an upper "house of skills" representing the various professional groups serving the neighborhood and a lower house of elected block representatives. Adjacent neighborhoods might combine to form a larger unit. These would merge further until eventually city and even metropolitan social units would be created. At the national level, the social unit would consist of a board of directors representing regions of the nation and a board of managers representing major occupations and professions. This all-embracing economic and social organization would then constitute the national government. In time, the social unit "might become a Social Union of Nations" (Phillips 1940, 352–53, 380).

Such was the grandiose vision of Wilbur and Elsie Phillips and their followers. In time, it would prove to be the Achilles heel of their Mohawk-Brighton experiment. In 1916, however, all eyes were fixed on the unit as an experiment in efficient democracy. Phillips presented it as a device for "getting divergent minds to work together," the generalized mind and the specialized public mind. Each professional group was to be the mind of the public "within its field," with "the public democratically using that mind," the key figure being the democratically elected worker who served as the channel of communication between the citizen and the expert (1940, 49).

Following their vision, the Phillipses appear to have achieved some successes in Mohawk-Brighton in neighborhood service affairs. Contemporary evaluators of the experiment avowed that ordinary citizens showed themselves quite capable of using the unit institutions for the management of their health affairs and of proposing imaginative extensions of the unit's functions. In fewer than three years, however, the entire undertaking was enveloped in public controversy and destroyed.

The collapse of the Cincinnati Social Unit has been attributed to the red scare following World War I (Haber 1964), but, in fact, more substantial forces were at work. The unit proved to be incompatible with the surrounding institutional and political environment. Dr. Edward Devine, an impartial investigator who studied the project at close range, concluded that the general acceptance of the unit principle would have provided a substitute not only for existing municipal departments and governments, but also voluntary social agencies (1919–20, 120). It was quite useless, therefore, for the unit's defender to argue that the experiment had brought improved health and sanitary services to the people of Mohawk-Brighton. "Let the regular city government do those things" was the mayor's retort and many public officials agreed (Dinwiddie 1929, 131). Consequently, the mayor denounced the unit as a government within a government and warned Cincinnatians that it was but a step away from bolshevism.

The Cincinnati Social Unit was a severe test of the theories of Wilbur and Elsie Phillips and those of Mary Parker Follett that the conduct of neighborhood affairs could be a cooperative enterprise of the people and the experts. The unexamined premise had been that the experts were indeed able and willing to share their power with the people. In Mohawk-Brighton, the physicians and clergymen may have been secure enough for this act of trust, but with other professionals, those of lower and less-assured status, the situation was quite different. At the time of the mayor's attack, the visiting nurses were already disaffected and other social workers were wavering, fearing the usurpation of their functions by those bright and aggressive laymen, the block workers. The Council of Social Agencies, one of the principal supporters of the unit, always denied the importance of this factor, pointing instead to their dependence for funds upon wealthy, conservative patrons. However, it seems probable that the failure of the social unit experiment was due not to red scares but to deeper causes—the opposition of mayors and other city administrators to this upstart social unit that challenged and would have replaced the ward as the duly constituted political unit of the city. It was due as well to the opposition of threatened proto-professionals. Whatever the case, when the cry of bolshevism was raised, the crucial financial support of the council was lacking, and the social unit quickly succumbed. Thus ended America's first experiment in efficient democracy.

"Those who ignore the lessons of history are bound to repeat them" goes the old saw. If knowledge of the Mohawk-Brighton experience had been more widely available one might have predicted the defeat of Indianapolis's "Minigovs" bill in the 1970s at the hands of threatened ward officials. Had Mohawk-Brighton been remembered and its lessons absorbed, one wonders if the framers of the Model Cities Act and the community action programs of the 1960s would have been so confident.

Reflections

The progressive ideas examined here raise a profound question: How to retain two fundamental but apparently mutually repulsive forces—democracy and technocracy, the authority of the experts and the people's wisdom. To let either go, to sacrifice scientific knowledge to its democratic political culture or vice versa, would constitute a calamitous defeat for Western culture.

For Taylor, the engineer, the solution seemed obvious. The claims of democracy could be satisfied in the workplace, paradoxically by totally eliminating the worker's voice in the conduct of his work. He argued that under scientific management, since both worker and boss were subjected to a common discipline, the requirements of the job, they were, in fact, equals, comrades. That workers might have something of their own to contribute to technological progress seems never to have occurred to Tay-

lor, or even to his critics. It took Follett to highlight the idea that innovation is a "group process," that is to say, a social process and not necessarily the deed of a lone hero, a Prometheus bringing fire to mankind. Modern scientific managers with their theory of the superior efficiency of the
small, alert, proactive work team are more the followers of Follett than
they are Taylorites, while Taylor's brand of scientific management is considered outmoded, a relic of the era of "Fordism" (Reich 1983).

The issue was joined more squarely when Taylorism entered politics,
brought there by Gulick and his confreres. Engineers may be presumed
to have the superior say in industry, but politics in America (at least in
those loftiest reaches of the national aspiration where myth is reality) is
the home ground of the man in the street. In the United States, the common man is not merely acceptable. He is considered to be the highest
type of citizen. His common sense is what protects the Republic from the
experts, with their intellectual excesses, their abstractions, and their one-
eyed perspectives. At the same time, it is also a part of the American
character to stand in awe of the expert and his technical prowess, even
while regarding him with profound mistrust. Fear of his wizardry, especially in the realm of the natural sciences, is evident today, as witness
the efforts to subordinate science to ethics (genetics, nuclear research,
etc.). The test of science used to be, Does it work? Today it is, Is it socially responsible?

The attempt to reconcile science and democracy has resulted in a
change in the meaning of social science. Follett, in particular, said something basic on this subject. The objects of the social sciences, unlike those
of the natural sciences, are not objects at all. They are subjects—men and
women. They are capable of observing their observers. Therefore, contrary to the imaginings of Merriam and his school, social science requires more than observation. It must partake of the nature of communication. To be scientific, social research must talk with the people. It
must test its knowledge against what the people know and the way in
which they know it. This is democratic dogma. Also implicit in Follett's
view, and that of the Phillipses, is the converse proposition: To be democratic, life must be lived scientifically. Any person or group, the quantity or quality of whose store of knowledge is seriously substandard,
stands in danger of sinking to the state of an object and being manipu-
lated by more competent neighbors. What is needed is a method that
facilitates contact between the specialist and the people and ensures the
interchange of the qualitatively different kinds of knowledge and intelligence that each group possesses. How is this to be accomplished? According to the Phillipses, the solution should take a political and territorial form. What better way of interacting with the experts—and of

controlling them—than that the people and the experts be neighbors, or if not actual neighbors, than equal collaborators in a neighborhood framework? But in this highly mobile, free-wheeling, and individualistic society, the democratization of expertise has taken a quite different turn from that envisaged by Elsie and Wilbur Phillips. Instead of uniting experts and people in one neighborhood, the tendency is to unite them in one person, to create the citizen-expert; hence, the incessant bombarding of laypersons with the minutest technical detail bearing on the conduct of their lives, from avoiding heart attacks to surviving in a snowstorm. This comports well with the antibureaucratic, antielitist cast of modern American society. Interestingly, the means for democratizing knowledge are themselves technical, mass-media techniques rather than political.

If education is one master tactic in the strategy for overcoming the tension between democracy and technocracy, the other is automation. In addition to the philosophy of the enlightenment, the roots of the American ethos are in the abundant natural resources of the country. Reason and bounty, together, constituted the foundation of economic and therefore of political freedom. Because no man could any longer starve another man out, no longer should one man have to serve another. This ideal was expressed with pride by St. John de Crèvecoeur at the very outset of the Republic in his definition of the American: "We have no princes, for whom we toil, starve and bleed; we are the most perfect society now existing in the world" (Chute 1964, 75).

A bountiful natural environment was the original guarantor of that ideal. If America has had a direction since de Crèvecoeur's time, it is toward the same ideal through the construction of an even more bountiful, man-made environment—an integrated, worldwide network of power and machinery, easy to use and freely accessible to all, that reduces to a minimum the need for a class of expert managers of whatever stripe, scientific, industrial, or political. In this new technical Garden of Eden, not only would no man be a slave to another, he also would be less of a slave to himself. Technical solutions would obviate the need for relationships of force and, by extending further the substitution of automated for human labor, it would lessen the split between the self as subject and the self as object. The liberation of man from servitude to himself as well as to others—this is the dream underlying American technology. It has a modern prophet of sorts in R. Buckminster Fuller (1969, 1976). Its most formidable philosophic adversary is environmentalism of the romantic variety, which preaches the curbing of the Promethean spirit of technology and teaches accommodation, if not total submission, to nature.

Notes

This essay is an expanded version of a paper delivered at the Second International Conference on Planning Theory and Practice, Turin, Italy, September 2–12, 1986. The theme of the conference was the distribution and redistribution of social resources.

1. The observations in this paragraph are attributed to Professor White by the conference reporter. They are not necessarily Professor White's own words.

2. Elsie Philipps appears to have been in all respects a full partner in her spouse's "adventures for democracy." Unfortunately, she has left no comparable autobiographical account. Elsie La Grange Cole was born in 1880 in Albany, New York, the granddaughter of that city's first superintendent of schools, and graduated from Vassar College in 1901. She was an important union leader with a particular concern for women workers and was a prominent member of the Socialist party. She died in 1961. For a sketch of her girlhood and young womanhood see Phillips (1940, 52–60).

References

Cabot, Richards C. 1934. "Mary Parker Follett, an Appreciation." *Radcliffe Quarterly* 18 (April): 80–82.

Chute, William J., ed. 1964. *The American Scene: 1600–1860.* New York: Bantam Books.

Croly, Herbert. 1965. *The Promise of American Life.* Cambridge: Harvard University Press.

Devine, Edward. 1919–20. "The Social Unit in Cincinnati, an Experiment in Organization." *Survey* 43 (Oct.–March): 115–26.

Dinwiddie, Courtenay. 1919. "Comment on the Report of Social Agencies on the Social Unit Organization." Unpublished typescript. July 7.

———. 1929. *Community Responsibility: A Report of the Cincinnati Social Unit Experiment.* New York: New York School of Social Work.

Exploratory Research Conference on the Reorganization of the Areas and Functions of Local Government. 1932. *Resume of Proceedings.* University of Chicago, May 7–8.

Follett, Mary Parker. 1926. *The New State.* New York: Longmans, Green.

———. 1924. *Creative Experience.* New York: Longmans, Green.

Fuller, R. Buckminster. 1976. *And It Came to Pass—Not to Stay.* New York: Macmillan.

———. 1969. *Operating Manual for Spaceship Earth.* New York: Simon and Schuster.

Graham, Otis. 1967. *An Encore for Reform.* New York: Oxford University Press.

Gulick, Luther. 1928. *The National Institute of Public Administration, an Adventure in Democracy.* New York: National Institute of Public Administration.

Haber, Samuel. 1964. *Efficiency and Uplift: Scientific Management in the Progressive Era.* Chicago: University of Chicago Press.

Hurst, James Willard. 1967. *Law and the Conditions of Freedom in the Nineteenth-Century United States.* Madison: University of Wisconsin Press.

James, William. 1936. *The Varieties of Religious Experience.* New York: Modern Library.

Kimball, Dexter S. 1914. "Another Side of Efficiency Engineering." In *Scientific Management,* ed. C. E. Thompson. Cambridge: Harvard University Press.

Lubove, Roy. 1962. *The Progressives and the Slums.* Pittsburgh: University of Pittsburgh Press.

Metcalf, Henry, and L. Ruwick. 1941. *Dynamic Administration.* Bath, England: Management Publication Press.

Mitchell, Wesley C. 1912. "The Backward Art of Spending Money." *The American Economic Review* 2 (June): 269–81.

Phillips, Wilbur C. 1940. *Adventuring for Democracy.* New York: Social Unit Press.

Reich, Robert B. 1983. *The Next American Frontier.* New York: Times Books.

Smith, T. V. 1962. *A Non-Existent Man, an Autobiography.* Austin: University of Texas Press.

Smith, T. V., and Leonard White, eds. 1929. *Chicago: An Experiment in Social Science Research.* Chicago: University of Chicago Press.

Referential Land Use Classification

This multidimensional land use classification system is of conceptual and historical interest because it stated and demonstrated, for the first time, the importance of carefully defining the dimensions or attributes of land use. Before its appearance in the 1950s, it was still standard practice to assign parcels to "impure" categories which included combinations of attributes. Instead, following this example, we now assign multiple attributes to each parcel and derive classifications from raw data as needed. Each mutually exclusive dimension is separately recorded as an attribute field. Modern database technology has facilitated this new method by enabling us to encode the most fundamental data possible so that we can create many classifications to serve any purpose as the need arises. There are, however, still impurities in the following lists. For example, rather than category 13 in the building dimension being "with both sewer and street service," it would have been better to construct such a category, if needed, from raw attribute data in which "sewers service" and "street service" would have constituted two distinct dimensions or attribute fields.

A Multiple Land Use Classification System (1959)

Land use is a key term in the language of city planning. Not only does its meaning continue to be uncertain, but it also grows more uncertain with time. This increasing ambiguity is due, in part to our efforts to probe more deeply into the use of land. As interest in the subject broadens and knowledge of relevant variables expands, we endow *land use* with more and more meanings. It seems clear that some effort should be made to replace the broader term *land use* with others that are more precise. But first it will be necessary to identify the individual components or dimensions of land use and to define them clearly.

In addition to trying to identify the different dimensions of land use, I have also tried my hand at classifying them according to their variable characteristics. The result is a set of parallel classifications, each based on a single dimension.

Two features of this system are worth noting. The system is expandable; as additional dimensions of land use are discerned and classified it will be possible to range them alongside the others without disturbing these in any way. It is also flexible; it will be possible to combine on punch cards the categories of different classifications (i.e., to cross-classify them). This is of special interest because many of the more urgent problems of planning, both practical and conceptual, have to do not so much with the individual dimensions of land use as with the relationships among them. The multiple classification of land use provides a way of studying these relationships.

The Major Dimensions of Land Use

Omitting ownership, the following five factors are typically involved in the use of land: 1) a site; 2) a site facility; 3) an activity; 4) an enterprise conducting the activity; and 5) an activity effect.

Corresponding to these factors, we can identify five distinct dimensions of land use: 1) general site development; 2) site adaptation as represented by building type or other special site facility; 3) actual use (i.e., the type of activity on the premises); 4) economic overuse (i.e., the type of economic function performed by the enterprise conducting the activity); and 5) activity characteristics (size, rhythm, realm, and material impact).

Classification of General Site Development Characteristics

The following classification can be used to give an account of the broad development characteristics of a community.

CODE	CLASS
00	Undevelopable land[1]
10	Undeveloped, unused
11	with direct sewer service only
12	with direct street service only
13	with both
14	with neither
20	Undeveloped, otherwise used
21	with direct sewer service only
22	with direct street service only
23	with both
24	with neither
30	Nonstructural development; development ornamental (e.g., landscaping)
40	Nonstructural development; development functional[2] (e.g., crops)
50	Developed with temporary[3] nonbuilding structure (e.g., a billboard)
60	Developed with permanent nonbuilding structure (e.g., a power pole)
70	Developed with temporary building[4] (e.g., a newsstand)
80	Developed with permanent building

Classification of Site Adaptation: Building Type or Other Structure

The following classification provides a basis for an inventory of the quantity and quality (not to be confused with condition) of internal space available in a given area, as represented by type of building. It also provides a classification of type of nonbuilding structure.

The principal problem in the use of the building-type classification is that alteration and addition and the construction of more than one building on a site often render building types indistinguishable.

In the following list, the category is meant to denote type of building, not the activity which takes place in the building. Thus, "church building" means a building built as a church, not a storefront used as a church.[5]

CODE	CLASS
00	*No structure or nonbuilding structure*
01	No structure
02	Irrigation facilities
03	Pavement
04	Sign or billboard
05	Power pole
06	Radio or television tower
07	Open wharf or dock
08	Storage tank
09	Other (e.g., special recreation equipment)
10	*Office and bank buildings*
11	Office building, 1–3 stories
12	Office building, 4–10 stories
13	Office building, 11 or more stories
14	Bank building
15	Combination bank and office building
16	Combination office and loft building
17	Multistoried office building over storefronts
20	*Specialized industrial buildings*
21	Open-sided, shed-type building
22	One- or two-story factory or warehouse building, nonfireproof
23	Quonset
24	One-story factory or warehouse building, fireproof
25	Multistoried factory or warehouse building, fireproof
26	Large area assembly plant
27	Specialized laboratory building
28	Power generation plant or transformer station
29	Other (e.g., incinerator, sewage disposal plant, etc.)
30	*Specialized buildings for storage and handling*
31	Produce warehouse (distinguished by covered platform)
32	Grain storage elevator
33	Rail and truck transfer sheds
34	Refrigerated warehouse
35	Small one-story distribution warehouse
36	Large area single-floor distribution warehouse
37	Trucking terminal dock building
38	Wharf and dock shed
39	Other specialized storage building

40	*Store buildings*
41	Free-standing one-story building
42	One-story store buildings in a row
43	Single supermarket building (distinguished by special treatment of parking)
44	Supermarket complex
45	Multistoried department store building
46	Two- or three-story building, store and residence overhead
47	Two- or three-story building, store and offices overhead
48	Two- or three-story building, store and loft space overhead
49	Other specialized store buildings
50	*Residential buildings*
51	Single-family house, detached
52	Single-family twin house
53	Single-family row house
54	Duplex house, detached
55	Duplex twin house
56	Duplex row house
57	Apartment building, 1–4 stories
58	High-rise apartment building or hotel
59	Other (e.g., dormitory building)
60	*Specialized public assembly buildings*
61	Theater building or movie house
62	Sports arena
63	Church building
64	Concert hall
65	Bowling alley
66	Skating rink
67	Terminal building (air, rail, or bus)
68	Stadium
69	Other specialized public assembly buildings
70	*Other specialized community buildings*
71	Hospital building
72	Medical clinic building
73	School building
74	Museum or library building
75	Fire station
76	Police station
80	*Garages and other buildings specialized for auto service*
81	Free-standing private garage
82	Private garage in a row
83	Multistoried public garage
84	Gasoline service station
85	Drive-in theater
86	Drive-in bank

87   Roadside stand
88   Motel building
90   *Miscellaneous buildings*

Classification of Actual Use (Activity)

Activity means what actually takes place on a parcel of land, as opposed to the type of structure on the parcel and to the overuse (i.e., the economic function in the service of which a parcel of land is enlisted). As "what actually takes place" consists of observable relationships among persons, goods, and vehicles, the categories of an activity classification should suggest in a word, or in a few words, typical differences in these relationships. I have experimented with several roundabout terms which might suggest the phenomenal nature of different activities without making use of the terminology of either economic function or facility type. But in a few cases the results were so ambiguous that I prefer to rely on the name of the facility to suggest the activity type with which it is usually associated. Thus the term *store-type activity* is not meant to denote any activity taking place in a store building, but rather a particular relation of persons and goods usually, but not always, found in a store building—people walk in, pay other people for goods kept on the premises, and walk out with them. Nor should the term *store-type activity* be equated with *retail trade*, a function term, because the description of store type activity given above could apply loosely to a man picking up shoes left for repair at a cobbler's or to a man purchasing a new pair of shoes. In these two examples, the economic function performed is different but the activity is similar.

For want of a better term, I suggest *shop-type activity* to denote an interpersonal transaction similar to that which takes place in the store-type activity, but not involving physical distribution of goods on the premises. A man's hair is cut, or his picture is taken, or perhaps he is shown some sample goods and makes a purchase of stock which will be delivered to him from a distant warehouse. Here again, we see one activity type straddling two economic functions, "personal service" and "retail trade."

The terms *office* and *school* should cause no trouble; common usage applies them as often to types of activity as it does to building types.

CODE	CLASS
00	*No activity*
01	Office activity, public-oriented
02	Office activity, non-public-oriented
03	Heavy goods handling and processing
04	Store-type activity
05	Shop-type activity
06	Storage, inactive (e.g., of water, fuel, etc.)
07	Eating and drinking (e.g., that normally occurring in restaurants, bars, etc.)

08   Residing family (i.e., with children)
09   Residing nonfamily (e.g., that normally occurring in hotels, dormi-
       tories, hospitals, asylums, etc.)
10   *Play and active recreation*
11   School activity
12   Mass assembly and spectatorship (e.g., at games or movies, etc.)
13   Passenger assembly (e.g., that normally occurring in terminal build-
       ings)
14   Other forms of public assembly (e.g., that normally occurring in
       parks, shrines, museums, etc.)
15   Pedestrian movement
16   Vehicular movement (on roads)
17   Vehicle parking
18   Nonsurface activity (for land not used at surface level)
19   Unclassifiable activities

Classification of Economic Over-use (Function)

A ready-made classification of economic overuse or function, both general and specific, is available in the Standard Industrial Classification (SIC) (Bureau of the Budget 1957). Groups of two-digit SICs constitute divisions which are comparable to what we have called general economic functions above. Specific functions emerge in the SIC at the second- , third- , or fourth-digit levels.

There are two reasons for preserving the SIC intact. First, it is capable of giving us what we are seeking in this classification, namely economic functions. Second, and more important, is the wealth of data available in that form. The SIC will become increasingly useful as more cities adapt it for land use classification, thereby making possible refined intercity comparisons.[6]

Certain modifications in the regular two-digit SIC code are suggested in order to adapt it to the approach used here.

1. Each division has been given a single, distinct code number.

2. A new division has been added called "nonfunctional land," to represent land which is undeveloped, unused, and held for speculative purposes. Used land held for speculation should be classified according to the function served by its use.

3. SIC 88, "private households," has been dropped and a new division, "residence," added.

4. SIC 93, "local government," has been renamed "city government."[7]

5. The unused code number SIC 95 is used to designate county government.

6. The division "wholesale trade and retail trade" has been broken into two divisions: "wholesale trade" and "retail trade."

All departures from the official [1957] SIC two-digit code are shown below in parentheses. For example, in the case of nonfunctional land, I have added both the class (nonfunctional land) and the code number (0). But in the case of mining, I have added only the code number (2).

CODE	CLASS
(0)	*(Nonfunctional land)*
(1)	*Agriculture, forestry, and fisheries*
01	Commercial farms
02	Noncommercial farms
07	Agricultural services and hunting and trapping
08	Forestry
09	Fisheries
(2)	*Mining*
10	Metal mining
11	Anthracite mining
12	Bituminous coal and lignite mining
13	Crude petroleum and natural gas extraction
14	Mining of nonmetallic minerals, except fuels
(3)	*Contact construction*
15	Building construction—general contractors
16	Construction other than building construction
17	Construction—special trade contractors
(4)	*Manufacturing industries*
19	Ordnance and accessories
20	Food and kindred products
21	Tobacco manufactures
22	Textile mill products
23	Apparel and other finished products made from fabrics and similar material
24	Lumber and wood products, except furniture
25	Furniture and fixtures
26	Paper and allied products
27	Printing, publishing, and allied industries
28	Chemicals and allied products
29	Products of petroleum and coal
30	Rubber products
31	Leather and leather products
32	Stone, clay, and glass products
33	Primary metal industries
34	Fabricated metal products, except ordnance, machinery, and transportation equipment
35	Machinery, except electrical
36	Electrical machinery, equipment, and supplies
37	Transportation equipment
38	Professional, scientific, and controlling instruments; photographic and optical goods; watches and clocks
39	Miscellaneous manufacturing industries
(5)	*Transportation, communication, and other public utilities*
40	Railroad transportation

41	Local and suburban transit and interurban passenger transportation
42	Motor freight transportation and warehousing
44	Water transportation
45	Transportation by air
46	Pipeline transportation
47	Transportation services
48	Communications
49	Electric, gas, and sanitary services
(6)	*Wholesale trade*
50	Wholesale trade
(7)	*Retail trade*
52	Retail trade, building materials, hardware, and farm equipment
53	Retail trade, general merchandise
54	Retail trade, food
55	Retail trade, automotive dealers and gasoline service stations
56	Retail trade, apparel and accessories
57	Retail trade, furniture, home furnishings, and equipment
58	Retail trade, eating and drinking places
59	Miscellaneous retail trade
(8)	*Finance, insurance, and real estate*
60	Banking
61	Credit agencies other than banks
62	Security and commodity brokers, dealers, etc.
63	Insurance carriers
64	Insurance agents, brokers, and service
65	Real estate
66	Combinations of real estate, insurance, loans, law offices
67	Holding and other investment companies
(9)	*Services*
70	Hotels, rooming houses, camps, etc.
72	Personal services
73	Miscellaneous business services
75	Auto repair, services, and garages
76	Miscellaneous repair services
78	Motion pictures
79	Other amusement and recreation services
80	Medical and health services
81	Legal services
82	Educational services
84	Museums, art galleries, botanical and zoological gardens
86	Nonprofit membership organizations
89	Miscellaneous services
(10)	*Government*
91	Federal government
92	State government

93	(City) government
(94)	International government
(95)	(County government)
(11)	*Residence*

Classification of Activity Characteristics

Of the various classifications which comprise this system, the set presented below are perhaps least satisfactory. They represent the working edge of the system, as it were. Despite their present primitive form, they are included because a comprehensive system dare not omit classifications whose subjects are of such central importance to planning. Suggestions as to how these subjects might be better handled or more fully developed will be welcomed.

In the first classification—that of activity size in terms of traffic generation—the relative terms *high, medium,* and *low* would correspond to class intervals whose limits could be determined only after the full range of quantitative variation in pedestrian, auto, truck, and rail traffic had been observed for a particular community.

The code numbers in the second classification, time shape, would represent curves describing the daily variation in each kind of traffic generated by the activity. Similar curves might represent weekly or monthly variation. To my knowledge, no such curves have yet been constructed.

The classifications in this set would be used to classify relatively few activity units or establishments in a community.

Activity Size in Terms of Traffic Generation:

CODE	PEDESTRIAN	AUTO	TRUCK	RAIL
1	high	high	high	high
2	medium	medium	medium	medium
3	low	low	low	low

Corresponding Daily Time Shape:

1	1	1	1
2	2	2	2
3	3	3	3

Realm or Range of Influence:
CODE
1	neighborhood
2	sectional
3	citywide
4	regional

Material Effect:
CODE
0	none

1   noise
2   glare
3   odor
4   vibration
5   smoke
6   other
7   combination
8   combination
9   combination

Machine Manipulation[8]

By means of punch cards we are able to adapt this system for machine manipulation. On a single card representing a single parcel of land[9] we can use one column or field for site development characteristics, the next for structure or building type, the next for actual use or activity, and so on. We can classify each parcel in several ways and thus analyze the use into its separable elements. The use of multiple land use classification in combination with punch cards would permit us to observe and record the quantitative and qualitative relationships of each dimension in the land use complex, quickly and accurately, parcel by parcel.

For example, consider a survey requiring the selection of all office buildings in a city which house the administrative operations of a manufacturing enterprise (for the purpose, say, of determining office-space inputs to the manufacturing function). The procedure would be to machine sort for the appropriate code punch along the field representing economic function or over-use (i.e., for a punch which stands for manufacturing). Having selected all cards bearing this punch, one would then sort through the activities column for office activity. A final sort along the structure field would yield all parcels having the three specified characteristics: manufacturing, office activity, and office building. Machine adding of the lot area or floor area recorded on each card would quickly produce the required quantitative data.

Notes

"A Multiple Land Use Classification System" is adapted, with permission, from the *Journal of the American Institute of Planners* 25 (Aug. 1959): 143–50.

1. This category refers to land which is undevelopable (except at great expense) only by virtue of some present or past physical development (e.g. unstable land over derelict mines, quarries, etc.).

2. There is a question as to whether development normally considered nonfunctional, such as an area planted with trees, is also functional in the sense that it may reduce noise and provide open space for neighboring areas.

3. The word *temporary* refers to the physical durability of a structure, not to its economic durability.

4. *Building* is used here to mean any three-dimensional structure, covered or uncovered, which persons normally enter, either for work or for some other purpose. In this sense, an oil storage tank is not a building structure even though it is three-dimensional and provides internal space.

5. This classification is made with only the most elementary knowledge of those differentials which distinguish one type of building from another in the structural sense. Doubtless, many criticisms are possible and should be made.

6. For a similar recommendation see Sparks (1958).

7. The term *government* may denote either of two things: 1) a distinct economic function, that of administering or regulating other functions; or 2) a type of ownership (public) under which certain services are dispensed and, rarely, goods (e.g. a state liquor store). In the classification below, the term is meant in the first sense only (i.e., to classify land used for the administrative or regulatory function, for example, the land occupied by city hall). A city playground, on the other hand, offers a kind of service. Accordingly, its economic function is not government but service. At this level of description, the only feature which distinguishes it from land used for other services is type of ownership.

8. When multidimensional land use classification was invented more than forty years ago, the method of activating it for large amounts of data was punch-card sorting. Now, database software is used. The technology has changed, yet the logic of the system remains unchanged. Indeed, it is mainly through the advances in computer technology that the system has come into its own.

9. One card for one parcel is a ratio possible only in the simplest land use situation (i.e., where one establishment occupies one building on one lot). In the case of mixed use (two or more establishments on the same unit of land which differ in their major activity, function, or type of building they occupy), each establishment would be represented by a supplementary or trailer card. The parcel card would then serve to record only those data characteristic of the whole parcel. One obvious difficulty is the apportionment of lot area among the different users of the same lot. The apportionment of floor area presents no unusual problem.

References

Executive Office of the President, Bureau of the Budget. 1957. *Standard Land Use Classification Manual.* Washington, D.C.: Government Printing Office.

Sparks, Robert N. 1958. "The Case for a Uniform Land Use Classification." *Journal of the American Institute of Planners* 24, no. 3, 174–78.

Prescriptive Classification

Types of Change

No change
Use (activities) change (e.g., replacement of residential by commercial activity)
Operational change
    In management practices:
        sanitation
        repair and maintenance practices
        refuse disposal
        pest control
        safety measures (e.g., lighting, firefighting equipment, etc.)
        use or abuse of natural site qualities (soil, cover, etc.)
        other
    In user practices:
        hours of activity
        parking habits
        loading practices
        emission of noise, odor, particulate matter
        floor loading
    Storage practices (as of combustibles)
    Other (as overloaded circuits)
Change in natural site characteristics
        clearing (of natural cover)
        draining
        grading
        other
Change in site facilities (site-readaptation)
    New construction
    Reconstruction:
        lot layout
        interior design
        mechanical equipment (e.g., power, water, light, air conditioning, etc.)
        major structural repairs (e.g., walls, foundation, roof, beams, etc.)
        minor structural repairs (e.g. doors, windows, stairs, etc.)

Means of Change

No means
  Available
  Possible
  Required
Purchase (voluntary sale)
  Of the fee
  Of certain rights:
    development rights
    use rights (as easement)
    other
Condemnation (mandatory sale)
  Total
  Partial
Regulation (control without compensation)
  Of the site facility (e.g. height, setback)
  Of the activity type
  Of user and management practices (as hours of activity)
Persuasion (change in attitude or motive of actor)
  Information and education programs:
    mass media
    neighborhood meetings
    individual consultation or instruction
    other
  Demonstration (as clean block program)
  Other
Tactical methods (change in environment of action)
  Change in physical environs of parcel:
    access
    community facilities or services
    other
  Change in legal and economic environment:
    loans
    credit
    write down
    tax subsidy
    relocation service
    other
  Other

Note

Appendix B is adapted with permission from *New Directions in Land Use Classification* (Chicago: American Society of Planning Officials, 1965).

Index

ALBERT GUTTENBERG was born in Chelsea, Massachusetts. He was graduated from Harvard College in 1948 after serving three and one-half years in the armed forces. He was a practicing planner in Philadelphia; Portland, Maine; and Washington, D.C. before joining the planning faculty at the University of Illinois in Urbana-Champaign in 1964. As a Guggenheim Fellow and a Guest Scholar at the Brookings Institution in 1970, he studied the history of American planning, with a special emphasis on the New Deal period. He is currently engaged in a collaborative study of geographic information systems theory with colleagues in Europe and North America.